Information Management in Health Services

Health Services Management

Series Editors:
Chris Ham and Chris Heginbotham

The British National Health Service is one of the biggest and most complex organizations in the developed world. Employing around one million people and accounting for £36 billion of public expenditure, the Service is of major concern to both the public and politicians. Management within the NHS faces a series of challenges in ensuring that resources are deployed efficiently and effectively. These challenges include the planning and management of human resources, the integration of professionals into the management process, and making sure that services meet the needs of patients and the public.

Against this background, the Health Services Management series addresses the many issues and practical problems faced by people in managerial roles in health services.

Information Management in Health Services

Edited by Justin Keen

U. M. C.
NEW CROSS
SITE

Open University Press
Buckingham · Philadelphia

Open University Press
Celtic Court
22 Ballmoor
Buckingham
MK18 1XW

and
1900 Frost Road, Suite 101
Bristol, PA 19007, USA

First Published 1994

A catalogue record of this book is available from the British Library

ISBN 0 335 19116 9 (pb) 0 335 19117 7 (hb)

Library of Congress Cataloging-in-Publication Data
Information management in health services/edited by Justin Keen.
    p.   cm.
Includes bibliographical references and index.
ISBN 0–335–19116–9 (pbk.) ISBN 0–335–19117–7 (hb.)
    1. National Health Service (Great Britain).   2. Information
resources management—Great Britain.   3. Communication in medicine—
Great Britain.   4. Communication in medicine—Government policy—
Great Britain.   I. Keen, Justin.
    [DNLM: 1. Health Services—organization & administration—Great
Britain. 2. Information Systems.   3. National Health Service (Great
Britain)   W 26.5 I427 1993]
RA412.5.G7I54 1993
362.1′068′4—dc20
DNLM/DLC
for Library of Congress   93–24065
                                                                                CIP

Typeset by Graphicraft Typesetters Ltd, Hong Kong
Printed in Great Britain by Biddles Ltd, Guildford and King's Lynn

Contents

The editor and contributors

Brian Bloomfield is a member of the Centre for Research on Organisations Management and Technical Change in the Manchester School of Management (CROMTEC). He lectures on management information systems; his research interests centre on the sociological study of technology, with particular reference to the development and use of IT in complex organizations. His research on the NHS has focused on the resource management initiative, IT strategy and the role of management consultants.

Andrew Brooks is Consultant Physician, and formerly Clinical Director for Medicine, at the Royal Hampshire County Hospital. He qualified in Sheffield and was Registrar and Senior Registrar in Edinburgh and Cambridge respectively.

Jane Clayton is co-ordinator for nursing and therapy audit at York Health Services NHS Trust. After taking a degree in geography she worked at the Foreign Office for two years. She then trained as a nurse and worked in the independent sector for several years before going to York in 1992. She has recently obtained an MSc in gerontology from King's College London.

Rod Coombs is Director of CROMTEC. He co-ordinates CROMTEC's contribution to the ESRC's national programme of research on IT (the PICT Programme). He teaches and conducts research widely in the area of management issues raised by technology, but with particular emphasis on strategic management of R&D and on the strategic use of IT.

Bob Galliers is Lucas Professor of Business Systems Engineering at Warwick University Business School. He is Director of Warwick's award winning Master's Programme in Business Management Systems, and is an Associate Chair of the Business School. In addition he holds the post of

Visiting Professor for Information Management at Hong Kong Polytechnic. He was previously Foundation Professor and Head of the School of Information Systems at Curtin University, Perth, Western Australia. He has consulted in strategic business and information systems planning and in executive information requirements determination on behalf of major multinational corporations and public sector organizations both in Britain and Australia.

Wally Gowing is Director of Information, South East Staffordshire Health Authority (SESHA). He joined in 1986 as Information Services Manager, after 14 years in local government. Following the initial task of implementing Körner for the health authority, a major part of his work was to develop and implement an information strategy for Burton Hospitals. This led to the selection of a hospital information system and the successful implementation of the first phase by March 1992. Wally is an Executive Director of SESHA and current preoccupations are implementing the District Information Systems Projects (DISP) for SESHA and developing cross agency data flows.

Mark Harrison is Consultant Urological Surgeon, and formerly Clinical Director for General Surgery and Urology, at the Royal Hampshire County Hospital. He qualified at Cambridge University and the Middlesex Hospital Medical School and completed his urological training in Leeds and Bradford.

John James is Chief Executive of Kensington, Chelsea and Westminster Commissioning Agency, comprising the District Health Authority and the Family Health Services Authority. Before joining the NHS he was a career civil servant, mostly in the Department of Health, but also including a secondment to the Treasury. From 1986 to 1989 he was a member of the NHS Management Board.

Justin Keen is a Research Fellow in the Health Economics Research Group at Brunel University. He has undertaken many research and consultancy projects in the NHS over the last few years, and was a member of the research team which evaluated the six resource management pilot hospitals.

Andy Kennedy has worked in adult education and development for the last 20 years. He has taught at universities in Canada and the UK, and has undertaken development projects in numerous large companies in Western Europe as well as in the public sector in West Africa and India. He worked for 3 years as a training and development consultant to a first-wave trust, where a particular focus for his work was the contribution of healthcare professionals to the management of the organization. He is now a Fellow at the King's Fund College, where his interests include conflict and collaboration in healthcare organizations.

Rebecca Malby is the Director of Nursing Practice at the Institute of Nursing at Leeds University. After nurse training she practised in several hospitals in the London area and undertook a variety of nursing management and research roles, most recently at Yorkshire Regional Health Authority. She won a Florence Nightingale Scholarship in 1990, and in 1992 obtained an MA in Public and Social Administration at Brunel University.

Margaret Marion is Unit General Manager, and formerly Director of Nursing Services, at the Royal Hampshire County Hospital. She qualified from St Bartholomew's Hospital and was Nursing Director of the Wessex Neurological Unit.

Jenny Owen is a Research Associate in the Centre for Research on Organizations, Management and Technical Change in the School of Management, UMIST, Manchester. Apart from her current research interest in IT strategy and use within the NHS, she has previously undertaken research into the development of 'human-centred' office systems in a local authority context, with specific reference to issues of gender equality.

James Raftery is a health economist with the Wessex Institute of Public Health. Previously he worked with Wandsworth Health Authority, where he was closely involved with the development of purchasing. He also works for the National Casemix Office, this following a secondment to the Department of Health. He has degrees in economics and recently completed a PhD in the economics of mental health services.

Ray Robinson is Professor of Health Policy and Director of the Institute of Health Policy Studies at the University of Southampton. Before moving to Southampton in 1993, he was Deputy Director of the King's Fund Institute in London. He has also held posts at the Universities of Leeds, Sussex, California and the Australia National University. This paper was prepared, in part, while he was a Visiting Professor in Health Policy at Emory University, Atlanta, USA.

Mike Smith is Professor of Health Informatics at Keele University and Director of Information for North Staffordshire Health Authority. He graduated from the University of Wales, obtained an MA from California State University and a PhD from the National University of Ireland. Prior to his appointment at Keele in 1990, he was Manager of Software Development, Petroconsultants SA, Geneva; lecturer in Computer Science at the University of Reading, Head of Research and Development for ISTEL; Director of Computing for the Robertson Group plc and Information Technology Director for several smaller businesses.

Andrew Stevens is a public health physician at the Wessex Institute of Public Health. Previously he worked for the South East London Commissioning Agency and the Department of Health where he had responsibility for developing 'needs assessment' and the public health Common Data Set.

Acknowledgements

In any edited book everything depends on the authors producing their chapters on time and to a good standard. The passage of this book into print has been greatly eased by the authors' ability to keep to deadlines, and to willingly undertake requested revisions. They have also produced texts of high quality: a great deal of thought and effort has gone into them, and the task of editing has been made much easier as a result.

The task of assembling the text fell to Nicky Gillard and Jo Holland, who worked with their usual speed and goodwill. Finally, to the staff at Open University Press who oversaw the publication, my thanks for their help and support.

Section 1

Overview: information policy and the market

In a period of rapid and turbulent change in the organization and delivery of health care, the potential value of good information would seem to be obvious. By extension, some would argue, information technology (IT) is a vital part of the armoury of any hospital. One might expect there to be agreement across the National Health Service (NHS) about the value of both information and IT. Yet the situation is not this straightforward. The NHS Review of 1989 brought information to the centre of the stage, but the spotlight revealed structural weaknesses in the way the NHS collects and analyses data, and problems in integrating information and management processes. Key processes, including contracting for health services, hospital management and professional review of services, all depend for their success not only on collecting accurate and relevant data but also on arriving at an understanding of the nature and role of information. Both of these are goals that the NHS has not yet achieved and must aspire to during the 1990s.

The problems with implementing IT would also appear to be serious. The NHS Review effectively committed the NHS to major investments in new systems, but evidence suggests that it has a moderate-to-poor track record in implementing them. If contracting and other elements of the Review are to be implemented successfully then the success rate will have to be improved, and sooner rather than later. Given this pressure, it is a sobering fact that the private sector and other areas of public administration have struggled to justify investments. For every documented success there seems to be a clutch of failures. Indeed, the wonder is that anyone retains faith in the ability of IT to improve organizational performance.

This book focuses on information and IT in hospitals and the purchasing environment surrounding them. Hospitals are complex organizations, which have witnessed a steady increase in the application of IT in recent years. The book examines the problems in using information and implementing IT successfully and points the way to better practice through extant examples of good practice and suggestions concerning the national and local changes that might be needed to bring the average nearer the best. In doing so, it emphasizes the essentially political nature of the topic, but does not lose sight of the very real technical issues that dog progress in many areas.

It is inevitable in a multi-authored book that a variety of opinions should emerge. At this stage in our understanding of the issues this is a plus – there are few absolute rights and wrongs to guide us. However, the editor has biased the selection towards contributions that are cautiously or actually optimistic about the value of IT in health care, but where the optimism is leavened with realism about the ability of the NHS – or organizations in general – to overcome problems. It thus attempts to steer between the technological utopianism of some authors and the outright cynicism of others: neither extreme is, in the end, likely to be all that helpful.

The book is organized in three sections. First, Section 1 deals with two substantial topics: the nature of the internal market for health services and the current status and future direction of central policies relating to IT. These set the scene for the treatment of specific topics in later chapters. The second and third sections present the views of two groups with distinct vantage points. Section 2 comprises five chapters from NHS staff – both managers and health professionals – who are at the forefront of developments in this area. Section 3 contains six contributions from academics who have undertaken research in the NHS, or into the application of IT, or both.

1 Hospitals in the market

Ray Robinson

Introduction

After over forty years of central planning, the NHS underwent a radical transformation on 1 April 1991. A new economic system was introduced in which power and responsibility for decision making were devolved to district health authorities, individual hospitals, community units and selected GPs. The mechanism for achieving this devolution is the internal market.

This chapter looks at the way in which hospitals can be expected to operate within this market. It starts with a brief review of the structure and organization of the internal market. This highlights some of the management issues and aspects of the external environment that can be expected to govern the way in which hospitals act within the market. The next section concentrates on one specific aspect of the internal market – the contracting process. It reviews the evidence on contracting as it has developed over the first year of the reforms; it describes the types of contract that have been negotiated and presents some evidence on the quantitative importance of these different forms of contract. The final section of the chapter takes a longer term view of contracting. It draws upon a particular branch of economics – the transactions costs approach – to make some suggestions about the forms of contractual relationship that are likely to be most appropriate for the NHS.

The internal market

The internal market separates the responsibility for purchasing services from the responsibility for providing them (Fig. 1.1). It involves the functional separation of supply and demand. It is 'internal' in the sense that it

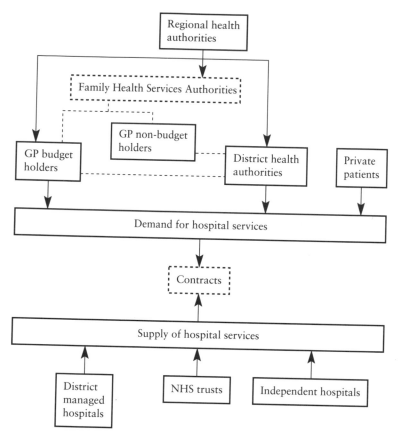

Figure 1.1 The separation of responsibility for purchasing and providing services in the internal market.

is designed to operate within the NHS, although trade between the NHS and the private sector may mean that this popularly used term is something of a misnomer.

The main purchasers within the market are district health authorities. Districts receive annual budgets, based upon weighted (i.e. community risk-adjusted) capitation payments, with which they are expected to purchase a range of services on behalf of their resident populations. The transfer of responsibility for the final deployment of these funds from regional health authorities to districts is a major change from the old style funding process, which was based upon the Resource Allocation Working Party (RAWP) formula. Previously, the majority of funding for district cross-boundary flows was allocated by regions directly to providers. Now this is a matter for the purchasing district's discretion and, in some cases, it is leading to major changes in the flow of funds. In particular, it has caused some well-publicized difficulties for London hospitals as many districts outside London have decided to have their patients treated locally and have withdrawn their funds (King's Fund Commission 1992).

Those GPs who apply and are accepted for fundholder status also have budgets with which they are able to buy a designated range of diagnostic and minor surgical treatments directly from providers on behalf of their patients (Glennerster *et al.* 1992). These budgets are top-sliced from district allocations by regions and are allocated directly to fundholders. At the beginning of 1993, there were just over 600 fundholding practices, and they account for about 4 per cent of the total hospital and community health services budget. However, this figure tends to understate the importance of fundholding practices, as their concentration in certain districts, and on particular elective procedures, already means that they represent an extremely important concentration of purchasing power in some areas. Furthermore, the expected large increase in the number of fundholders as third-wave practices join the scheme in April 1993, and the Government's aim of extending the opportunities to smaller practices and to those in inner cities – and for extending the range of services that fundholders can purchase – suggests that the proportion of the hospital and community health services budget covered by these arrangements can be expected to rise quite markedly in the future.

On the supply side of the market, there are three main types of providers – NHS trusts, directly managed units and independent providers. At the beginning of 1993, there were 156 NHS trusts, with another 128 due to be formed in April 1993. This will mean that over 60 per cent of hospital and community health service revenue is spent on trust services. It is the Government's intention that eventually all NHS providers will acquire trust status. As such, they will all possess the degree of local autonomy considered necessary to enable them to function efficiently within the internal market. A major instrument for promoting greater efficiency will be supply-side competition between providers for services commissioned by districts and GP fundholders. Competition between NHS providers and the private sector may also be expected to develop in the future, although this is very limited at the moment (see below).

As Figure 1.1 shows, however, the market between purchasers and providers will not exist in isolation. Regional health authorities will continue to carry out a range of functions, including regulation of various aspects of the market. And, above regions, sits the NHS Management Executive (ME). The ME can also be expected to regulate the terms on which trusts and other parts of the market operate. Although some aspects of this regulation are already in place, there is still a good deal of vagueness about the precise form it will take in the longer term (Ham 1992).

Despite this uncertainty, however, it is clear that the separation of purchasing and providing, and the encouragement of supply-side competition, represents a totally new environment for the NHS. Hospitals and other providers are now required to earn revenues through the sale of clinical services, and to balance these revenues against the costs of providing services. The ability to exert influence over revenues through the marketing of services constitutes a major change from the old-style financial regime, where the delivery of an acceptable volume of services within a fixed budget constraint was the primary management objective. Set against this extra dimension of managerial freedom, however, is the removal of certainty over guaranteed levels of funding. This has been replaced by an environment in which revenues must be secured in the face of competition from other providers.

Quite how this market will develop over time is still difficult to predict. There are, however, issues relating to the internal organization and management of hospitals, and to the external environment within which they operate, that can be expected to be of major importance.

Internal organization and management

As the 'steady state' requirements that applied during the first year of the reforms are relaxed, so a certain amount of expansion and contraction can be expected to take place as successful hospitals gain business and unsuccessful ones lose it. The move to weighted capitation funding will reinforce this trend. The ability of hospitals to adjust to these changes will depend upon their management systems. How well these will perform is uncertain. Part of this uncertainty arises because hospitals are complex institutions that pursue multiple objectives, many of them non-financial (McGuire et al. 1988). In most organizations, managers can be expected to specify objectives in terms of sales, profits, growth or other financial variables, and to devise strategies to meet them. However, the division of professional responsibilities within a hospital, especially the presence of doctors with clinical responsibilities, makes it far less easy to ensure that everyone works towards a common financial objective.

The Government's answer to this problem has been to devolve more responsibility to hospital managers, especially through the establishment of NHS trusts. But while managers have overall responsibility for financial performance, doctors continue to make clinical decisions which determine the way in which money is actually spent. They also have ultimate responsibility for meeting any changes in workloads, either upwards or downwards.

Recognition of the pivotal role of doctors in committing expenditure has led to successive attempts to include them formally in management decisions about the use of resources; the latest such attempt is the Resource Management (RM) initiative. This has been adopted for nationwide application as part of the NHS reforms. RM involves the introduction of organizational structures – usually based on clinical directorates – that involve doctors and nurses in management decisions, including budgetary control.

This is seen as a key requirement if hospitals are to be able to respond to the incentives offered by a competitive external environment. Progress with RM to date has, however, been limited. The three-year evaluation of the six experimental sites carried out by the Brunel University researchers suggested that 'it is still not possible to provide a definitive assessment of RM as an ongoing working process for hospital management' (Packwood *et al.* 1992).

External environment

The other area of uncertainty facing hospitals concerns the nature of the external environment within which they will be expected to operate. Two issues related to this environment are considered here – the degree of competition that hospitals will face and the extent to which their behaviour will be regulated by regions or the NHS Management Executive.

It is well-known that hospital markets often display elements of monopoly. These arise for a variety of reasons. Barriers to entry to, and exit from, the market occur because of heavy investment costs. Spatial monopolies arise because patients' reluctance to travel for treatment, coupled with hospitals' need for a minimum patient/population catchment area, prevents hospitals locating in close proximity to each other outside of densely populated urban areas. This process has been reinforced in the UK because NHS planning has proceeded on the basis that the district general hospital should be largely self-sufficient and should serve a defined area. For all of these reasons, the absence of nearby rivals means that many hospitals are not subjected to competitive pressures. Evidence from the USA suggests that, in such markets, hospitals concentrate on non-price competition, usually through product differentiation (Robinson and Luft 1987; McLaughlin 1988). The result is prices above minimum, long-run costs and excess capacity.

While it is likely that many market areas within the UK will have elements of monopoly, this prospect is sometimes overstated. One empirical study of the degree of competition facing 39 NHS hospitals in the West Midlands Regional Health Authority found that only one-quarter of them were faced with degrees of market concentration that might necessitate antimonopoly measures (Appleby and Little 1990).

Even if the degree of competition between existing hospitals is insufficient to be relied upon to encourage efficiency, it is still possible that the threat of potential competitors might act as a spur to efficient behaviour. This is the essence of a contestable market. In such a market, competitors do not have to be actually present if they can be expected to enter the market when existing firms fail to operate efficiently or when they make excess profits. However, it is likely that even this possibility will be difficult to sustain in the case of competition between hospitals because the heavy sunk costs of existing providers will constitute a powerful barrier to new entrants. In the light of this restriction, some commentators have suggested that contestability could be applied to hospital managements. That is, the NHS Management Executive, or some other regulatory body, should be prepared to replace hospital managements if they fail to perform satisfactorily (Culyer and Posnett 1991). This arrangement would pose problems if doctors were involved in management, as replacing them would be more difficult than replacing non-medical managers. This prospect might also act as a disincentive for doctors to enter management, as required by the RM model.

The second aspect of the external environment about which there is uncertainty is the extent to which hospitals' activities will be regulated or managed. Already, the degree of regulation that will be placed upon the market has been extended some way beyond that envisaged originally, with the result that the system is now often described as an example of managed competition. The experience of NHS trusts provides a vivid example of increasing regulatory control. When the NHS reforms were introduced, trust status was presented as a means of offering greater freedom and autonomy for individual hospitals to manage their own affairs. The freedom to borrow from both the public and private sectors in order to fund capital expenditure was seen as an important element of their newly acquired autonomy. From the potential trust's perspective, this was seen as a means of addressing a longstanding problem, namely, the tight restrictions imposed by the Department of Health on their ability to undertake capital programmes.

However, granting greater freedom over borrowing was always likely to be problematic. As part of the public sector, trusts' borrowing forms part of the Public Sector Borrowing Requirement (PSBR). This means that the Treasury is bound to maintain a close interest in trusts' activities. In the event, each of the units that became first-wave trusts in April 1991 had their borrowing limits – known as external financing limits (EFLs) – set by the Department of Health in a way that exerted tight control on their ability to raise funds. Even stronger constraints were applied to the borrowing powers of the second-wave trusts. It is most unlikely that these controls will be relaxed so long as macro-economic management of the economy requires the government to be able to regulate public sector borrowing.

Elsewhere, subsidies for providers with especially high capital costs and restrictions on the freedom of GP fundholders to take out contracts which benefit their patients at the expense of non-fundholders' patients represent two more examples of strengthening regulation (Robinson 1992). All of these restrictions can be justified on the grounds that planned change is more likely to meet the multiple objectives of the health care system than a purely market-led approach. However, the tendency to introduce additional regulation on an *ad hoc* basis makes it difficult to predict how the market will perform. Moreover, over-rigid regulation could pose a threat to greater efficiency if it stifles the local freedom upon which the internal market is supposed to be based.

Hospitals and contracting

No matter what long-term uncertainties face the internal market, one area in which systems had to be developed rapidly during the first year of the reforms was in relation to service contracts. Contracts constitute the formal link between purchasers and providers of health care. They are the mechanism through which providers make clear the services they intend to supply and the terms and conditions on which they will be supplied. In essence, they are about the exchange of data, and about discussion and negotiation. The details of contracts agreed between purchasers and providers during the first year varied a good deal according to local circumstances. However, they were all based upon three main categories – block, cost and volume, and cost per case.

Under a block contract, access to a defined range of services and facilities is provided in return for an annual fee. Block contracts were particularly suited to the first year requirement of steady state, because they were able to reflect, albeit in contractual form, levels and patterns of activity that were already taking place. They were also the least demanding in terms of information requirements. Many purchasers simply took out block contracts with their local provider which reflected levels of activity and funding that were previously provided by the district general hospital within the pre-reform, unitary health authority. At the same time, however, even block contracts have been more specific than the old-style arrangements in terms of the requirements placed upon providers.

For the most part, block contracts have been used to ensure access to a defined range of facilities. However, it has usually proved necessary to forecast expected levels of activity. Variations in activity around indicative volumes were expected to be one of the main problems in operating block contracts. Providers might fail to use capacity to the full or treat more cases than had been agreed and funded. To cope with this problem, most block contracts specified ceilings and floors, which permitted some variation around the expected level of activity. If actual activity fell outside this range, cost and volume arrangements came into operation.

A cost and volume contract specifies that a provider will supply a given number of treatments or cases at an agreed price. It allows the service specification to be made more explicit than is generally the case with a block contract. Greater emphasis is placed upon services defined in terms of outputs, i.e. patients treated, rather than in terms of inputs, i.e. the facilities provided. If the number of cases exceeds the cost and volume agreement, extra cases have usually been funded on a cost per case basis.

Cost per case contracts are defined at the level of the individual patient. Because they obviously involve a considerable level of transactions costs, health authorities have mainly used cost per case contracts to fund treatments that fall outside of block or cost and volume contracts. Referrals by GPs to providers with whom districts did not have prospective contracts, i.e. extracontractual referrals, have been the main form of district purchasing

Table 1.1   Contracts for acute services 1991/92

Contract type	Number	Value (£m)	% of number	% of value
Block	1131	4346.5	40.7	60.4
Block with ceiling and floor	1179	2434.5	42.4	33.8
Cost and volume	169	314.1	6.1	4.4
Cost per case	108	17.6	3.9	0.2
RHA agency contracts on behalf of DHA	191	85.9	6.9	1.2
Total	2778	7198.6	100.0	100.0

Note: Based upon returns from 101 DHAs.
Source: NAHAT, Purchasers Survey, 1992.

Table 1.2   Providers for acute services contracts 1991/92

Type of provider	Number of contracts	Value (£m)	% of number	% of value
NHS provider within district	488	5610.1	17.8	78.6
NHS provider outside district	2161	1503.4	78.6	21.1
Private sector	13	1.5	0.5	0.0
Voluntary sector	67	9.4	2.4	0.1
Other	19	12.0	0.7	0.2
Total	2748	7136.4	100.0	100.0

Note: Based upon returns from 101 DHAs.
Source: NAHAT, Purchasers Survey, 1992.

covered by cost per case contracts. Many services bought by GP fundholders have also been covered by cost per case contracts.

As might be expected, the overwhelming majority of contracts taken out in 1991/92 were block contracts. Table 1.1 shows that 83 per cent of contracts taken out for acute services, by volume, were of this type – either simple block contracts or block contracts specifying ceiling and floor levels of activity. In value terms, the dominance of block contracts was even greater – representing 94 per cent of the total value of contracted services.

Table 1.2 shows that large, block contracts placed with NHS providers within the purchaser district accounted for the bulk of services by value in 1991/92. The size of these contracts – at an average value of £11.5 million – meant that they accounted for nearly 80 per cent of the total value of contracted services, even though they only represented about 18 per cent of the total number of contracts.

The dominance of block contracts placed within districts reflects the requirement of steady state contracting. Guidance offered by the NHS Management Executive (NHS ME 1991) stated that:

> Dramatic changes in activity would be likely to disrupt patient services, so that service specifications in 1991/92 will need to describe activity based on the current pattern of services, except where planned changes have been agreed with providers.

In the light of these requirements, the first year's contracting process on the part of most health authorities was mainly about developing the mechanics of a contracting system. Over time, however, as costing and pricing systems become more sophisticated, less reliance will be placed upon block contracts. Tariffs based upon more refined specialty costings, or even some form of diagnostic-related groupings, can be expected. This will increase the precision of pricing but may also lead to steeply rising transactions costs. This raises questions about the most appropriate contractual arrangements for the longer term.

Hospitals and contracting: the longer term

It has already become clear that the contracting process has incurred substantial costs. Setting up systems for recording, costing and billing has involved large investments in information systems. Many of these items of expenditure are non-recurring and will not be a source of higher costs in the future. But other costs will persist, particularly those associated with continuing transactions between purchasers and providers. These will constitute an additional source of costs that were not incurred under the pre-reform system.

Within the economics profession, fears that excessive transactions costs may be a substantial source of inefficiency has led to an approach which seeks to identify those factors which, if present, mean that market contracts will be expensive to write, complicated to execute and difficult to enforce (Williamson 1975, 1986). If these conditions apply, firms may choose to bypass the market and rely upon internal, hierarchical forms of organization instead. Hence, transactions that would otherwise have taken place in the market are dealt with internally through administrative processes. Put another way, firms and markets can be viewed as alternative methods of economic organization for handling transactions. The choice between them should depend upon their relative efficiency.

Three features which, taken together, can be expected to favour internal organization over market transactions are bounded rationality, opportunism and asset specificity.

Bounded rationality means that decision makers, while seeking to act in a rational manner, can only be expected to do so to a limited extent. The bounded nature of behaviour arises because the capacity for individuals to formulate and solve complex problems is necessarily limited. These limitations become particularly important when faced with uncertainty about the future. If it becomes very costly or impossible to identify all future contingencies and to specify adaptations to them, it may be more efficient to replace contract arrangements with internal organization.

Opportunism refers to behaviour whereby individuals can be expected to pursue their interests through devious means. They may seek to derive advantage from the selective or distorted disclosure of information, or by making false promises. Information may be manipulated in a strategic fashion and intentions may be misrepresented. The existence of opportunism means that uncertainty is introduced into contractual arrangements as neither party can rely on the other one honouring non-legally binding promises. In such a world, internal organization may be a more effective means of controlling opportunism.

Asset specificity arises when transactions require investment in assets – both physical and human – that are specific to these transactions. As such, the parties to a contract have a continuing interest in each other because the nature of the commodity being traded depends upon an ongoing supply relationship. This arrangement is a converse of a spot market, where deals are struck by anonymous buyers and sellers. With asset specificity, market competition is liable to break down, as existing suppliers will enjoy advantages in relation to new entrants.

Hence, the transactions cost approach suggests that when bounded rationality, opportunism and asset specificity are all present, internal organization is likely to be a more efficient method of economic organization than trade between separate firms. In the context of the NHS reforms, this consideration raises the obvious question: will transactions involving clinical services display these characteristics?

On the first characteristic – that of bounded rationality – there seems to be little doubt that this applies to the NHS. The nature of health and social care is highly complex, with major areas of uncertainty regarding, *inter alia*, the cost of individual services, their quality and, most important of all, measures of their outcome.

Whether opportunism will be a problem is less clear. The NHS is traditionally viewed as embodying a set of values – based upon collective responsibility and caring – which might be expected to exclude self-seeking and opportunistic behaviour. On the other hand, it would be naïve to suggest that the strategic pursuit of self-interest has not always represented an element of NHS behaviour, whether through corporate or professional vested interest. Whatever else it achieves, it seems extremely likely that the introduction of a more commercially-based approach will increase the incidence of this behaviour.

Asset specificity is another characteristic which seems to apply with particular force to health care services. Few services correspond to the simple type of consumer good which allows a person to enter a store, choose an item from the shelf, pay for it and disappear into the anonymity of private consumption. Much health care is a continuous, or at least a long-term, process involving treatment by a variety of agencies in many different contexts. This is especially true of long-term care and the treatment of chronic conditions. Even in the case of elective surgery, however, there is a complex chain stretching from pre-admission assessment to inpatient or day case treatment and through to postdischarge care. All of these considerations suggest that continuity in relations between purchasers and providers is likely to be important.

Taken together, therefore, there are strong reasons for believing that the conditions highlighted by the transactions cost approach are present in the NHS. One interpretation of how it might be expected to influence the contracting process between purchasers and providers has been put forward by Bartlett (1991). As he points out, block contracts have been the dominant form of contract in the short run. These specify an annual fee in return for access to a defined range of services. They are broad brush and do not endeavour to specify prices for every eventuality. For this reason, they are necessarily incomplete and subject to opportunism. In particular, Bartlett believes that, despite the creation of mechanisms for measuring performance, opportunistic behaviour could lead to reductions in the quality of service provision, to an overemphasis on prestige treatments and to an increase in organizational slack in the form of increased perks and side payments to staff. These can all be expected to raise the cost of services above the efficient level.

All of these considerations may be taken to suggest that efforts to create an internal market through the separation of purchaser and provider functions might be misplaced. However, before reaching this judgement some additional considerations need to be taken into account. Most notably, there is the role to be assigned to incentives. Much of the case for an internal market rests upon the belief that supply-side competition between rival providers will be a source of increased efficiency. It is recognized that there may well be extra transactions cost. However, the Government believes that efficiency gains in service delivery will more than offset these. Whether they will or not is an empirical question that cannot be answered with certainty at the moment. But the case for introducing an incentive structure for increased efficiency is a powerful one.

How can these apparently conflicting requirements be resolved? How can incentives be preserved but, in the light of transactions costs, the most efficient form of purchaser/provider organization be devised? Consideration of the theoretical literature and available empirical evidence suggests that one approach would be to encourage purchasers and providers to enter into long-term, stable relationships rather than to view their task as one of making spot market deals. Certainly, modern approaches to industrial organization and marketing emphasize the essentially collaborative nature of purchaser/provider relations (Davies 1991). Collaboration is a prerequisite for the effective sharing of information. In practice, this takes place far more widely in the private sector than is generally realized. The NHS should draw on this experience. At the same time, however, mechanisms for ensuring efficient behaviour will be necessary. If the market is to be regulated, this could be a responsibility of the regulatory body. In this connection, the concept of yardstick competition may be drawn upon. Yardstick competition is a device used by regulators which enables them to encourage efficiency in monopoly industries (Kay and Vickers 1990). It offers a means of defining clear standards of performance in terms of which both purchasers and providers may be assessed. In recent years, NHS performance indicators have been developed for a similar purpose. It is, however, unlikely that performance indicators in their present form, i.e. measures based primarily on inputs and activities, will provide the necessary information. New systems will need to be developed which, in the longer term, emphasize outcomes data.

With a system of yardstick competition in place, improvements in standards should be achievable through negotiation and mutually agreed action between purchasers and providers. However, there may be some cases where purchasers and/or providers believe that the comparative performance of the other party is substandard and where they are unable to reach agreement on strategies to rectify a situation. In such cases, the concept of contestability might be appropriate as a strategy of last resort. In short, the regulatory body may wish to retain the option for replacing management on either the purchaser or provider side of the market if it believes that there is no other way in which to encourage improved performance.

Conclusion

The internal market has been in existence since April 1991. During the first year of its operation, steady state requirements were imposed to prevent disruptions resulting from sudden change. These restrictions are being lifted slowly, although regulation is likely to remain a permanent feature of this market. Striking the right balance between greater freedom for hospitals and other units to manage their own affairs, and regulating their behaviour in the interest of wider objectives, will be a demanding task. The role of regulatory agencies in balancing objectives – whether as part of the NHS Management Executive or regional health authorities – is likely to prove particularly important if the lessons of the transactions costs approach lead to long-term contractual relationships between purchasers and providers rather than short-term competition between rival providers.

References

Appleby, J. and Little, V. (1990) 'Measuring Competition'. Paper presented to the Health Economists Study Group, Dublin, Summer.
Bartlett, W. (1991) *Quasi Markets and Contracts: A Market and Hierarchies Perspective on NHS Reforms*. Bristol, School of Advanced Urban Studies, University of Bristol.

Culyer, A. and Posnett, J. (1991) 'Hospital behaviour and competition', in A. Culyer, A. Maynard and J. Posnett (eds), *Competition in Health Care*. London, Macmillan.

Davies, G. (1991) 'Picking a philosophy', *Health Service Journal*, 7 March, 101, 20–1.

Glennerster, H., Matsaganis, M. and Owens, P. (1992) *A Foothold for Fundholding*. London, King's Fund Institute.

Ham, C. (1992) 'What future for the regions?', *British Medical Journal*, 305, 130–1.

Kay, J. and Vickers, J. (1990) 'Regulatory reform', in G. Majone (ed.), *Deregulation or Re-regulation? Regulatory Reform in Europe and the United States*. London, Pinter.

King's Fund Commission (1992) *London Health Care 2010*. London, King's Fund.

McGuire, A., Henderson, J. and Mooney, G. (1988) *The Economics of Health Care*. London, Routledge and Kegan Paul.

McLaughlin, C. (1988) 'Market responses to HMOs: price competition or rivalry?'. *Inquiry*, 25, 207–18.

NHS ME (1991) 'Working for Patients: Starting Specifications'. A DHA Project Paper. London, Department of Health.

Packwood, T., Keen, J. and Buxton, M. (1991) *Hospitals in Transition*. Milton Keynes, Open University Press.

Robinson, R. (1992) 'Health policy in 1991', in F. Terry and P. Jackson (eds), *Public Domain 1992*. London, Chapman Hall.

Robinson, J. and Luft, H. (1987) 'Competition and the cost of hospital care', *Journal of the American Medical Association*, 257(43), 3241–5.

Williamson, O. (1975) *Markets and Hierarchies: Analysis and Antitrust Implications*. New York, Free Press.

Williamson, O. (1986) *Economic Organisation: Firms, Markets and Policy Controls*. Brighton, Wheatsheaf Books.

2 Information policy in the National Health Service

Justin Keen

Introduction

The National Health Service (NHS) is on the horns of a dilemma. On the one hand it is committed to considerable investments in information technology (IT), principally as a consequence of the NHS Review (Secretaries of State 1989). Good data is crucial to the success of the new arrangements, and the speed of assimilation and transfer required demands that IT be used. On the other hand, there is increasingly open questioning within the NHS of the value of existing investments in IT, and it has become clear that the creation of an infrastructure for information exchange is a long-term goal rather than a short-term project. This questioning is complemented by external bodies such as the Audit Commission (1992) and national and NHS press. How should the NHS, particularly at national level, respond to this dilemma?

This chapter addresses the question by considering national information and IT policies and local experience of implementation, particularly in hospitals. As elsewhere in the public sector, the relationship between the centre and periphery has been analysed from a management perspective (Klein 1989; Ham 1992), but to a much lesser extent in terms of information and IT policy. The chapter has two main elements. The first outlines past and present national information and IT policies, by tracing the development of data collection systems and the gradual merging of thinking about management and IT. The second speculates on the future role of the centre in shaping information-related events out in the service, and considers some of the desirable characteristics of an information policy.

To begin, then, at the top. For strategies in the NHS to be implemented they must be communicated to the periphery, and this generally occurs by

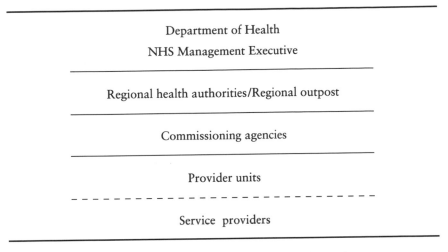

Department of Health

NHS Management Executive

Regional health authorities/Regional outpost

Commissioning agencies

Provider units

Service providers

Figure 2.1 'Building blocks' of information policy for hospitals.

either of two routes. One is to pass them down through successive administrative levels (Fig. 2.1). Before 1989 this was the usual route, reflected in the creation of central data collection systems and in the appropriation of different aspects of IT policy at each level. For example, many regional health authorities ran large IT systems for functions such as finance and personnel. Districts were the focus of Körner-related (see page 32) data collection activities, particularly relating to activity and finance data and, during the 1980s, individual hospitals increasingly implemented their own systems for assimilation of data. Within hospitals there was often a further distinction between systems for senior managers and those for professionals, with the different parties having their own 'languages'.

The other route is to engage directly with professional groups. In the 1970s and 1980s the Department of Health met doctors' representative groups to discuss and negotiate on many issues, though IT was not generally among them. The situation changed, though, with the advent of policies which combined management and IT: the negotiation of terms for the Resource Management initiative between the Department and Joint Consultants Committee (DHSS 1986) is good example. After a hiatus following the NHS Review, the NHS Management Executive and medical royal colleges are now negotiating again on issues such as 'common clinical languages' (that is, data definitions).

The second route emphasizes the singular nature of the NHS, where much power is concentrated at the periphery, most obviously in the hands of doctors. There are, not surprisingly, tensions between the centre and doctors – and to a rather lesser extent between nurses and other service providers. These have been reflected in the formulation of many policies down the years. It is a basic truth of policy-making that the best-laid plans can be subverted or simply fail, but the problem in the NHS seems particularly acute. In relation to IT, hospital staff will often have their own priorities, and these may differ from those of the centre. Thus doctors might argue for better operational systems for departments such as pathology and radiology, whereas the Management Executive backs systems to aid central monitoring or professional review. As IT becomes more (obviously) important in clinical and management processes, local negotiation about information and IT will influence the outcome of central policies.

The development of NHS Information policy to 1989

The development of information and IT-related policies in the NHS comprises three main strands. The first is the national data collection infrastructure, which has grown larger and more complex over the last decade. Second, there are policies specific to the implementation of IT, and third there are policies which combine management and IT issues.

Data collection

There has always been some form of data collection in the NHS, suggesting that someone somewhere has been thinking about data and information ever since its inception. Important milestones in the formulation of an explicit information policy were the Royal Commission on the NHS (1979), and the Griffiths Report (1983). The Royal Commission's report led to studies on a national data collection system and of mechanisms for calculating budgets; Griffiths built on the budgeting work. These reports remain important for two reasons. First, they represented concerted efforts to address some aspects of information policy, even if they were limited to formalizing data collection. Second, they left a legacy which is still with us today. Many hospital finance systems were designed to reflect the management budgeting approach advocated by Griffiths. This effectively committed hospitals to a top-down department- or specialty-based approach during the 1980s.

Perhaps the most important legacy is the national data collection system, originally devised by the Steering Committee on Health Service Information chaired by Edith Körner (DHSS 1982–4). Körner's system is still with us, and forms the basis of the national performance indicators. These have been widely criticized – perhaps condemned is a better word – principally on the basis that they reflect input and process measures, and largely omit outputs and outcomes. Moreover, though intended for local use they reflected a centralized view of the world, and so were of limited use to those who collected them. The practical consequence for local sites was that most of their data collection efforts went on data of little local relevance, and most felt they could not commit substantial extra resources to the collection of other, more relevant data.

IT-driven policies

The idea that the NHS should have a formal, national information policy seems to have surfaced first in the mid-1980s, with the publication of a small booklet by the IT Division of the DHSS outlining the need for a national strategy (DHSS 1986). The document marked the start of work at the centre in a number of areas. One was the development of a set of common data structures which could be used throughout the service to facilitate system design. The Common Basic Specification (CBS), as it came to be called, involved the construction of entity-relationship and other formal diagrams which were claimed to capture the essence of information flows throughout the NHS. The CBS was typical of the prevailing centre-led and data/IT-driven approach at the time: work on it has since been seriously questioned. The advent of open systems has rendered the approach obsolete and the NHS Review has radically changed information flows, emphasizing the need for flexibility in this area.

More generally, the document focused on data and systems, suggesting that the task in hand involved the identification of an appropriate IT infrastructure. There is no hint of any potential problems in implementation or use of systems. It is difficult to trace direct impacts on the wider service, though it does seem to have stimulated action in a number of areas where the centre could argue it had a legitimate concern, such as communications standards. But in retrospect IT policy was rather marginal to the NHS during the 1980s and did not appear high on the agenda of most managers and service providers.

Management processes and IT

To a striking degree, managers and service providers have always tended to generate their own information. Doctors and nurses have their own patient records and managers have developed finance and other information systems. That these divisions were not helpful was recognized by the DHSS and a number of attempts have been made to encourage sharing of information. The Griffiths Report led hospitals to implement new finance systems, with the intention that managers and doctors discuss financial information together. However, by 1985 it was already clear that while they were useful to finance managers, these systems were not popular with doctors, who felt that the reports they received were either unintelligible or inaccurate, or both. The centre felt that it was crucial to involve doctors in resource allocation decisions, so rethought its approach. In 1986 the Finance Division at the DHSS launched the Resource Management (RM) initiative at six pilot hospitals. RM had three distinct strands (Buxton *et al.* 1989): (1) collaboration between managers, doctors and (to a lesser extent) nurses in management processes; (2) new information systems and technology for managerial and clinical decision-making; and (3) the capacity for intentional change. With regard to information systems, the original thrust appears to have been to collect and use data, according to a simple mechanistic model: collect, analyse, interpret, act. Interestingly, however, RM turned out to be a mixed blessing. On the positive side, the pilot sites began to link management processes to information systems, and also learned a great deal about systems implementation. Less positively, RM threw up a series of intractable issues, which sites struggled to deal with. In particular, databases containing patient-based data proved difficult to implement, and service providers protested that data was incomplete or irrelevant. Most interesting of all, though, was that in the hands of hospitals RM ceased to be financially-driven and became concerned more with collection of accurate data on activities. Still, these developments were not replicated elsewhere until after the NHS Review, so that up to 1989 information was divided on a tribal basis.

This brief account emphasizes a number of points. First, the persistence of pre-Review structures, such as Körner, reminds us that the NHS Review has not swept the board. Rather, it is a superstructure built on what was there already. Second, the lack of any co-ordination of policy between the Finance and IT Divisions of the DHSS exemplifies the fragmented nature of information and IT policy in the 1980s. The centre did not speak with a single voice, so that co-ordinated implementation was unlikely. Third, policy was top-down in nature – policies were imposed rather than support provided. As subsequent events have shown, the desire for central control over data and IT remains powerful.

The NHS review and related developments: 1989 to 1993

The NHS Review of 1989 currently dominates the NHS policy agenda. The most striking element of the Review was the introduction of an internal market for health services, with purchaser and provider functions split formally. In addition to these headline-grabbing changes there were many other proposals, including endorsement of professional review of services (medical audit) and the formal involvement of service providers in management (in the Resource Management initiative and other policies).

In the immediate aftermath it was thought that a new infrastructure for data collection broadly consistent with the concept of an 'internal market' and with specified within-hospital activities needed to be implemented. Greater attention would have to be paid to the collection of quantitative data, as the operation of an internal market and activities such as medical audit required collection of volume, cost and quality data by providers, to a level of detail not previously countenanced in the NHS. Realizing this, the government made available considerable sums for the purchase of new computer systems. This went into supporting the new contractual relationships between purchasers and providers, and to both sides to support internal management processes.

Important investment decisions were made early on during the first flush of enthusiasm for the new arrangements. At that time there was no explicit, integrated information policy, so that IT was endorsed on a policy-by-policy basis. Hence money was made available for systems under the banners of purchasing, RM, medical audit and other policies, but it was not clear how the systems should be co-ordinated. For example, were RM and medical audit two sides of the same coin or two different coins? In addition, it was noted in Chapter 1 that the ultimate destination of the reforms is unclear. As a result IT was at best purchased on the basis of predictions about that destination, at worst to satisfy immediate perceived needs: the opportunity for error was great.

More recent government initiatives are also influencing data collection activities in hospitals. One is the Patient's Charter, which has led to a flurry of surveys to measure 'performance' against the standards laid down. The Charter focuses on process measures such as time spent waiting in out-patient clinics: it appears that data will have to be collected on a regular or even routine basis to monitor compliance. Again, the link between the Charter and other data collection activities has not been made explicit: hospitals seem simply to have added it to existing duties, rather than integrated it into them.

Hospitals have also made moves to monitor their own affairs more closely. One example is British Standard 5750: a number of hospital departments, notably those with high concentrations of technology, have attained or are seeking to achieve the standard. Similarly, many hospitals have signed up for the King's Fund Organizational Audit. One effect of the Review, then, has been to encourage hospitals to review their own internal information flows.

So, on an individual basis information and IT policies can be discerned. What is less clear, however, is whether these individual policies form a coherent whole. The Framework for Information Systems (Department of Health 1990) published after the Review makes no attempt to do so, and there is no obvious unifying objective (such as 'improving patient health outcomes') which could be used to fit policies together. Indeed, information policy in the three years following the Review lacked overall coherence, with particular policies being modified seemingly on the run. The Framework reflected this, in its attention to detail in individual areas while at the same time offering little to bind them together. It seems that the deep assumption driving policy at this time was that IT is both necessary and valuable. And underpinning this assumption was another, namely that all activities of interest could be described as numbers or in alphanumeric codes.

The effect of the Review on the selection of systems can be analysed in terms of explicit or implicit effects on information policy (Fig. 2.2). Perhaps the most striking characteristic of Figure 2.2 is the variety of different policies, each with their own objectives and effects, that contribute to NHS information policy. An extensive critique might point to any number of inconsistencies and omissions, but suffice here to say that information

		Scope	
		NHS-wide	New initiatives piloted at few sites
Impact on information policy	Explicit	Contracts for health services Resource management Medical audit Patient's Charter	Hospital information support systems
	Implicit	Value for money	Total quality management

Figure 2.2 Examples of post-Review policies.

policy lacked internal consistency or any clear relationship to broader policies. (Of course, many would argue that these broader policies are the problem: their fragmented nature makes a fragmented information policy inevitable.) The deep assumptions held centrally about the value of data and IT left no room for alternative notions. Yet it is difficult to maintain them and explain simultaneously why system implementation has so often been problematic or why available data is not used.

The Information Management and Technology strategy: something old, something new

The NHS Management Executive published its post-Review Information Management and Technology (IM&T) strategy at the end of 1992. It continues with some elements of previous policies but also points to a radical departure from the past. The strategy offers a five-point vision of future developments (Fig. 2.3). The continuity is reflected in four of the five, which suggest that local and national networks will be the focus of central initiatives. In particular, the encouragement of further integration of systems so that any data item is collected only once, and the assumption that management information will be derived from operational systems, confirm the key role of developments started under the RM and Hospital Information Support Systems (HISS) banners. The sharing of data across the NHS acknowledges the impact of contracting on data flows.

The commitment to a comprehensive national infrastructure has the same general flavour as past policies, but it is interpreted in a more concrete form. Each patient is to have a 10-digit NHS number (for the first time) and clinical data will be captured using new common clinical terms. A

- Information will be person-based
- Systems may be integrated
- Information will be derived from operational systems
- Information will be secure and confidential
- Information will be shared across the NHS

Figure 2.3 Strategic vision in the IM&T strategy.
Source: IMGME 1992

network of shared administrative registers holding basic patient details will be developed to replace existing isolated databases, and there will be an NHS-wide network for data, voice and radio communications.

In contrast, the endorsement of person-based systems is new to the NHS, although the idea has been around for several years in other organizations. Many private sector institutions have moved away from systems which hold data by function (e.g. banks holding separate data on current accounts, loans and mortgages) towards systems which hold all data about an individual in one place. In principle at least this enables them to tailor marketing and services to individuals. In the public sector the individual focus has been stimulated by the Citizen's Charter, which similarly promotes the idea of the individual as the focus of public services. This implies major change, not just in the organization of service delivery and in IT, but in the culture of the public sector. The move to person-based systems in the NHS is thus part of a more general trend. In broad terms, it suggests that collaboration between professionals in delivering services should be the norm, that the needs of individuals will be addressed directly, and that IT will be designed to promote integrated services.

Elements of this vision can already be discerned in hospitals, notably in nurses' preoccupation with providing information to patients, and the development of multidisciplinary care profiles. But enshrining it in national policy changes the scope of what might be possible. The potential advantages of person-based systems would seem to be obvious. Patients would see a service which has, in the main, been monolithic and unresponsive, transformed into one which treats them as individuals, offers integrated services and holds detailed personal medical records which are always easily accessible.

However, important problems will need to be resolved if this element of the strategy is to be successful. One lies in the tension between systems designed for command and control and those for supporting operational service delivery. It is simply not clear how person-based systems will be squared with those used for monitoring. It may be, for example, that the data recording needs of the two are rather different (Chapter 5 emphasizes this point). Another lies in the collection of large amounts of sensitive personal data in one place. It is possible to imagine a continuum of possibilities, from simple local and largely manual systems through to a complete medical record being available at a computer terminal. In the latter case, an individual's complete medical history might be available. This raises many questions, including patient access to information: will patients be able to review all data held on them? How, in practice, will this be reconciled with the need for security? A third problem (explored in Chapter 9) is that local political factors may militate against successful implementation. Although progress is being made in delivering co-ordinated multidisciplinary care in hospitals, powerful political forces will have to be overcome if all professionals are to share information routinely. These concerns should not be taken to imply that person-based systems are a bad idea. Rather, they are a potentially exciting development which will need a very great deal of careful thought before proceeding too far.

Can the strategy work?

Just as there are possibilities and problems with specific elements of the IM&T strategy, so there are with the strategy as a whole. Given that it is likely to evolve over time, it is sensible to consider issues in general terms. On the positive side, the centre has enunciated a strategy with some clear priorities, which should help both the NHS and suppliers formulate their own strategies. The strategy deals with themes such as networking, and so offers a means of linking hitherto isolated initiatives; the place of those initiatives in the larger scheme of things should be clearer. There are also signs that the relationship between information and management processes is recognized, though the focus remains on data and technology rather than information.

   To set against these points, though, are five areas of concern. The first relates to the tensions inherent in the stated policies, noted earlier. The relationship between person-based and management information systems needs close attention.

   The second concern is the vagueness of the prescription. To set a broad framework for developments, particularly in an era of trust hospitals, would seem to be sensible but it does leave a great deal of room for error. For example, the place of finance data is not clear. Will it be linked to person-based data, with a view to costing episodes of care? Or does it fit in at a higher level? Another example is imaging data, on which the strategy is silent. It is already possible to foresee a time when radiology departments are fully computerized, with conventional X-rays replaced with screen-based images. This offers the possibility of concentrating radiology services, with images taken in one place and reported on in another: radiologists could report on images for a large geographical area from a central location. This would depend on networks capable of handling image data – they would have to be high speed and high capacity. At present it seems that networks are being planned to carry other types of data: failure to consider imaging data now would greatly add to the cost of wiring up for it later.

Third, the strategy both endorses existing IT developments and proposes a radical departure. The task of bridging the old and the new points to a need for a change strategy. While the need for better training and development is recognized, it remains to be seen whether this will bring the understanding required to make the bridge: and the likely difficulty of this task emphasizes the problems that the vagueness of the strategy may bring. Additionally, the legacy of existing IT needs to be addressed: to what extent can HISS, RM or audit systems be harnessed to provide person-based systems? Or should some of them be ditched?

Fourth, the focus of the IM&T strategy is still largely on data and IT. Consideration of political issues is absent, as in earlier policy statements. This raises the concern that political barriers will not be tackled and system implementation will become an end in itself: like Körner and the CBS, the mere existence of the infrastructure is counted as success. Perhaps the landscape will simply be covered with IT. The hope here must be that the success of the strategy in practice depends on the co-ordinated efforts within and between organizations, and that any problems that arise will have to be treated as management issues rather than narrow technical ones.

The fifth area of concern is that the centre is seeking to control local investments. Notably, all purchases over £0.5 million are to be vetted by the NHS Management Executive. It could be argued that this is consistent with the strong regulatory framework that may evolve (see Chapter 1). However, it rests on two beliefs – that controlling procurement processes will help to ensure good use of ITs, and that the centre has a legitimate management role in the information-related affairs of purchasers and trusts. Both beliefs are open to challenge. The policy may be a response to head-line-grabbing computer failures, but if so it is not clear that it will work: it is difficult to think of examples of systems where the centre has both kept a tight lid on costs and made a decisive contribution to a successful initiative.

The value of an IM&T strategy

The potential problems with the new IM&T strategy raise a deeper question: what is the likely success of any such strategy? In the NHS, with change occurring in a mix of the planned and unplanned, the need for good strategy formulation would seem to be unarguable. To an important extent the NHS remains a centralized organization, with the Review, if anything, strengthening the hand of the centre. The government and NHS Management Executive continue to set priorities, particularly on politically sensitive topics such as waiting lists. There is also a more general political overlay, for example the Patient's Charter and the concern with quality. But the Review was supposed to be about devolving responsibility for decision-making. Given this, is a clear national IM&T strategy desirable? And is it possible, or is policy doomed to be fragmented and subject to ever-changing priorities? Two questions seem germane.

First, what are the goals of information strategies? Explicitly to improve patient outcomes? Inform and educate patients? To cement trust between managers and professionals? To get systems in place? The answer might be any or all of these. Merely asking the question highlights the problem: how can a centrally determined strategy work if it depends on local sites pursuing multiple goals, where those goals may not be shared between centre and periphery?

Perhaps the problem lies in the word strategy. It could be viewed as introducing a new *framework* for the collection and exchange of data. Thus one role for the Management Executive is to set a national framework which helps to ensure a variety of standards are adhered to. Interfaces between systems are one area, clear data definitions another. There is, therefore, a broad choice between attempting to impose or negotiate policy from the centre and helping to provide an infrastructure. In the latter case, it is left to local sites to exploit the infrastructure to their own ends. And if they are to exploit it properly, they may also need help in understanding what it can do for them: they need to be become 'informated' (Zuboff 1988), i.e. understand their role and how to use information to deliver services effectively. Such a focus on local understanding would place the strategy firmly in the management domain.

One problem with a strategy that seeks to enable local initiatives is that it runs the risk of becoming an end in itself. Those responsible for (say) a national network may rightly be satisfied with implementing it: but it would be an island, not part of the main. The key is to have local sites use it, and this will require a merger of management and technical interests. Another problem concerns the ownership of a strategy. To take a concrete example, who owns a national data network? One answer might be British Telecom or Mercury, were they to provide the infrastructure; or the NHS Management Executive might retain control. Whoever owns the physical network, someone will have to take responsibility for data-flows. These issues hint at a need for a network regulator, who would monitor network owners and users: a regulator might be part of or separate from the NHS Management Executive and be responsible, *inter alia*, for protecting patient interests. In determining the goals for the IM&T strategy then, issues of ownership and regulation must be addressed.

Second, what are the effects of national initiatives on the ground? We know remarkably little about the impact of earlier initiatives, though some clues can be gathered together. These suggest allocating central monies to particular systems is no guarantee of success, at least as defined by the centre. On an anecdotal level, it seems that several post-Review IT-related initiatives have run into trouble: empirical evidence would be very helpful.

It is tempting to suppose that the information and IT elements of national initiatives go the way of other initiatives, with local sites finding ways of subverting or ignoring them. It might also be that national initiatives have a tendency to remove the scope for local discretion, and so may reduce the incentives for local ownership and understanding. But the fact is that we don't really know.

The question of the relative merits of a top-down national strategy and an enabling framework reflects the wider debate over the nature of the changes taking place in the NHS. It is not possible at present to take the argument further without more information: but unfortunately it is not possible to wait until the dust settles before deciding on what to do next. What might be the desirable characteristics of a national information policy? Many could no doubt be listed: a few are outlined here.

1 *Address existing problems.* An information policy must recognize and address the problems the NHS faces in defining what it does, implementing systems and integrating information and management. Policy concerns would thus include, *inter alia*, the technical skills base and project management.
2 *Impose where necessary.* There seems to be no alternative to simply handing down such things as common data definitions if contracting and other processes are to work. Of course, these need to be negotiated with representatives of relevant groups first.
3 *Enable where necessary.* In circumstances where imposition would not work – or be counterproductive – the centre needs to encourage the periphery. This might take various forms, such as undertaking to develop and maintain a national data network or supporting promising local initiatives (without meddling in them). But enabling requires a merging of management and technical concerns.
4 *Use incentives and exploit governance structures.* The 'internal market' can be viewed as a mechanism for changing incentives to hospital managers and clinical staff and for imposing new governance structures, notably in determining the composition of trust boards. The extent to which they encourage people to enter into discussions using quantitative data should be reviewed, as should their likely impact on IT implementation.
5 *Examine the relationship between information, IT and management.* This is linked to the last point, but is also a major training and development issue. To a large extent the remainder of this book is a commentary on this relationship.
6 *Be consistent.* This can be difficult in the public sector, but there seems no reason why (say) person-based systems should not remain a central plank of policy for the rest of the decade. The NHS often seems like a dress shop, with particular ideas in fashion for a few months which then disappear from sight. This needs to end, and the centre can help by persisting with core policies.

In the end, the long-term outcome of current policies will depend less on the form of words in documents than on how the Management Executive and the wider NHS handle the strategy. If it is allowed to evolve in a sensible way, it is reasonable to hope that things will get better. If imagination and insight are lacking, then the future will mirror the present.

Conclusions

The NHS has a modest track record in using information and implementing IT. Early national policies largely failed to address these problems, and in particular focused on ITs rather than integrating information and management. The IM&T strategy takes steps in the right direction, but there are a number of areas that will require close attention if it is to be successful. The balance between benign imposition of standards and enabling innovation will be difficult to strike, but certainly worth the effort if it can be achieved.

References

Audit Commission (1992) *Caring Systems*. London, HMSO.

Buxton, M., Packwood, T. and Keen, J. (1989) *Resource Management: Process and Progress*. Uxbridge, Brunel University.

Department of Health (1990) *Framework for Information Systems: The Next Steps*. London, HMSO.

DHSS (1982–4) *Steering Group on Health Service Information* (Chair: Edith Körner). London, DHSS.

DHSS (1986) *A National Strategic Framework for Information Management in the Hospital and Community Health Services*. London, DHSS.

Griffiths, R. (1983) *NHS Management Enquiry* (The Griffiths Report). London, DHSS.

Ham, C. (1992) *Health Policy in Britain*, 3rd edn. Basingstoke, Macmillan.

Klein, R. (1989) *The Politics of the NHS*, 2nd edn. London, Longman.

NHS ME (1992) *IM&T Strategy Overview*. London, Information Management Group/NHS ME.

Packwood, T., Keen, J. and Buxton, M. (1991) *Hospitals in Transition*. Milton Keynes, Open University Press.

Royal Commission on the NHS (1979) Cmnd 7519. London, HMSO.

Secretaries of State for Health, Wales, Scotland and Northern Ireland (1989) *Working for Patients*, Cm 555. London, HMSO.

Zuboff, S. (1988) *In the Age of the Smart Machine*. London, Heinemann.

Section 2
The practitioner perspective

In an organization as large as the NHS examples of good and bad practice can be found in any area of endeavour. This is certainly true of information and IT, where some sites seem determined not to use what is available to them but others are finding new and creative ways to examine their management and clinical practice. Section Two presents evidence from the latter group, on topics ranging from large system implementation to the development of inter-professional collaboration.

In Chapter 3 Wally Gowing describes his experiences in implementing a hospital information support system (HISS). HISS serves as an example of the essential truth that one hospital can implement a system successfully and another fail completely with identical technology. It is naïve to talk of 'good' or 'bad' IT – rather there are good and bad projects in more or less favourable environments.

Andy Kennedy discusses training and development in Chapter 4. So much guidance on these issues – both generally and as they relate to IT – is vague and impossible to translate into local practice. Andy shares some hard-won experiences from the front line, and relates them to current thinking about good practice in developing organizations. Chapters 5 and 6 provide clinical input to the arena of information. The fusion of management and clinical concerns is reflected in Chapter 5, where three members of the Royal Hampshire County Hospital, each of whom has served in both management and clinical positions, discuss the ways in which they have integrated information into management processes. They show that the concept of defining information requirements is not an arid academic activity but at best a positive exercise in developing an understanding of how a hospital works and devising systems to monitor its workings. Chapter 6 examines an area which has proved frustrating in many hospitals: nursing systems. Rebecca Malby and Jane Clayton discuss the failures of past systems and point to a rather more hopeful future where nurses have a positive role in co-ordinating service delivery. Finally, in Chapter 7 John James takes a different perspective, that of the commissioner of health services. Commissioning agencies now have a major role in shaping the nature of services that hospitals deliver. The chapter explores the nature of the relationship between commissioners and hospitals, and discusses the information that should flow between them to underpin that relationship.

3 Operational systems

Wally Gowing

Introduction

Operational systems are a basic necessity for most organizations in operating their businesses. They serve the purpose of supporting the day-to-day operations of an organization by recording the details of transactions, events and staff activity happening within that organization. They also support staff in undertaking their work and this applies in most business sectors; examples of use of operational systems are real-time manufacturing systems, stock control systems, point-of-sale systems and bank finance systems. Such operational systems also provide information to support the management of the particular area of activity and for input to the overall management of the organization.

NHS hospitals have a diverse range of activities, covering direct patient treatment; patient administration such as outpatient appointments; running departments, such as radiology, pathology, catering, sterile supplies and works; and financial and administrative functions. Information systems can contribute much to the operation of these and other areas, but it has only been recently that such operational systems have been considered a normal part of the NHS. The basic tenets are that:

1 Information is a key element in running hospitals, in that it is vital to all activities and operations undertaken in hospitals.
2 Technology is an enabling mechanism to process, more efficiently than any other means, data into information to support the operations of staff, departments and hospitals.
3 Information technology (IT) brings the ability to collect, store and recall information at many points and times, well beyond the traditional manual and case-note methods.

Just as the introduction of IT has had profound effects in many industries and businesses, so IT can be harnessed through good operational systems to significant advantage for the NHS.

The background – Körner, resource management and contracting

Computer systems have developed within the NHS along the lines common to many other businesses. Basic financial processes, such as payroll and general ledgers, were computerized first. Use of computer systems in patient areas was restricted to pioneering enthusiasts, until major developments of systems for patient administration commenced in the 1970s. The costs of such systems were high and there was considerable resistance within the NHS to this use of resources. This resistance is naturally strong, as this reduces funding available to direct health care. However, three major initiatives, namely Körner, Resource Management (RM) and the 1989 NHS reforms, have led to increased requirements for operational information systems.

Körner

By the early 1980s, there was considerable pressure on the NHS for comparative information on performance. However, there was little relevant standard data for making comparisons. Data has been collected within the NHS since its inception, but ensuring standards across the NHS has proved difficult. A Department of Health (DoH) committee under the chairmanship of Dame Edith Körner was set up to address these issues and significant steps were taken in the period 1984–8. The original aims of the Körner Committee were to:

1 Ensure that standard data was collected within particular sectors, such as acute hospitals, across the NHS to a common set of definitions.
2 Provide local and national management statistics and information from data collected as a byproduct of operational activities.

These aims were admirable and, if achieved, were to support the development of general management in the NHS. However, the real outcome was that 'implementing Körner' became an end point in itself. Whilst Körner returns may have been helpful to the DoH, their usefulness within health authorities, in hospitals and for doctors has been extremely questionable.

Körner did, however, ensure that information and IT were put on the management agenda and the realization that operational systems in areas such as radiology were needed to enable staff to cope with the resulting volume of data collection. The need for systems in turn led to resources being assigned to this area and particularly to the establishment of information and IT departments.

Resource management

The Resource Management Initiative was primarily a cultural development for acute hospitals, concerned with bringing doctors, as major initiators of resource usage, into the management process. To achieve this, significant improvements in management information were required. Funding was available for key systems, namely a Case Mix Management System (CMMS) and ward nursing, but such systems required feeding from other operational systems, such as laboratory, theatres or radiology and required links to financial systems. As this and other chapters show, the RM Initiative added to the pressure for suitable operational systems and associated developments in information systems and their use.

Contracting

The 1989 NHS reforms brought fundamental change to the operation of the NHS with concepts of purchaser and provider organizations contracting with each other for the provision of healthcare services. This structure requires, ultimately, that each item of healthcare activity is recorded and costed in some form. Therefore, with contracting came the need for providers for:

1 Improved definition of what services are available and provided, stated in terms of what the service is, how much is provided and at what cost.
2 Understanding, monitoring and management of volumes and types of activity undertaken within the contracts.
3 A reduction in the reporting time cycle so that data are available speedily, in as accurate and reliable a manner as possible and in a form suitable for analysis and presentation to enable the business to operate effectively against contracts.

To achieve this across the large volumes and the wide range of activities undertaken within hospitals requires sophisticated and robust operational computer systems and has led to IT being a key component in provider management.

Internal initiatives

As has been outlined above, many developments took place in information-related work because of requirements placed upon hospitals. However, developments also took place more locally, mainly stemming from a bottom-up approach as individuals saw the potential for information systems in their area of operation. Whilst many staff may have seen the need for systems at a grass roots level, the efforts of the enthusiastic amateurs and companies addressing specific department needs (like blood banks) were restricted until the advent of minicomputers and, more particularly, microprocessors enabled computer systems to be financially and practically

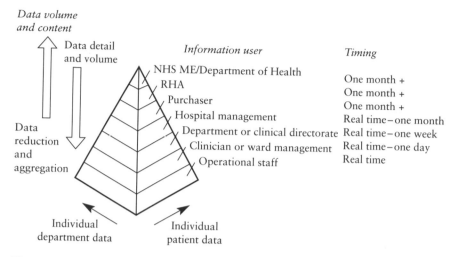

Figure 3.1   The information pyramid.

within the reach of most hospitals. Due to the high costs, during the late 1970s and early 1980s, of developing software and of suitably sized hardware to cope with hospital computing needs, consortia were formed for the development of systems such as the Inter-Regional Collaboration (IRC) Patient Administration System (PAS) or the Financial Information Project (FIP) Association for developing community, paramedic, theatre- and ward-based systems. In other areas, standard regional systems were developed, such as the Trent PAS or the South West PAS. These initiatives were aimed at providing solutions, which were not commercially available, for a restricted niche market which did not appear to be sufficiently funded or commercially viable. These developments took place in 'third generation' development environments and necessitated a significant workload in system maintenance. However, further developments were hampered by the consortia mechanisms, fund-raising problems and the development environments themselves. Such systems tended to be geared to providing good on-line transaction processing capabilities, with limited ability to utilize data beyond standard statistical reporting through batch processing. These systems are now being further developed or redeveloped in fourth generation environments.

Data collection, operational systems and management information model

From the lessons learned from earlier operational systems, a model (Fig. 3.1) can be developed of the relationship between different users, their need for information and the levels of aggregation and data filtering. This model is based upon:

1 Full sets of data on patients and associated activities being collected and used for operational purposes by 'front line' staff in all departments, such as medical secretaries, doctors, nurses, technicians and administrative staff.
2 The data set being reduced in content on a need basis (a physician may need only to know an X-ray on a specific patient was reported as 'normal', whilst the radiologist requires a full set of data to make that decision).
3 The data set being aggregated to aid the operation of ward, department or clinical directorate.
4 Further aggregation and reduction across the hospital to provide hospital management with information to manage the whole organization.
5 Subsets of data being provided in aggregate and contract minimum data set (CMDS) form, such as individual finished consultant episodes (FCE), to purchasers.
6 Aggregated subsets of data are required for external monitoring by the Regional Health Authority (RHA) and by the NHS Management Executive.

The model has a time dimension. Essentially the bottom layer must operate in real time, whilst for the layers above, the time lag between data entry and information receipt moves from real time to reporting on a regular periodic basis, such as monthly.

The essential difference between real-time use of operational systems and postevent use is that the latter tends to be a retrospective examination of mainly aggregated data. This is to enable comparisons between individual or cumulative group activity against standards or norms, similar to examining expenditure against budget levels. A key point is that clinicians and managers are operating from the same set of base data.

Hospital operational systems

Patient-based systems

The primary focus of hospital operational systems needs to be the patient. It is the patient who provides the rationale for a service, and therefore data and information about patients should be the basis of any system. Patients relate to staff and facilities (such as outpatient clinics), which in turn need to feed into resource use files: patient data can then be linked to resource use. Some facilities, such as a sterile supplies unit may have no direct relationship to patients but may be related to staff and other facilities.

Systems and their user departments

All hospital departments can utilize information systems to support their operations. The list below identifies systems applicable to hospital departments. Hospitals are organized in a variety of ways, so it is more straightforward to link system requirements to functions, rather than departments:

1 *Patient administration*, covering master patient index, referral letters, waiting lists, outpatient scheduling and clinic administration, inpatients (providing admissions, discharges and transfers (ADT) facilities), clinical coding, contracting, billing and Patient's Charter monitoring.
2 *Clinical systems*, covering care planning, pharmacy, radiology, pathol ogy, maternity, accident and emergency (A&E), genito-urinary medicine (GUM), theatres, therapies, clinical and medical audit, and systems for specialist departments, such as electrocardiographic service (ECG) or intensive treatment units (ITU).
3 *Support Services*, covering results reporting, order communications, nurse management, catering, hospital sterile supplies unit (HSSU), works departments, materials management and stock control.
4 *Financial Services*, covering general ledger, accounts payable, accounts receivable and fixed assets.
5 *Management Systems*, covering CMMS for resource usage and management information reporting, decision support systems (DSS) and executive information systems (EIS).

Information systems can be created to meet all the functions outlined above. This can be achieved on an individual function basis, through a collection of linked systems or through one integrated system. The first approach can be termed the standalone departmental systems approach, the latter two by the collective name of Hospital Information Support System or HISS. Ideally, HISS should incorporate all functions to provide a whole hospital system, but the term is more usually used to cover patient administration, clinical, elements of support services and management systems. (This is covered more on pages 45–49). HISS systems are derived mainly from products developed for hospitals in the USA, which tend to look for complete solutions from one supplier.

Characteristics and principles of operational systems

A checklist of desirable characteristics of operational systems can be derived from empirical study. Hospital systems operate in a difficult and unusual environment in that many are required to be in action 24 hours per day, every day. Ideally, operational systems should have:

1 *Data collection facilities*, which are easy to use and based on facilities (such as windows and use of colour screens) and should be menu-driven. The use of light pens and bar code devices reduce keyboard use and minimize potential transcription errors. Data entry facilities should include facilities for mandatory fields and routine validation checks between data elements. With complex modules, facilities such as 'hot

keys' to allow rapid transfer between screens in different parts of the system, should be available. Data collection should be reduced to once and once only and should be available to all modules, e.g. change of address affected across the entire system, if linked multiple module systems are used.

2 *A consistent user interface*, with the same style of interface for all users and modules. This decreases training requirements and maximizes the access points to the system.

3 *Flexibility of presentation, operation and capability built in*. The way systems are used varies from hospital to hospital and over time. It is vital, therefore, that the systems are capable of being adapted to local and other changing circumstances. Examples are the need to provide facilities to shape a system to local hospital organization and practice, such as moving clinical coders out to wards and consultants' offices. These can be achieved in system presentation to users through the use of appropriate 'look-up' tables or dictionaries or by ensuring that a system function can be fulfilled by staff operating centrally or on a distributed basis. Systems need to be able to be adaptable to changing requirements, such as new data collection and information demands. An example of this would be for PAS outpatient modules to allow Patient's Charter monitoring information needs to be coped with.

4 *Sufficient system capacity to enable the system to operate effectively*. This means that there must be enough terminals and more than adequate processing capacity and memory storage. For the system to be seen in a positive light by users, there must be rapid response times, normally required to be subsecond, and minimal downtime.

5 *Reporting facilities on all data items*. This is vital to ensure that all information requirements can be met and as an aid to optimizing data quality through the production of standard 'delinquency' reports.

6 *Parallel training database facility*, so that staff can be trained without affecting the live system.

7 *Good security facilities*, to ensure that access to data is controlled with user types linked to specific system facilities and, if necessary, to specific terminals. Audit trails to link data entry and editing to users are required to enable security checks to be undertaken and to enable assessment of training issues to be undertaken.

8 *Technical robustness built in*, with features like mirror discs or fault tolerance, to ensure that the system will provide the consistent operational support required by hospital staff, if necessary for 24 hours per day.

These operational characteristics are individually important but collectively essential for a system to have credibility. For example, if a system once loses credibility through being unreliable or incapable of producing relevant data, then it is an uphill task to gain acceptance and to make any efficiency gains through the use of the system, as users will look to other methods of supporting their activities. However, it is likely that not all features are built into systems as technology may not allow this or costs may prohibit meeting all requirements.

There are inevitably tradeoffs between the different characteristics and local circumstances which will dictate priorities. For example, in selling a system a vendor will meet specific requirements, but will offer a lower price to reduce the levels of flexibility built into the system, so that the hospital has to return to the vendor for changes to meet small variations in the use of the system. Another example is that hospitals often compromise on system capacity by purchasing the minimum number of peripheral devices possible in order to be able to afford a system, but with the intention of purchasing more terminals when funds permit. This is fine, so long as the processor or key communications devices are also capable of being upgraded.

Any compromises that may have to be made must be seen in the light of the long-term development of the system, in that such compromises should not preclude extending the use of the system. The various factors listed above can be prioritized in their impact on the selection of an operational system for a particular requirement. Obviously if the compromises are too great, for example if there is no upgrade path or the system cannot perform key functions, then the system should not be purchased.

Operational systems must be designed for use with the following principles in mind:

1 Data required for management purposes must be an integral part of data required to undertake day-to-day activities.
2 Data collection must act as and be seen as a natural part of the work of staff involved.
3 Data collected must be relevant to or affect the data collector or user in such a way that an adequate feedback loop exists. This is needed to ensure data is collected, to maximize opportunity for data accuracy and to improve timeliness of producing information.
4 Operational systems must be designed with online transaction processing optimized to minimize the impact on frontline staff. Operational systems must have facilities to enable appropriate information to be generated through reports which select or aggregate data; preferably facilities should be available to allow some interactive analysis, rather than total reliance on overnight batch runs.
5 The only data medical staff will believe is that data collected from or by medical staff directly. It has long been part of the game for doctors and management (with information staff in tow) to sit on opposite sides of the table and describe each other's information as 'rubbish'.

The operational characteristics outlined above should form part of a description of the requirements of any operational system for a hospital. The requirements will vary and should reflect the differences, especially in organization and culture, between hospitals. These requirements should be complemented by the technical standards for the system and an indication of the changing NHS systems environment the new system will be working within.

Technical standards and fitness for purpose

The NHS has a commitment to comply with computer industry standards, in particular the use of open systems and OSI (the International Standards Organization's Open Systems Interconnection). To enable separate systems to interwork, this approach is the obvious route to remove many of the problems created within the NHS by developments in totally disparate operating environments. This approach should also reduce the cost of hardware by ensuring that any of a number of standard Unix-type processors can be purchased to provide the 'box' on which the system can operate.

It is vital to ensure that the capability to communicate electronically through standard mechanisms, such as EDIFACT (the United Nations standard for Electronic Data Interchange for Administration, Commerce and Transport), over OSI-based networks is available with systems that are to provide data to other NHS bodies. With the advent of the NHS network providing a national network backbone from the mid-1990s, the ability to transfer data electronically will be a requirement for hospitals and their computer systems. Much of this messaging may be handled by other computers, normally PCs, acting as a translator between the hospital system and the outside world.

When purchasing computer systems, however, the primary issue has to be the fitness for purpose of the system to provide the necessary functionality to enable the hospital or department to operate effectively, with standard compliance on operating systems as a secondary issue. The reasons for this are twofold. First, operating systems are used within the closed environment of the hospital. It is more appropriate, therefore, that the hospital determines its own strategy on how its systems will work co-operatively, and this could be through an operating environment which is proprietary, but is comprehensive within the hospital. Second, open operating systems, such as UNIX, are not necessarily optimized for online transaction processing, nor do they necessarily meet the stringent security requirements for hospital operational systems. If a non-standard route is chosen, assurances are required from the software supplier that they will migrate their software to an open platform as soon as is feasible and effective.

Facing future needs

Whenever specifying and examining systems, allowance must be made for the imminent introduction of some new areas of information systems development within the NHS. These areas include linking operational systems to external systems, such as GP systems and to the NHS Administrative Register (NHSAR). Additionally, allowance must be made for the revised unique patient identifier in the form of the new NHS number, and the capacity to record data about the outcomes of NHS treatment needs to be considered.

The GP links should bring significant benefits to the operation of the NHS in providing mechanisms for reducing the time taken to communicate between GPs and hospital doctors on reporting test results, for making referrals and seeking appointments. The NHSAR offers the prospect of improved basic information about individuals and their demography, by enabling basic patient data to be checked against or collected from the local AR.

These developments will place demands on hospital operational systems in ensuring that such communications can be handled and the data utilized appropriately. There are also likely to be significant organizational impacts as the protocols for using external systems to book outpatient appointments, for example, will need to be worked through. This emphasizes the need for flexibility in the design and structure of operational systems and a clear understanding with the system vendor of how such developments are to be implemented. These should be covered in any contract for the supply of a system.

Developing a strategy

Starting out

In determining whether to undertake any large-scale information systems development, a strategy is required in which to frame potential developments. A strategy has to be local and is dependent upon the systems currently installed. It should cover all the functions of a hospital and be related to the purposes of developments. In turn, these developments have to be seen in the light of the hospital's overall business needs and there should be a clear relationship between the hospital's business strategy and operational systems strategy.

A strategy for hospital operational information systems must recognize that a hospital is a large organization, and systems to support its operation are major undertakings. One option is to implement a HISS (Fig. 3.2). HISS is defined by the HISS Central Team as 'an integrated patient-based IT environment covering applications of both a hospital-wide (for example PAS) and departmental (for example pathology) nature, together with a terminal and data communications network and an order communications system'. Applications in a HISS environment must operate in an integrated manner ensuring that data is entered once and once only and is then made available wherever required in the system, to be retrieved from any other terminal on the hospital network. The HISS Central Team argue that HISS can be worked towards on an incremental basis through three levels:

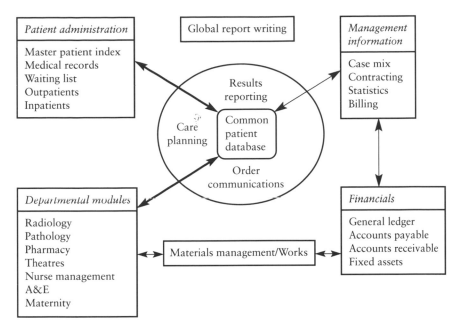

Figure 3.2 The integrated hospital information support system.

1 Linkage of patient demographic data between systems.
2 (1) plus results enquiries across different systems.
3 (2) plus order communications to allow orders to be placed from wards.

The cornerstones to either standalone systems or HISS are the PAS and networking facilities. This is because the PAS master patient index and functions are utilized to drive the systems, with the communications network providing the links to all users. Many strategic reviews of operational systems take place when the use of local PAS systems is examined. Whilst it may not be possible to gain access to sufficient funding for implementing a whole new set of operational system facilities, it is important to determine the strategic direction at this time. A particular direction or solution should be chosen and the implementation can follow a 'big bang' or incremental approach. In either event, the first steps should include PAS replacement and networking. If possible, results reporting should be included in this step.

HISS versus departmental standalone systems

As indicated earlier, there are basically two approaches to providing operational systems across hospitals, either through departmental standalone systems or through HISS. There are arguments for and against each approach. However, whilst departmental systems can provide a focus for the well-being of, and aid the efficiency of departments, unless the systems are linked in real time to other systems, they do not provide any additional contribution to the overall efficiency and effectiveness of the hospital. There are high levels of interdependence between the different operational areas of hospitals, such as X-ray with A&E departments, with wards, and with outpatient clinics, such that there is a significant need to share information between departments.

Within hospitals, therefore, there is a need to share data to aid efficiency and effectiveness of systems, to remove duplication of data and to provide value for money. The volumes of data held within hospitals and the related computer systems are large and, if systems are not integrated, much of it can be held in several different systems. For example, an average district general hospital may have a master patient index of 400,000, which in itself requires significant storage, and much of which may be held repetitively in several departmental systems. There is also an increasing need to produce patient data summaries across departments, so as to aid care processes and access to data by staff and GPs.

Investing in a HISS ensures that departments do not operate as islands, and indeed forces different parts of hospitals to talk to each other in the development and implementation of systems. From this, integration of systems assists in the integration of the organization, as there is a need for common language, such as agreement on descriptions of procedures, for example X-rays, in order to ensure that there are no ambiguities or misunderstandings. Following a HISS route may cause one or more departments to compromise on solutions in their area of operation, as the system may not be the optimum solution for that department, but is contributing to the overall increase in the effectiveness and efficiency of the hospital.

Justifying HISS and bringing benefits

When computers were first introduced, they were used in supporting tasks and automating processes, such as large-scale ledgers or payrolls. Where computers are used in 'robotic' mode, such as in car construction or in computer-controlled manufacturing, such as metal milling, there can be reductions in numbers of staff as the processes are automated. However, in hospitals, such staff reductions are likely to be minimal. This is because the computer systems are not taking the place of anyone, but rather the systems are there to support staff in labour-intensive activities, which are not capable of being automated. So, justifying operational systems on a pure cost–benefit basis in terms of direct savings may not be feasible. It is possible to assign monetary values to some benefits of HISS, which can then feed into a cost–benefit calculation, but it will not necessarily release cash.

There are many examples of benefits accruing from operational systems (which are covered in more depth in Chapter 12). Some examples of HISS benefits are given below:

1 *Organizational benefits* – examples of benefits to the organization include the introduction of a common interest in the system, including the use of common language, which in turn aids the integration of organization.
2 *Management benefits* – examples of benefits include the opportunity to gain additional 'business' through better understanding of the workload and improved organization. This arises from such things as being able to predict theatre workload and enabling waiting lists to be better managed.
3 *Clinician benefits* – clinicians, whether they are doctors, nurses or paramedics, depend on information in their work; the whole process of assessment, treatment and follow-up is dependent on information about patients and their condition.
4 *Patient benefits* – benefits to patients accrue from those outlined above in improved quality of service and generally better organized services, such as outpatient scheduling or reduced time spent giving name, address and other administrative details a multiplicity of times; reduced testing, such as having the results of blood tests conducted for GPs available to hospital doctors on-line, thus avoiding a duplicate test. The chances of errors in relating information, like test results, to the wrong patient are reduced. Benefits can arise from correlation of data within systems, such as contra-indications between drugs and laboratory tests.
5 *Cost avoidance* – the above examples indicate areas where costs can be saved or avoided. For example, reducing the numbers of blood tests saves money, whilst that and the time saved on dealing with telephone enquiries provides some leeway for additional activity to be undertaken.

Operational systems as infrastructure

Major operational systems, such as HISS, need to be recognized as fundamental items of infrastructure and as such are as vital as the buildings in which hospitals are housed and the staff that work in the hospitals. The same 'approval in principle' process should be undertaken internally on major operational systems as on building development; that is showing benefits and costs, but not on a strict cost–benefit justification, as such systems should be an investment to provide improved services. Emphasis should be placed upon the appropriateness of the system to the particular requirement and on fitness for purpose of the system to ensure that good value for money is obtained.

Operational systems will need to be updated and changed, and must not be seen as a one-off purchase at a particular point in time. Changes will occur because technological developments bring greater capabilities, such as the wider use of optical mass data storage and of RAID (redundant arrays of inexpensive disks) technology, the ability to handle high resolution radiology imaging, the development of document imaging technologies and the development of cordless hand-held devices for remote data collection and dissemination. Changes will happen because equipment wears out, and better methods are conceived of tackling problems, all leading to new or more advanced systems becoming available. The current state of the UK hospital market resembles that of the US several years ago. Now, in the US, major operational systems are bought and utilized over a particular time span, normally seven years, and then replaced with a more advanced version of the existing system or an entirely new system.

Whilst it can be expected that hardware and software prices may well fall in future, it is likely that some revenue consequences of such systems will increase as they become more sophisticated and complex, and that large-scale capital investment or leasing will still be required. This raises some potential problems for hospitals with the purchaser–provider split and the impact of the capital charges regime on capital developments. This seems at present to militate against development of large-scale operational systems, which flies in the face of the NHS Management Executive's intention of improving information systems.

Choosing systems

The procurement process

As part of the NHS, hospitals buying computer systems must comply with the European Community directives. Therefore systems likely to cost more than 100,000 ecus (December 1992 equivalent to £88,000) must be purchased following the appropriate guidelines. The procedures which must be undertaken, known as POISE (Procurement of Information Systems Effectively) are specified in detail. However, there is a danger that the process itself can become too mechanistic – just as implementing Körner became an end in itself, so the procurement process can take over and the original purposes of the system lost. This can be avoided if users are kept regularly involved in evaluation and other elements of the process. The main steps in the selection process are shown in Figure 3.3.

The cultural issue is extremely important. Different organizations operate in different ways, have different structures and different management styles. This appears to be particularly so in the NHS, where every hospital appears to be unique! Therefore, whilst a system may be successful in one hospital it does not mean that it will transfer into another hospital easily or successfully. This is of particular relevance given the stress on creating consortia to procure systems. The hospitals joining in consortia need to be clear on their cultural similarities and differences before attempting to buy together, or a system inappropriate to one or more hospitals may be chosen. The important cultural issue between the vendor and the hospital is whether or not the vendor is prepared to understand or is capable of understanding the hospital's organization, values and priorities. If the vendor does not understand what is important to the management or medical staff of a particular hospital, the chances of a successful implementation must be reduced.

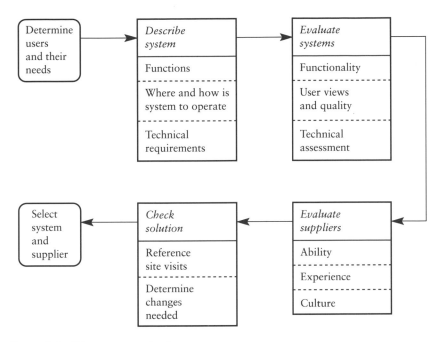

Figure 3.3 The system selection process.

Case history: Burton Hospitals' HISS

On 1 April 1992, Burton Hospitals went 'live' with Phase I of a HISS system. This represented the culmination of three and a quarter years work, with the prospect of another year and a half to implement the remaining two phases.

Procurement

In early 1989, Burton Hospitals and South East Staffordshire Health Authority (SESHA) attempted to procure a CMMS, being a Resource Management roll out site. At that time it was apparent that case mix systems were in their infancy and the procurement was abandoned as it became clear that data accuracy and currency were major issues which could be better addressed through a HISS solution. SESHA joined with three other districts in the West Midlands Region to form the West Midlands HISS Consortium and a successful bid was made to the HISS Central Team to gain Pilot Project status and funding support.

Individual hospitals developed Operational Requirements and a consolidated version was produced for the official procurement process. Following complex selection procedures between the four hospitals, a short list of four suppliers was drawn up. During 1990, the suppliers demonstrated their systems against predefined scripts to examine their suitability and functionality. Technical discussions were held to understand the products and how they operated and communicated. Reference site visits were made to hospitals in the USA to see the systems in operation. Standard sets of questions were asked, with an emphasis on talking to users. Reports from US-based hospital information systems consultants were used to supplement this process. Examination of the suitability of the products at this stage reduced the short list to three suppliers.

Memorandum of Specification (MoS) discussions followed, in which the suppliers indicated how they would address shortfalls between existing functionality and that required by the Consortium and how they would plan and carry out the implementation process. At the end of these discussions, three members of the Consortium were prepared to sign-off an MoS with two suppliers and invite them to tender for supply. However, SESHA was prepared to sign off with all three suppliers. This brought to a head the difficulties of operating a consortium approach. There were considerable differences of opinion within the project team on how processes should be carried out and the weight to assign to different factors in the evaluation processes. These differences of opinion were not about rights and wrongs, but about different approaches and ways of working reflecting the very different cultures of the organizations involved. The outcome was that SESHA withdrew from the Consortium and pursued its own route without external financial support for the HISS approach. SESHA decided to continue the procurement. A bid from Data General/Meditech won on the grounds of cost and quality and a contract was signed in April 1991.

The operational system

The operational system is based upon the Meditech Hospital Information System running on a set of five networked Data General Aviions. The software required extensive development to meet the UK requirements, with new software for activities such as waiting lists and contracting. A list of the modules and the hardware is given in Boxes 3.1 and 3.2. Some of the significant strengths of the system are the response times, normally subsecond; the use of a standard user interface at all terminals (also available on PCs), involving colour and being menu driven and easy to use; the ease of changing screen layout; the tailorability through being a dictionary-based system; an extremely easy to use read-only patient care enquiry facility, including results reporting available from day one of operation; high levels of system security with audit trails; a test database; reporting possible on all data items within the database and the reliability of the hardware, with mirror-discs and interchangeable discs allowing continued operation in a degraded mode if any of five processors is out of action.

Box 3.1 Software modules

Phase I – April 1992	*Phase II – January 1993*	*Phase III – September 1993*
Master patient index	Care planning	Nurse management
Patient administration	Pharmacy	Theatres
Contracting	Billing	Departmental module*
Radiology		Order communications
Pathology		and results reporting
Case mix management		
Patient care enquiry		

* The departmental module is for specialized clinical requirements, such as Maternity, A&E and therapies, specialized clinical and medical audit and small departments, such as electrocardiographic service (ECG).

Box 3.2 Hardware

Five Data General 16 Megabyte RAM Aviion 6200 computers with 24 Gigabytes (Gb) disc storage memory comprising 11 Gb master memory, 11 Gb shadow memory on mirror discs and 2 Gb archive.

300 Data General colour terminals with 80 HP Laserjet III and 90 Facit dot matrix printers linked via 70 terminal servers over a core fibre optic based Ethernet network.

Implementation

Implementing the system involved creating a project team from staff within the hospital and recruiting a project co-ordinator. Each project team member was a subproject manager for an area of implementation, whether hardware or a specific software module. The project team reported to a project board under PROMPT methodology. Additional technical support staff were recruited to strengthen SESHA's IT agency supplying the technical support to the project.

Software development was based on observation, discussion and prototyping, using the Operational Requirement and Memorandum of Specification as a documented baseline and as guidance to the overall objectives. Important factors on meeting the project plan timetable were detailed planning, good teamwork, facing up to problems, the Unit Management Board, having a highly committed hospital consultant lead a project assurance team and a common purpose between vendor and hospital staff. The latter was strengthened by a classic situation of common external challenge and a sense of adversity. In this particular case, the challenges were other hospitals undertaking similar ventures in a similar timescale and the removal of central funding leading to a mutual determination to succeed.

The unit management board members had been involved with the developments on information systems, and hence HISS, from the outset of the RM initiative and there was a strong belief in the need for HISS in the development of the hospitals. During implementation the project manager had access to the management board when significant organizational issues arose, which were then dealt with rapidly.

Teamwork was strengthened by setting frequent short-term goals, which engendered a sense of achievement, and by strong social links between the sets of staff involved. Meditech staff worked from their Boston base with one- or two-week work sessions in Burton. This visiting process helped planning and aided the concentration of minds on tasks to be completed between visits. During visits, the working days tended to be intense, followed by planning and 'wrap-up' sessions (in more relaxed environments!). The meeting of different cultures, both organizational and societal, taking people out of their normal working environments, together with a sense of adventure and of fun resulted in high quality and generous contributions from a wide range of staff. Underlying the contributions from SESHA staff were three factors: (1) the knowledge that the system could be very effective, as it had been seen in operation in extremely well run hospitals in Canada and the USA; (2) a high standard of professional and technical competence in information system matters in the IT staff; and (3) a co-operative culture of management and clinicians in Burton Hospitals.

Implementations are never smooth and easy; there were many problems and issues, some of which are still in the process of resolution, but the major objectives were achieved and the system was operational, and on budget on schedule following a ten day parallel run.

Current position and future steps

At the time of writing (December 1992) the first phase of HISS has been in operation for nearly 9 months. As was to be expected, there have been teething problems, especially in the area of ensuring the accuracy and validity of statistical reports, which can only be carried out fully when the system has data in it and the system is being used. Operational aspects have been modified as experience has been gained and better methods have been found and, perhaps inevitably, unexpected problems have occurred. However, no over-riding operational or system problems have so far been encountered, and many minor issues have been resolved through use of the system.

Whilst major challenges still lie ahead, such as fully realizing benefits and rolling out the use of order entry functions across all departments, the project remains on schedule both in terms of cost and time. Already further use of the system is being examined in terms of GP links and a new executive support system module, and an examination is under way on how best to run financial systems alongside the Meditech system.

Successful systems

Fundamentals for success

Our experience suggests that the fundamental requirements for the successful utilization of operational systems in hospitals are:

1 Understanding and recognizing that operational systems are a normal part of running hospitals.
2 Determining what is required to suit the local circumstances; what are the important factors about the hospital, its organization and operation; what can be gained from experience in other hospitals.
3 Developing a strategy, which as a minimum should start from the PAS function, networking and results reporting.
4 Involving users in the whole process, and particularly those users actively wanting the system.
5 Ensuring that the system brings benefits over and above existing methods.
6 Training and communications.
7 Engaging management commitment for all aspects of the systems impact, namely, financial, operational and organizational, especially the recognition that jobs will change and that stress and strain will be put on staff.

People: the most important factor

When deciding to purchase, select and implement operational systems, it must be recognized that hospital operational systems are ultimately about people, i.e. patients and users. The people aspect can easily be lost sight of when technical issues are being discussed, when the complexities and the drive of the procurement process take over, and the realization of the length of time taken to undergo this process comes to the fore. This perhaps applies more to hospital operational systems than most other systems in that there are patients to be cared for; there are patients who can be delayed by the system not working properly and there are the staff who have to use the system, who need confidence in the system and must not be impeded in carrying out their work. Above all, hospital operational systems should not come between health care practitioners and the people they are trying to help, but should be there to help both parties.

4 Managing development: developing managers' information management

Andy Kennedy

Introduction

The world of those who manage in the NHS is complex. The impact of the tension that exists between the Government's espoused intentions for health care and the constraints on public sector borrowing is felt daily. Public attention follows as the media, with increasing accuracy, scrutinizes medical and managerial practice in the NHS, and brings issues such as prioritization and rationing into the public arena.

Managers, clinical heads and professional leaders find themselves confronted with an imposing list of pressing issues, none of which is simple to address and all of which appear to require sophisticated information and consummate managerial ability. These issues are likely to include strategic business planning, external relationships, marketing and the development and maintenance of client-focused services.

Managers' agendas are also likely to include attempts to deal with overlapping organizational development initiatives from the centre, such as Resource Management (RM), Total Quality Management (TQM), Medical Audit and the Patient's Charter. This takes place alongside local initiatives, which may include major projects on skill mix, job profiling and contracting procedures – to say nothing of performance measurement and budgetary control.

The context for this managerial activity is one in which parts of the NHS may be isolated from each other, and where there is an established tradition of looking inwards. Management structures and reporting arrangements may often be confused and unclear, and it may be difficult to sustain the view that a hospital, say, is one coherent organization, rather than several. From the background of this complex and rapidly changing management context emerge particularly thorny issues such as the involvement of professionals – especially doctors – in management, and the management of professionals and clinical activity.

In this context, general and clinical managers often say that they have both too much and too little information. Too much, they say, about large-scale intentions and local idiosyncrasies, not enough about underlying directions and unifying values. Training and development is looked to for support by managers as they seek to address this complexity, both for their own development, and for the development of their staff. Providers of training and development seek to make appropriate services available, to enable the hard-pressed managers of the NHS to do their jobs as well as possible. This chapter is about the sometimes difficult relationship between managers and providers of training and development. In what follows, I shall try to present a picture of NHS attitudes to management and training and development. Within this picture information management is considered as a creative process, central to any management practice, or at least, to any management practice that seeks to promote the ability of the employees of healthcare organizations to contribute to the greatest extent of their potential.

Before proceeding, I want to address some possible confusion in terminology. Non-specialist workers may be surprised to learn that, among practitioners in training, development and education, it can be difficult to find an acceptable term for what lies at the heart of their job. The 'teaching–learning process' was a contender for some time, and was felt to capture quite well the two-sidedness of the 'training' relationship. More recently, however, it is not much used because of the connotations of the word 'teacher'; many practitioners would rather describe themselves as facilitators (of learning or of group processes), for example.

This difficulty is not trivial, I believe, and variability in terminology and usage among practitioners reflects deeply argued differences with regard to theoretical orientation, preferred style, classes of desired outcome, process interventions and so on. In view of the debate within the professional community, I use the term 'T+D' – training and development – as the name of the function recognizable in most NHS organizations. I want this phrase to be neutral with regard to the extent to which the learning outcome is planned and to the degree of control, authority of direction of any particular participant such as a group leader.

Additionally, I observe that there is no uniformity or regularity in the way in which members of the T+D community decide to call themselves developers, trainers or facilitators. This means that it is not possible to predict that someone calling herself or himself a Management Developer would plan to execute work in any particular way, or that that way would be utterly different to that of someone who called herself or himself a Management Trainer. Most T+D professionals are, on the one hand, eclectic in their methodology and, on the other, sensitive to the terminology of those who they hope will commission them.

I shall attempt to show later that NHS managers' attitudes to T+D are multivariate and sometimes contradictory. First, however, in order to illustrate the context for T+D in the NHS, I include these statements, some from T+D practitioners, and some from managers:

> Training should have clear outcomes. For myself, there should be some 'answers' which I can apply. For my staff, there should be some change manifested in their performance.

> Managers' attitudes to training and development change over time and with familiarity with the processes of learning. Paradoxically, those who are least sophisticated will come to me asking for something highly specific. My some sophisticated clients often come with ill-defined problems and open minds about best processes and likely outcomes.

> I recognize the significance of the impact of training. I know that it is a strategic tool for ensuring organizational development. I also expect it to be able to solve an employee's attitude problem.

> Clients tend to believe that there is a training solution for everything, even when they have great difficulty in articulating what the problem is, or what changes are desirable. And when they've been ignoring the problem for years!

> I've got about 30 part-time staff. Would two half-hour sessions over lunch be enough to do customer care?

> It is unrealistic, quixotic, to think that 60 medical secretaries could be taught word processing with no training centre, in a couple of weeks. Oh – and on a budget of £10,000.

> Some organizations spend 5 or 6 per cent of payroll on staff development. For us, that would be about £1,000 per person per annum. Actually, I have £13.20 to spend on each member of staff.

Attitudes to management and to T+D

It is quite obvious that different managers in the NHS have different views at different times. This is true of their understanding of the nature and task of T+D and also of the nature of the management task itself. Indeed, an individual may hold, simultaneously, distinct views which actually contradict each other. Additionally, both individuals and groups may be unaware of differences between the way they discuss the world and the way they conduct their affairs in it. This contrast has been elegantly captured by Argyris and Schon (1978); they write of the differences between managers' 'talk about openness of communication and the participative approach of their organizations (what is called their 'espoused' theory) [and] what they actually do (their theory in use)'.

Box 4.1   Position A

The manager should ensure that workers' work is broken down into its constituent parts. Planning should be separated from execution, workers should be isolated from each other and work practices should be completely standardized.

The manager should enforce standards and enforce co-operation. The manager should supervise and control work and ensure that the best implements and work tools are adopted.

In this position, superordinates tend to believe that workers cannot be trusted, and there are many specific rules. Tight co-ordination is applied through routines and schedules, and communication tends to be in the form of directives. Inadequate performance is attributed to negligence or insubordination. Disagreements are hard to reconcile because of essentially divergent goals. People are inherently lazy and would not come to work if they could avoid it (Blackler and Shimmin 1984; Pugh and Hickson 1989).

The way in which attitudes to management on the one hand and to training and development on the other impinge on each other, can be shown on a matrix. This matrix is made by the intersection of two dimensions, seen as continua; the two axes represent attitudes to management and attitudes to T+D. Along the first axis are arranged all sorts of ideas about management. In recognition of the eclecticism of management writers and practitioners, we would expect to find insights from sociologists, anthropologists and psychologists alongside the aphorisms of the management gurus and the hard-won nuggets from lifetimes of experience. At one end of this continuum is position A (Box 4.1) and at the other is position B (Box 4.2).

Along the second axis are arranged all aspects of practice and thinking about T+D, including the thinking of non-specialist NHS managers. At one end of the continuum is Position C (Box 4.3) and at the other is position D (Box 4.4).

A matrix

Combined, these two continua form a matrix (Fig. 4.1) on which can be plotted attitudes towards management and T+D. I have labelled the top right-hand quadrant 'creative contribution' and the bottom left-hand quadrant 'control' in order to characterize distinctly the contrasting positions which may be found. The matrix highlights a number of points, and I list some of them below:

1 It may be the case that managers have different expectations for the outcomes of T+D, depending on the staff groups involved. I hope it is

Box 4.2   Position B

Bearing in mind that every organization has to prepare for the abandonment of everything it does, managers have to learn to ask of every process, every product, every procedure, every policy 'If we did not do this already, would we go into it now, knowing what we know now?'

Managers must be researchers who study their own organization and create a learning process. This is essential to effective performance in a world characterized by perpetual novelty and change. In this position, the commitment of subordinates is taken for granted. There is no close supervision or detailed regulation, and there is an emphasis on joint problem solving. Communication is in the form of consultative discussion, and inadequate performances are seen in terms of honest misjudgement or mistakes. Disagreements are worked through, and learned from. Given meaningful and challenging work, people will commit their energies willingly (Blackler and Shimmin 1984; Drucker 1992; Freedman 1992).

Box 4.3   Position C

The purpose of T+D is to make individuals fit the system better so that they are fit for work. Tasks can be clearly defined and, in order to carry them out well, individuals should conform to established patterns of behaviour. One task of T+D is to impose this conformity. T+D tends towards convergence and in its objectives and procedures addresses itself to what is similar about people. It relies on established techniques and, although it is willing to work towards greater efficiency, it does not encourage participants to question its own methodology or the ways of working found in the organization.

Box 4.4   Position D

The purpose of T+D is to provide for creativity; specifically, it helps individuals contribute actively to the development of the network of social interactions, which is at the heart of the organization. What is learned includes analytical frameworks and practice in their application; also included are procedures for modifying frameworks to enable participants to cope with problems that do not have a ready-made solution. T+D tends towards divergence and values whatever it is that makes people different from each other. It is ready to experiment in its own ways of working, and encourages participants to break from the confinement of prescribed practices – both within the T+D setting and in the wider organization (Widdowson 1983).

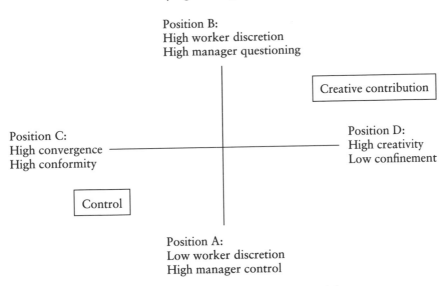

Figure 4.1 Matrix: attitudes to management and T+D activity.

not cynical to suggest that managers themselves want to make a more creative contribution to the organization as a result of development work they 'do', but expect others to be more compliant and amenable to managerial control as a result of training they 'go through'.

2 There may be considerable disjuncture between the rhetoric of business plans, for instance, when they speak of empowering the staff to make a full contribution, and the reality of opportunities for experiment and divergent thinking and practice back in the workplace. This disjuncture may also be made manifest through the unrealistically small amounts of money typically made available for staff training, or the common practice to 'send difficult people' on courses such as 'handling difficult people'. The heavyweight symbolism of such practices is usually not lost on participants!

3 This matrix can also help to highlight the apparent contrast between managers' desires for a creative, enjoyable, questioning *process*, and their expectation of a well-defined, deliverable *product*. This product may be difficult to specify, but is often characterized by the words 'knowledge' or 'skill', and implies quite high levels of conformity and convergence, I believe.

This matrix also brings into focus the fact that there is quite often tension between T+D practitioners and those managers who commission T+D work – whether they themselves will be the primary clients, or whether these are members of their staff. This conflict may be expressed in judgements about the extent to which the encounter should be process-dominated or topic-dominated, with many T+D practitioners tending towards a process orientation. Alternatively, this tension may be expressed in the degree to which the T+D practitioner is expected to present herself or himself as a knowledgeable 'master' to whom participants should (convergently) submit.

In concrete terms, T+D practitioners may find that in order to gain or maintain access to a client group, they have to agree to deliver work that is, in their view, not really appropriate or not the best use of resources. For example, an agreement might be made to 'teach' clinical directors 'information planning' – in quite a traditional way, perhaps – when the T+D practitioner's judgement is that 'conflict and collaboration' would be more useful, especially if delivered in an exploratory, non-didactic way. There can be very good outcomes of such work, of course, whatever its genesis; thoughtful T+D practitioners and committed participants seem able to create important learning experiences from almost any source.

Negative outcomes also accrue, however. For example, the process may be self-defeating in that a didactic style only proves to the clients that the course was redundant or that the motives of the organizers were suspect, and certainly not aimed at open discussion. Alternatively, a less directive style may elicit accusations of incompetence or 'navel gazing'. But the data which may flow from encounters such as these can be very interesting, and although in the short-term may appear negative, they may make a useful contribution to subsequent relationships. The difficulty for T+D practitioners is that, by being insufficiently challenging, they may help to perpetuate the view that the learning enterprise is essentially to do with acquisition of knowledge or 'skill'. This may encourage people to value institutionally approved routines more highly than reflection, thoughtfulness or responsibility. If the aim of T+D is to help develop systems which enable participants in the organization to contribute to the best of their capability, then it should presumably contribute to the development of 'a culture of tolerance, listening and intellectual curiosity, not intellectual arrogance' (Kanter 1991: 130).

T+D practitioners are, of course, subject to variability and fashion no less than managers, and they tend to value as sophisticated those managers who themselves value 'creative contribution', and to be critical of those managers who seek to use T+D as a social control mechanism. I am suggesting, then, that a real problem can emerge for managers and T+D practitioners as, with the best of intentions, they seek to work together; the former may tend to value the steady evolution of the status quo, while the latter may wish to upset the apple cart. One way of understanding this problem is to recognize the impact of education itself on our subsequent educational endeavours, whether as consumers (such as commissioners or course participants) or as providers.

I suggest that many persons now in senior positions in the NHS may have had educational experiences reminiscent of the following:

Children moved from grade to grade through a pre-planned sequence of standard subjects, as if on a factory conveyor belt. At each stage, certain facts were poured into their heads. Children with the greatest capacity to absorb the facts, and with the most submissive demeanour, were placed on a rapid track through the sequence; those with the least capacity for fact retention and self discipline, on the slowest . . . Standardized tests were routinely administered at certain checkpoints . . . and 'product defects' were taken off the line and returned for retooling. As in the mass-production system, discipline and order were emphazised above all else. (Reich 1991: 59–60)

Of course, I am not saying that people are immutably bound by their early experiences of education; they may have important subsequent learning passages, whether formal or not. I do suggest, however, that much mainstream education inculcates a widespread expectation that T+D will have a preplanned sequence, a curriculum of standard subjects, and some sort of capability test, probably at the end. Some managers would additionally assert that an objective is to promote the development of values such as discipline and respect for the paramountcy of the organization's objectives. I am sure that many NHS managers would regard any form of T+D that did not 'improve the quality of the workforce' as unnecessary and wasteful – if not likely to sow the seeds of discontent and instability.

This attitude to education is also carried over into much thinking about management itself, I believe. Although the historical trajectories of education and management have been quite different, there are similarities attributable to large-scale cultural and economic trends in Western society at large. Thus, management theorizing over the last hundred years or so has seen employees either as susceptible to control by manipulating systems, or as social beings whose emotions, attitudes and beliefs could be shaped (Barley and Kunda 1992: 384). Although some approaches to education since the Industrial Revolution have had an emancipatory tendency, the mainstream has been oriented to a social control function (Fagerlind and Saha 1983: 31ff). Much education, in short, has focused on an employment perspective, where necessary at the expense of the personal development of future employees – the participants in the educational endeavour.

Among educational practitioners, however, particularly those concerned with adult learners in contexts such as management development, a critical response has emerged which stands in sharp contrast to the quality-controlled conveyer belt mentioned above. This alternative view, in part no doubt itself the product of specialist education, tends to disparage a process in which the recipient is subjected to a cyclical process of diagnosis, prescription and treatment by specialized personnel using specialist equipment to achieve rational objectives (made explicit in the curriculum). The problem, it is suggested, is that any predetermined curriculum – expressed in terms of teaching objectives or of performance outcomes, as in the case of competence frameworks – brings a risk of disempowering the users.

This exacerbates a situation in which many adults – particularly those with limited experience of academic success – attempt to hand over responsibility for learning to the teacher, much as the 'classic' patient relates to a doctor.

Thus, T+D practitioners may really feel compromised by a tightly written, results-oriented syllabus:

> Faculty cannot engage in limited empowerment of learners . . . It is contradictory to empower learners within spheres of action which have been previously determined by the educator . . . (T)aking control . . . will inevitably involve learners in setting aside various aspects of institutionally prescribed curricula and operational procedures and criticising them for their irrelevance, autocratic nature or the perpetuation of inequity. (Brookfield 1986: 87)

Against the output measurement tendency, then, there is a strong, articulate lobby for the role of T+D in facilitating creative – and reflective – contributions to management:

> [Managers need] to be helped to an awareness of their own significance and responsibility by encouraging in them a consciousness of the difficulties with which they are engaged. They must be encouraged to think about the unprogrammable complexities which face them without the specious assistance of codes, competencies, catch phrases, and mission statements. Managers must begin to reflect upon the real world which they know they inhabit. (Reed and Anthony 1992: 609)

In the above, I have tried to draw out some of the difficulties which emerge when managers and T+D practitioners seek to work together to enable members of NHS organizations to work more effectively. I am suggesting that there is still a powerful tendency to regard educational endeavours as appropriately having a normative tendency. This involves people in learning the routines of the organization and in becoming 'competent' in certain well-defined areas. I have also suggested that there may be a discrepancy between an organization's espoused view of T+D, which emphasizes emancipation and participation, and the 'theory in use', which has as one function the delivery of accommodating employees, deferential to the prevailing managerial view of the world.

Certainly, experience suggests that while statements in business plans for example emphasize T+D's role in enabling the individual to make a possibly dissonant contribution to the organization, resources are often spent on those most amenable to managerial control. Alternatively, individuals may be asked to submit to T+D activity in preparation for demotion or dismissal, or at least so that 'the rough edges can be knocked off'.

To a 'commander' model of management, which 'assumes that the top manager is the rational actor behind the strategic plan, implemented according to his intention throughout the entire organization' (Alvesson 1991:

210), the conveyor-belt view of education is quite palatable. A persistent problem for T+D practitioners is to present a strong alternative to this established model. This is despite the fact that there is widespread acknowledgement that it is extremely difficult to design standardized learning procedures for very varied staff groups.

Information, training and development

So far, I have made little mention of information. At this point, it is interesting to note that in courses concerned with learning about the technology of information management, there appears to be a strong tendency to produce highly standardized packages. Some certainly have a 'personalizable' facility, and may prove useful for instructors and trainees alike.

I suggest, therefore, that the managers and others do not register passively all the information provided by the world of organization, but instead, through a process of selective attention, construct a unique awareness of the environment. From such constructs, managers and management teams choose interactions with the world and become the active creators of their experience of the organization (Korb *et al.* 1989: 19). It is an important function of T+D workers to ensure that managers and management teams interact with their environment as it is, not as they wish it to be. In this way, they are in a position to try to adjust their practices and the practices of those who work for them to the needs of the organization in its environment. The relationship of a healthy organization with its environment is – like that of a healthy individual – characterized by change, flow and mobility (Korb *et al.* 1989). By contrast, resistance, lack of change, rigidity and overcontrol are signs of ill-health. Unhealthy organizations, groups (such as managerial teams) and individuals may stop attending appropriately to the environment by disrupting the flow of information. Thus, the organization may not be able to take effective action in respect of such feedback as is available and, instead, may start to spend much energy on the maintenance of a (false) sense of security (Merry and Brown 1987: 209). In such a situation the management team may become out of touch with the internal information systems of the organization, as well as with the external environment of clients and patients. The management team may seek information which confirms its version of reality, and may devalue or neglect other information that might disconfirm it.

For example, a manager may fail to attend to complaints and anxieties of subordinates in a team meeting, or of an individual in an appraisal interview, regarding them as deviant or 'whingeing'. A T+D practitioner would consider that such a manager had deprived herself or himself of the chance to gain feedback from the encounter and so modify his or her understanding of the organization.

At an organization level, managers spend much time on collating information about matters such as:

- waiting times
- performance against budget
- revenue
- staff turnover
- bed occupancy
- theatre utilization
- length of stay
- comparative case mix costs
- asset utilization.

All are no doubt useful, but noticeable by their absence are these:

- health outcomes
- health of workforce
- participation of workforce in service planning
- top management time available to workforce
- time spent in education
- patients' relatives.

I am suggesting that the picture of reality that a management team develops will incline them to collect certain sorts of data, and not to collect other sorts. Unless this procedure is reviewed consistently, the management team may continue to spend time and energy collecting information about a situation which no longer exists.

It is a crucial role for T+D to encourage and enable management and other teams constantly to review their information gathering and interpretation practices. Thus, for example, questions might be asked about the responsiveness of the management team of a hospital to information being offered by those working in the community. Alternatively, attempts might be made to raise the level of management's awareness of information available within the organization. A focus for such questions might be the identity of management's own clients, and the nature of services offered them. In this context an important role of T+D is to constantly bring to awareness the possibility of questioning the information gathering process of the management team, and the related world view. This leads to a focus on renewal rather than on the maintenance of the status quo.

It is reasonable to ask, in conclusion, what would be the appropriate characteristics of a useful and fully functioning training and development service in an NHS organization. I suggest that organizations need a T+D function which emphasizes the particular, rather than the general. That is to say, it does not seek to impose universal solutions on essentially disparate situations and groups of people.

Such a function is likely to act opportunistically, rather than in pursuit of a well-defined, global implementation plan. The analysis of development needs should therefore be iterative rather than 'once and for all'. It is commonly known among T+D practitioners that the business of delivery brings with it a good deal of information about the subsequent development requirements of the clients. Needs analysis is thus best seen as an aspect of a wider management process of making sense of the world. The guiding principle for educational design and execution should be 'trying things out', rather than aiming for a replicable system of mass implementation.

I suggest that the T+D function should accept its limitations, as well as the expectations heaped upon it, and avoid the temptation to take on the burden of 'fixing' whatever it is that management cannot manage. T+D may be best thought of as servicing an organization's information requirements. It can do this in a variety of ways:

1 By unblocking communication bottlenecks and by challenging and attending to distortions in the flow of information.
2 By providing frameworks that enable groups and individuals to recognize as significant a wider range of information than their current world picture permits; this might be done by modelling absent behaviours, or by pointing out their absence. It might also be done by providing space for the articulation of difficulty, and by observing the extent of congruence between words and actions.
3 By facilitating a reflective process which honours all the expertise of all participants as they make sense of the world of the organization.
4 By offering a context of expert facilitation which inspires confidence and a sense of security.

In this way, T+D can honour the diversity of the ways in which information is created, used and managed in the organization, and so facilitate a wider, more creative contribution to the organization.

References

Alvesson, M. (1991) 'Organizational symbolism and ideology', *Journal of Management Studies*, 28, 3.

Argyris, C. and Schon, D. (1978) *Organisational Learning: A Theory of Action Perspective*. London, Addison Wesley.

Barley, S.R. and Kunda, G. (1992) 'Design and devotion: surges of rational and normative ideologies of control in managerial discourse', *Administrative Science Quarterly*, 37, 363–99.

Blackler, F. and Shimmin, S. (1984) *Applying Psychology in Organisations*. London, Methuen.

Brookfield, S.D. (1986) *Understanding and Facilitating Adult Learning*. Milton Keynes, Open University Press.

Drucker, P.F. (1992) 'The New Society of Organisations', *Harvard Business Review*, Sept–Oct, 95–104.

Fagerlind, I. and Saha, L.J. (1983) *Education and National Development: A Comparative Perspective*. Oxford, Pergamon.

Freedman, D.H. (1992) 'Is management still a science?', *Harvard Business Review*, Nov–Dec, 26–38.

Kanter, R.M. (1991) 'Championing change: an interview with Bell Atlantic's CEO Raymond Smith', *Harvard Business Review*, Jan–Feb, 119–30.

Korb, M.P., Gorrell, J. and Van de Riet, V. (1989) *Gestalt Therapy: Practice and Theory*. Oxford, Pergamon Press.

Merry, U. and Brown, G.I. (1987) *The Neurotic Behaviour of Organisations*. New York, Gardner.

Pugh, D.S. and Hickson, D.J. (1989) *Writers on Organisations*. Harmondsworth, Penguin.

Reed, M. and Anthony, P. (1992) 'Professionalizing management and managing professionalization: British management in the 1980s', *Journal of Management Studies*, 29, 5.

Reich, R.B. (1991) *The Work of Nations: Preparing Ourselves for 21st Century Capitalism*. London, Simon and Schuster.

Widdowson, H.G. (1983) *Learning Purpose and Language Use*. Oxford, Oxford University Press.

5 Clinical management

Mark Harrison, Margaret Marion and Andrew Brooks

Introduction

Clinical management was introduced in Winchester at the Royal Hampshire County Hospital following the Griffiths Report in 1983, against a background of a strong medical staff committee and a district general manager who saw it as important to involve professionals, but particularly doctors, as they were the major initiators of clinical activity (Buxton *et al.* 1991; Packwood *et al.* 1991). This close relationship has continued, though it has been viewed as too cosy by the Regional Health Authority in recent times. However, it was extremely helpful in fostering the beginnings. Our first Unit General Manager (UGM) was an orthopaedic surgeon and the then Chairman of the Medical Staff Committee, and our second and present UGM was the Director of Nursing Services when clinical management was introduced.

The District Medical Officer had a particular interest in information technology and produced a plan for an ambitious integrated IT system within the hospital. This was progressed as part of a regional initiative. A complex and sophisticated IT system has now, in the main, been implemented and although not designed for the NHS 'marketplace' has been of enormous benefit.

There has been an unusual constancy of personalities throughout this period of intense change. The medical staff are relatively young and most of the key players involved have known and worked with one another over the last ten years: working relationships have been close.

This is all set to change with our application for trust status, which is designed to bring acute and community units together. New faces will now appear in senior positions of management. We shall discover just how robust and durable the changes are that we have made to the organization and our management style.

Organizational issues

It is now widely recognized that the active involvement of clinicians in the management process is an essential component of successful resource management: collectively planning, managing, delivering and evaluating services for patients. The aim must be to secure more effective and efficient use of the resources available for the benefit of patients. This in turn is dependent upon the availability of relevant, accurate and timely information which is used, within a devolved management structure, as close to the point of delivery of care as possible. Indeed, the long-term survival of a devolved organization depends on the effective exchange of information, both vertically and horizontally. This constitutes a major cultural shift, which requires changes in attitudes between professional groups who have been used to working in a unidisciplinary way. Building this new-style management structure takes time and requires faithful adherence to the principles of devolved management. Responsibility for quality of the service, achieving activity and maintaining income and expenditure balance must be accepted by the clinical director. Equally, levels of authority must be explicit and honoured by the general management team (Fig. 5.1). It would certainly be speedier at times to respond to external demands for information or produce major documents such as the business plan by undertaking most of the work centrally and simply consulting at directorate level. However, for clinical management to succeed, all issues must be addressed through the line management structure. Similarly, information must be collected, validated and used at directorate level if it is to be credible to clinicians and used to improve the effectiveness and efficiency of the service provided to patients.

The development of a multidisciplinary approach is not easy and progress varies across specialities. These variations are hardly surprising as they reflect the historical nature of working relationships, but directors need considerable help to use vehicles such as business planning. There is no doubt that the harder edge of the business processes which have resulted from the development of the purchaser–provider relationship have created the impetus for rapid change. However, if this change process is not managed effectively key staff may retreat into their professional roles in an increasingly pressured atmosphere.

There are inevitably risks associated with this degree of delegation. It can begin to appear that six or eight hospitals (directorates) are functioning with an alarming degree of independence. This can be seen as a stage in the development of a fundamentally different management structure. Vigilance is necessary as rigorous management approaches must not be allowed to impinge upon professional responsibilities and standards.

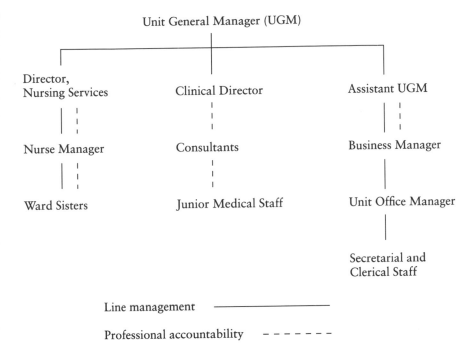

Figure 5.1 Management structure.

For example, many benefits can be achieved in devolving medical records functions to directorate level; but central professional leadership must remain in order to ensure that the integrity of the patient record is not threatened. Standards must be set and monitored, with appropriate staff being recruited and receiving relevant training. Similarly, nurses working within a directorate structure and accountable through their senior nurse to the clinical director must have professional leadership and be accountable on professional issues to the director of nursing. There will be occasions when their professional responsibilities will, at the least, not be in total harmony with business objectives. There will be times when the true strength of the structure will be tested within the directorate, within the unit as a whole and between professional groups. The careful use of information will sometimes help in the debate which must ensue, but this will be primarily a test of working relationships and corporate strength.

It is important that information is clearly understood to be as valid in identifying the healthcare consequences of financial constraints as it is in identifying areas of waste and inefficiency. In both instances the information gained can only be used effectively in a sound devolved management structure.

The place of information in the management process

To manage without information is to sail an uncharted sea but information without management is never to go to sea at all. (with apologies to Sir William Osler)

Simply presenting data does not usually enable management decisions unless an organization is highly receptive to the ideas that the data is to support. (The term 'data' in this discussion refers to quantifiable and measurable information. Consideration is given to the role of non-quantifiable information in the next section.) Indeed, data can both guide *and* confuse these decisions. Whatever the nature of the data, it should fulfil the general criteria of accuracy, timeliness and relevance; and it should also be presented in a clear and easily comprehensible form.

How does one achieve these ideals? The answer is with some difficulty, especially as you collect more and more data. Once you reach a certain level of data in an organization (and one can argue about that level) computers become essential to handle the large volumes in a structured and rapid way. However good the data is thought to be, it requires validation by someone who understands the process to which it relates. An advantage of a directorate system is that this means a member of the relevant directorate who is familiar with that particular data, usually a business manager in conjunction with a department head or clinical director. Ownership and confidence in the data can be achieved, which is important if decisions are to be both based upon it and implemented.

Initially, central management collected and presented data for directorate and board meetings and much time was spent challenging the accuracy and validity of the data. Although quite legitimate, it deflected the meeting from discussing the real issues that the data described.

With the increasing complexity of the NHS, the demands for data have increased at all levels. Providers, purchasers, regions and the Department of Health all have their different data needs. Computerization should aid this process but in reality the perception that data is now easy to collect has increased the demand and continues to do so. Körner and minimum data sets expand, and there are (for example) now Accident and Emergency data sets. The coding of operations and inpatient diagnoses will be expanded to include accident and emergency attendances and perhaps ultimately all outpatient attendances. Yet some data is still difficult to collect. For instance, if you wanted to look at the management of patients with haematuria from the time their GP refers them until they have been treated, as part of an audit, it would still be easiest to return to the clinical notes of all those with relevant diagnostic codes.

There is so much data available that clinical managers are easily overloaded. Considerable energy, staff time and money are expended in collecting and collating this data and only a modest proportion is of use at provider level. Indeed much of the Körner data set is of little value or apparent relevance to the management of a provider unit, and is viewed by many as an albatross.

There is a need to look carefully at data needs at all levels. Too much data can paralyse the management process. It is important that clinical managers have a clear idea of what information they require. Clinical directors and board members need monthly statements of expenditure against budget allocations and clinical activity against targets. Other reports on staffing, staff sickness, waiting lists and waiting times are needed less regularly at this level but are used constantly by business managers and nurse managers. Most other information can be produced as necessary to support the management agenda of the board or directorate. Business managers have an important role in obtaining and providing this information, particularly in helping to produce business plans and use them within the planning cycle.

Quantitative versus other data

All information, from whatever source, must be viewed as potentially valid. The full range from computerized data to professional judgements or even random information collected on the ubiquitous grapevine should be considered as possible sources in addressing specific issues. The belief that computer-gathered information must be the most valuable ignores the fact that unless processes are managed to ensure consistently high quality inputs, the data collected from the system will not be reliable.

The 'database' available within the directorate teams is invaluable, if not always readily accessible. Every organization identifies those who hold great stores of information about the history of service developments, relationships, how to get things done and so on. A welter of information is of limited value if the factors which will influence the response of individuals to a particular situation are not known and taken into account. This is all self-evident to an experienced manager, but the more rich in information an organization becomes, the more significant these factors become.

There is no doubt that a comprehensive and integrated hospital information system (HIS) can be a major source of information. This can serve to describe the relationship between individual patients or groups of patients and individual consultants or between groups of patients and a clinical speciality. Similarly, data can be merged and analysed for contracting purposes, financial projections, comparative analysis, resource utilization review or quality audit. However, discovering what will be of value and identifying presentational formats which will allow, indeed encourage, clinicians across all professional groups to utilize the information available in developing and improving services, requires considerable effort.

A first reaction to quantitative data frequently involves rejection of its content and challenges to its accuracy. However, this can be the beginning of the networking of this hard data with local knowledge and professional views. The effectiveness of theatre utilization is a good example of the complexity of such a process. Data gathered through a theatre computer can provide list start and finish times, calculate the session under- or over-run timings and quantify emergency theatre time utilized. This might appear to be sufficiently limited in its parameters to be acceptable to the users of the theatre services. However, factors such as delayed starts due to an over-run of the last list, unforeseen clinical issues, availability of key staff, portering delays, delay in availability of specific equipment, incorrect computer entries and many other explanations will be proffered in justification of performance which is under scrutiny within a directorate seeking to improve its efficiency.

It is probable that as many issues could be cited to counter the objections raised, but within this apparently rather futile exercise hard data can be used as a powerful debating tool and lead to change. In order for this to happen peer influence is necessary within a 'safe' environment and the financial implications of behaviour must be directly relevant to the individuals involved. This will allow the debate to lead to appropriate changes which individual clinicians feel they have influenced. It then becomes equally important to continue to monitor the relevant data to ensure that proposed changes are implemented, assess their impact and consider possible additional quality improvements. The collection, utilization and acceptance of the full range of relevant information is a powerful catalyst for change.

In discussion of theatre usage we have explored different ways of working: there is no doubt that financial pressures were also a catalyst for this rationalization. An outlying theatre has closed and special surgery (ophthalmology, ENT and oral surgery) incorporated into the main theatre suite. The theatres are now staffed more effectively and, by reducing registrar lists in other specialities, it has been possible to introduce regular trauma lists. More day work has been achieved in a separate day unit and in all the total number of surgical cases performed has increased. The outlying wards that accommodated special surgery also closed and a combined 5-day ward opened in the main surgical block. This was made possible by a reduction in general surgical beds and by rheumatology moving to a new facility.

Data and contracts

The relative value of data has inevitably been heavily influenced by the development of the contracting process. In a devolved management structure this is as significant within directorates as it is at management board level. The drive is to involve directorate teams in the contracting debate to gain true ownership of the commitments made, including activity, prices, waiting list targets and quality standards.

The volume of data required to manage the multiple contracts which will exist in the average hospital is very considerable. The financial viability of the hospital is dependent upon providing relevant and timely information. Minimum data set data for out- and inpatient activity must be available for each episode of treatment and assigned to an individual contract. This is dependent, in turn, upon internal systems, which ensure the collection of accurate demographic details including, for example, postcode and GP code; coding by diagnosis and procedure is essential.

It is clear that the data required to manage contracts is crucial to the well-being of any provider organization. However, the additional benefits to be gained from this database are considerable if the technology is in place to manipulate the data. Clinical audit can be facilitated through this data, drawing on clinical information and also on the 'management' information related to aspects such as comparative length of stay and total cost of care which in itself may point to wide ranges in practice. Quality of service and cost effectiveness can walk side by side, for example when considering use of out-of-hours services such as pathology and radiology, and more generally the number and nature of investigations. Work has been undertaken at the Royal Hampshire Hospital to produce protocols of practice, which have been instrumental in reducing levels of radiological investigation very significantly across specialities.

A major challenge to clinicians and managers is to use data creatively to feed a range of activities and to resist the temptation to adopt a task-oriented approach to using information. This emphasizes the need for the cultural shift, which is required to gain maximum benefit from the changes taking place in the management of health care. Clearly a key determinant of success in this strategy is the availability of information technology, which can be used to respond to the demands made upon it by clinicians and managers (between whom the distinction is rapidly becoming artificial). The danger is that the inability of the technology to respond adequately to these demands may stultify any initial enthusiasm to be radical in the use of information and will ultimately reduce its use to feeding the specific business demands of the organization.

The value of IT as a source of data

Information technology (IT) cannot produce information, it can only process it. By that we mean that the data entered into a system in clinical management must be accurate in the first place, and capable of manipulation by a computer system into meaningful forms of display.

Clear instructions about what clinical information must be put into an IT system are vital, especially if the information gathering is done by non-medical personnel or by junior medical or nursing staff. The senior clinicians wanting to use the information must be responsible for quality control of the information at the input stage. They must also know what format reports will be in and when the data has been processed, rather than assume that the programme will 'generate the data' by itself – if you do not know what has gone in you will not know what can come out. For example, data processing using IT from diagnostic coding may be used to convey trends in acute admission patterns and outcomes. However, it cannot be accurate or useful, however sophisticated the technology, unless there has been clear inputting of information and accurate instructions from clinical managers as to what they want to try to demonstrate.

It is easy to blame IT for producing poor data or unintelligible reports when the real faults are at the input and manipulation levels and are due to failure to appreciate the above concepts. When information has been put into an IT system accurately, and reports carefully thought out, then the strength of IT in data manipulation and display can be seen. Clinical managers must decide whether they are looking at general trends or particular instances. IT can store and manipulate information on many individuals or individual instances. A good IT system can be asked to produce general information, e.g. the number of acute admissions per month, but should be capable of being interrogated to display more individual instances, e.g. the number of people with a particular diagnosis each week, when required.

Although IT cannot produce information in terms of new facts, other than those inputted, it can merge data sets, to display seemingly 'new' information. An example would be merging of a medical unit's acute admissions data, with the month's elective operating list of the Orthopaedic Unit, to identify readmissions with medical postoperative complications. The ability of IT systems, suitably set up, to look back into a series of data on a timescale, and to project forward for future trends, is potentially very powerful. This may also be seen as production of new data, although in the latter case it must be recognized for what it is — a prediction which may not become reality.

The key issue at present seems to be the accurate inputting of relevant information into an IT system, to be processed into meaningful data for the clinical manager. If such inputting could be done as a byproduct of another routine function in everyday work it would be more likely to be accurate than when it is a special, separate function. For instance, diagnostic information for counting clinical activity, produced as a byproduct of a structured clinical letter in which diagnoses are clearly set out by a senior clinician after outpatient consultations, is more likely to be accurate than that gleaned from notes by a relatively untrained non-medical person.

The role of standards in management and clinical processes

A care profile is a record of those events and actions in the care of a patient, or group of patients, which occur during clinical management for a given condition. Such a care profile may be built up to include medical activities and treatments, nursing activities, the work of professionals, such as physiotherapists, and investigative procedures, on a day-to-day basis (Brooks 1991). Care profiles can be either diagnosis-, problem- or procedure-oriented, as appropriate.

Diaries of care, which include all these elements, may be built up for a large number of medical conditions seen in a hospital, or operations performed, and may be extended into primary care. They are more comprehensive than both guidelines (Haines and Feder 1992) – which concentrate on medical care – and anticipated recovery patterns. The diaries of care are not static and should be built up whenever possible on the results of audit and incorporate results of clinical trials (Chalmers *et al.* 1992), although there are inevitably many areas of practice where the results of both audit and clinical trials are scanty. If the profiles are derived from what actually happens in clinical practice, they will reflect the usual level of care being aimed for, and not some idealized standard which cannot be regularly achieved. These realistic standards can then be used to test how often subsequent patients with the same diagnosis receive that desired level of care.

Where a full care profile is seen as 'cumbersome' in its total form, selections of certain parts may be more useful. One particular area where this may be the case relates to the investigation and treatment of patients. From a full care profile, an individual clinician may build up a personal order set, through which junior staff, or the clinician, may order particular tests and treatments, and retrieve the results. Where a group of clinicians are working together, a departmental order set may be produced in the same way. While there are obvious advantages in all this group using the same order set, some individual variations may be possible, although too many variations defeat the purpose.

If a care profile is on a Hospital Information System (HIS), and can be accessed readily, it can be used in everyday clinical management. Junior doctors may check their clinical actions in respect to a particular patient group against the relevant care profile. It may guide their actions in diagnosis and treatment. Nurses may check their patients' progress notes against the profile, and use IT to write such notes if patient care corresponds to the profile.

How do care profiles fit into the clinical management process? Where a standard has been set and defined, it is easier to judge a clinical process against it and to more clearly define the outcome. Exceptions should be easier to detect and, once identified, subsequent interrogation of the database, facilitated by IT, may make understanding the reason for the exception easier. A logical extension of this process is into the use of profiles and standards in clinical audit: an audit cycle using a care profile is illustrated in Figure 5.2.

Clinical managers should therefore find profiles useful in measuring work done and identifying exceptions in terms of process and outcome. These may be studied in detail using an audit system linked to the profile. Profiles and standards might be criticized by clinicians as being inflexible and of potential danger in medicolegal situations. But flexibility can be built into profiles, and individual practices accounted for, by personal order sets. A profile is a guideline and not an absolute standard against which all is

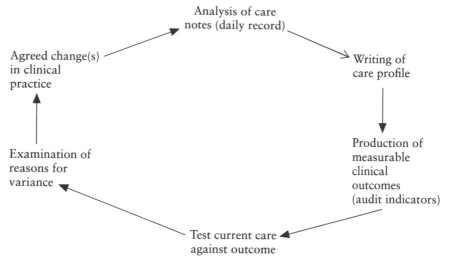

Figure 5.2   Use of care profiles in the audit cycle.

measured. Room for clinical discretion must always be allowed. Indeed, it could be argued that having a profile and order set may reduce errors (e.g. through better routine monitoring of certain drug levels) by promoting appropriate actions to be taken.

Conclusions

Many senior health professionals, particularly doctors, are involved in management and spend considerable time away from clinical work. At the same time, pressure on managers through the region and from the centre has increased considerably. There are many more high quality managers in the NHS than ever before. We would hope that new managers with limited experience of the provider function at the clinical interface will take the time to try to understand the problems and seek to resolve them in a constructive manner. Whilst the pre-Review arrangements were perhaps too cosy, there is a need for interchange of information between purchasers and providers relating to the contracting process not just at managerial level but also at the clinical level. Shroud-waving by doctors and 'macho management' are unlikely to produce the desired results in the long term.

Our experience of a devolved management structure suggests that this allows an organization to respond more effectively to the constant and increasingly rapid changes that we are now experiencing in the NHS. There has been a more constructive dialogue between managers and professionals. However, managers need a clear idea of the information needs of the organization and data should be collected as part of the process of delivery of care. This data should be validated by those whom the data describes before it is used in decision making.

References

Brooks, A.P. (1991) 'Care profiles of acute myocardial infarction and status asthmaticus', *Clinical Profiles of Care*. Workshop proceedings published by Resource Management Unit, NHS Management Executive, pp. 111–34.

Buxton, M., Packwood, T. and Keen, J. (1991) *Final Report of the Brunel University Evaluation of Resource Management*. London, Department of Health.

Chalmers, I., Dickersin, K. and Chalmers, T. (1992) 'Getting to grips with Archie Cochrane's agenda', *British Medical Journal*, 305, 786–8.

Haines, A. and Feder, G. (1992) 'Guidance on guidelines', *British Medical Journal*, 305, 785–6.

Packwood, T., Keen, J. and Buxton, M. (1991) *Hospitals in Transition*. Milton Keynes, Open University Press.

6 | Nursing information

Rebecca Malby and Jane Clayton

Problems and opportunities

Nurses, it could be argued, are the largest group of information collectors and providers in health care. This reflects their numbers, the particular role they play as information brokers for patients and their role as co-ordinators of care teams. In the past these roles have not been recognized. This chapter reflects on past problems and outlines ways in which nurses can play a positive role in informing good clinical practice.

In the last few years, nursing information has in significant part been concerned with information technology (IT). For example, the introduction of a nurse management information system (NMIS) was tacked on to the Resource Management (RM) initiative as an afterthought (Keen and Malby 1992). As RM systems concentrated on the process of care, so NMIS tended to follow suit, collecting data to support existing care delivery rather than looking ahead to ensure that they could support the nursing practice of the future. The purpose of the NMIS remained unclear to nurses and managers alike, and this was pivotal in the difficulty in instigating NMIS across all areas of nursing. More generally, implementation was hindered by the complex nature of the decisions surrounding nursing care and by the inability of the profession to articulate its expectations in relation to its information requirements.

The attractiveness of information technology (IT) to nurses has been a direct result of their perceptions that it would be a solver of problems. Nurses thought that it would demonstrate how hard they worked, would simplify care planning, and would save them time currently spent on clerical or management activity, such as drawing up the duty rota. Implicitly this assumes that nurses' information requirements are captured by the IT, that nursing practice stands still and that ward nurses have control over the use of information in a system. None of these assumptions bears scrutiny. Perhaps most importantly, nurses have become the data inputters and not information users. Where sisters do not control their stock and staffing budgets, they are in no position to be creative in using information to match the skills of available nurses to the needs of patients. In some hospitals the daily display that patient care demands outstrip nursing supply is a source of irritation or grief, as the hospital management is unable or unwilling to address the problem. The purpose of NMIS are rarely stated clearly, but appear to include:

1 To cost nursing care in order to price services.
2 To support nurses in decisions they make about the mangement and delivery of care.
3 To support the mangement prices in the review of efficiency and effectiveness of care.

Often the purposes are a mixture of all three, without any agreed priorities. To set against these problems, though, there are signs that the way that nurses approach their work is being rethought. 'New nursing' was a phrase coined by Beardshaw and Robinson (1990) in a King's Fund Institute research report on nursing developments. New nursing is grounded in the concept of partnership, in which a client's individual personal needs for nursing are identified and in which nurses attempt to offer them informed choice in their care. It centres on the 'clinical role of the nurse as care giver, and the unique contribution of nursing care to healing'. The report cites innovations in nursing that have real potential for improving quality of care, and states that developing these approaches will be a critical test for health policy over the next decade. Beardshaw notes that features of this direction include developing systems for organizing nursing care that take decision making as near to the patient as possible (e.g. Primary Nursing) and developing nursing teams who lead the research and development of practice (e.g. Nursing Development Units).

The focus for these innovations is empowerment. This direction in nursing has been welcomed variously by political leaders, patients and leaders of nursing. Empowerment involves enabling the individual to take control (power) over his/her own person, in order to exercise choice. The essence of this empowerment is information, and an environment that facilitates patient choice. In order to empower patients, professionals themselves must be empowered. Staff who are not empowered will be reluctant to take responsibility for their actions, to seek new ways to meet new situations or better ways to meet usual situations or to offer a personalized service. This empowerment has two prerequisites – decentralized decision making and individual professional accountability (Pearson *et al.* 1989). In turn, these are dependent on an ethical code of practice and commitment to staff development. Nurse empowerment is dependent on nurses having access to information that supports their practice decisions and contributes to the delivery of nursing care. Any information system must start from the practice of nursing itself, and the related desire for achieving patient empowerment.

Currently, nurses do not usually receive the information they require at a time when it is most useful to their clinical and managerial decisions, nor do they receive it in a form which they can understand and use quickly in a pressured environment. Notwithstanding this problem, there is a rationale for focusing on the nurse–patient relationship. Nurses are accessible to patients more easily than other health professionals. Patients tend to remember the information given to them by nurses, because they tend to receive it when they need it, and usually in terms that they can understand. In practice this means that information about patients should reflect the identity of the patient's care giver (the named nurse in the Patient's Charter), should enable critical review of that patient's nursing care and should ensure that the nurse–patient relationship is fostered by maximizing the time the nurse has with the patient. The primacy of the patient is the central feature of Patient-focused Hospitals in the USA (Box 6.1).

These new developments mean that there are many opportunities for addressing the roles nurses play in care delivery, in such areas as the Junior Doctor's Hours Initiative, the advent of Patient Hotels, the decreasing length of stay of patients and studies demonstrating the cost effectiveness of the new Nurse Practitioner. These, combined with the move towards more community-based services, emphasize the need for information on the cost and benefits of new developments from the patient's perspective, for the service as a whole and for the contributing professions. Future developments in service organization need to go hand in hand with consideration of management and operational information requirements.

Clinical nurse information requirements

In the guidelines for assessment in one hospital's individual patient care programme for mental health, it is suggested that in order to pass on information which is completely accurate and can be discussed directly with a patient, direct quotes should be used. For example, 'I feel terrible' is preferred to 'Patient seems depressed and despondent', because the latter introduces the professional's interpretation into the information that is recorded. This example illustrates the tension surrounding nursing information and its use in the current political climate of the NHS. There is a need:

1 To distinguish between 'hard' data required to support operational and management decisions and the 'softer' information which contributes to patient care decisions.
2 To determine how to evaluate the contribution of both kinds of information to local health service provision.

There seem to be three salient points in this context. First, when nurses are asked about their need for information, and the way they process that

Box 6.1 Patient-focused Hospitals. Case Study: Lakeland Hospital, Florida

The Lakeland Hospital has grouped nurses and their support staff into teams, with a team leader. These teams are responsible for the care of a small group of patients (usually six) assigned to one doctor. The teams ensure a registered nurse is rostered for their team on every shift, with a mixture of other nurses and support staff. *All* team members are multiskilled; in practice this means that they undertake the many tasks that nurses in the UK undertake already as well as new tasks such as phlebotomy and respiratory therapy. The teams are supported by a ward-based pharmacist, laboratory technician, radiographer and a (three-ward) unit-based clerk and admitting officer. All are managed by the ward clinical manager (a ward typically being 40 beds) and supported by the unit Clinical Nurse Specialist and Advanced Practice Specialist.

The most vital support to the team comes from the Master Scheduler. This person visits every team on the unit and is responsible for workload. They talk through patients' progress and discharges and inputs this information into a computer to calculate the team's workload. If the team's doctor wishes to admit a patient, they must first contact the Master Scheduler, who will agree an admission date based on team's workload. If the workload is too high to admit another patient, the Master Scheduler will look at the doctor's 'secondary team': each team has a primary and a secondary doctor. The Master Scheduler has a copy of the off-duty rota for each team, and the geographical location of patients on the computer. Thus patients can be admitted to beds that enable the teams to work within a small geographical area.

The location of computers by the bedside for rapid ordering and use of test results and the close proximity of the support services means that patients do not spend their day travelling between departments, and neither do the nurses spend unnecessary time chasing around after other services. It also contributes to improved morale, as the dedicated services feel part of a team and will help with ward activities when they are not busy with their main tasks. The nurses are thus supported in the management of their workload, and enter hardly any data into the computer.

Care in the unit is carried out against protocols that are agreed by a Nurse Practice Committee. Any doctor admitting a patient must agree in principle to these protocols. Nurse reporting takes the form of exception reports, which are examined by the unit Quality Improvement Team. The Patient-focused Hospital combines total quality management, with an order communications system, decentralized services and nurse empowerment.

information and pass it on to others, their responses tend to reflect not only their specific role within the organization, but also the degree of contact they have with patients, families, other professionals and managers. Most nurses would agree with the distinction between data (e.g. a series of observations, measurements of facts) and information defined as knowledge acquired through experience or study of specific events or situations. When asked what data they use, the majority will give examples from resource management and audit, for example to measure workload and work out rosters. Senior nursing management may comment on the use of statistics that could support them in their operational roles in day-to-day delivery of care, and in their management role to plan care, manage budgets and monitor services. In contrast, nurses who are most directly involved in patient care (staff nurses, enrolled nurses) tend to talk more about the need for patient-focused information, such as care plans and aids to communication, which are qualitative rather than quantitative. When asked to describe the sorts of phrases they would use in describing their care, terms such as 'empathy', 'touch' and 'being with the patient' come up time and time again. (When asked, very few clinical nurses feel that a computer could assist them at this level of information gathering or dissemination.) Sitting between these two groups are Clinical Nurse Specialists and Sisters who, when asked, speak most about professional information – that concerned with specific knowledge about their practice, which should ideally be research based. There are, then, likely to be quite stark differences in information requirements for different groups of nurses.

Second, nurses at every level seem to have developed a 'squirrel syndrome' for information gathering. This runs counter to good information management. A great difficulty for nurses is to know how best to use any information to inform their management and practice of nursing, or how to facilitate its use by other nurses, managers, health care professionals and patients. If nurses are to turn this roadblock into a stepping stone, they will need to learn how to use information to identify their level of performance through audit, and go on to use this information to make changes that will benefit all parties. One way to do this would be to record systematically what they learn from their *experiences* and use this information to inform, support and evaluate both managerial and clinical processes in nursing.

Third, nursing is very process-oriented in its information gathering and appraisal. Frater (1992) argues that if it is agreed that all those involved in the care of patients are likely to influence the outcomes of care, it is also crucial that substantial incentives are employed for the collection and use of information on outcomes. Such information would have direct relevance to clinical processes in which nurses are involved, be central to decision making by nurse managers and enable patients to comment on the merits of the care they are receiving.

There are currently few available measures for assessing the consequences or outcomes of nursing interventions. Information systems are not geared up to collect this information and, whilst there is considerable enthusiasm to develop methods for measuring outcomes in relation to functional health status, research is needed to assess how:

1 To bring about the organizational and cultural changes required to ensure routine collection of information on outcomes.

2 Methods of analysis and presentation of that information will ensure its effective use by all clinicians and managers.

Developing a model for information

Any contract for services will incorporate what the purchaser offers in terms of finances and what it expects to get out in terms of outcomes and productivity for particular patient groups. This requires providers to be able to turn those inputs into the required outputs. There are many studies of inputs and outputs in health care, but very few link the two. It is clear, though, that a defined sum of money does not guarantee a specific output, and this explains in part the variation in contract prices for instance, the cost of similar orthopaedic stays can range from £250 to £2,500. This is true of nursing. Studies such as Skill Mix In District Nursing (NHSME 1992) look at the grades of staff and their costs without linking them to quality of output. Output measures such as throughput and pressure sore prevalence rate are rarely linked to inputs, though these vary widely from hospital to hospital. As Buchan and Ball (1991) state, 'There is no "body" of literature on the costs and benefits of nursing, but rather a series of often incompatible parts . . . There is a requirement for more UK research which formulates and validates methodologies for measuring cost in relation to outcome.' The imperative for nursing in the current managerial climate is to demonstrate the costs and benefits of different models of nursing practice. At present we have studies investigating the effects on patient care and costs of a reduced or increased skill level (Bagust and Burrows 1992); we have resource management attempting to relate the costs of nursing through care plans or workload measures; we have the equivalent of the doctor's Read Codes (Read and Benson 1986) being developed for nursing and we have nursing audit attempting to demonstrate nursing outcomes. All of these are tackling different aspects of the problem. To ensure that the financial input achieves the best output, the process of care must be examined, as must the factors that affect this process. Thus each patient group requires a tracking system that can pick up professional groups' contribution to care, and a system for evaluating the effectiveness of that process within the context of the care environment. The Value for Money equation attempts to link resource management, quality and audit into one patient-focused information system (Fig. 6.1). Below we consider each element.

Costs

There are several ways to measure the costs of nursing care. These include:

1 *Cost per day/diem.* This is the average nursing cost per patient day, i.e. the total nursing cost of the service divided by the number of days the patient was an inpatient.

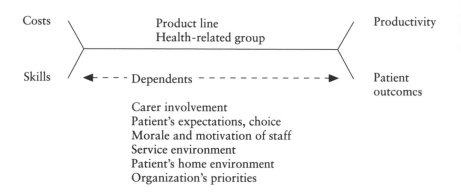

Figure 6.1   The value for money equation.

2 *Cost per diagnosis*. This is the standard nursing care cost per patient diagnosis. For this method, a standard multidisciplinary care profile is agreed, which incorporates the resource most commonly used. The profile is costed (by analysing the activity specified within it) to determine the average time spent on delivering the nursing component of the profile, and the nursing costs of that time. The relation to a medical diagnosis is useful in ensuring consistency and compatibility with costing systems for medical inputs, but does not necessarily reflect the nursing needs of the patient, or properly classify those patients whose primary requirement is for nursing.

3 *Cost per relative intensity measure*. This was developed because of inadequacies in the previous method to accurately reflect differences in patient acuity. It calculates the time spent on nursing and non-nursing tasks for the entirety of the patient stay, dividing patients into homogeneous groups based on the use of nursing resources (Edwardson and Giovannetti 1987). Length of stay was found to be the single best predictor of nursing time required. This work has been undertaken predominantly in acute units.

4 *Cost per nursing workload*. This links costs to diagnosis or cost centre by assigning the patient to a dependency category, for each of which there are determined nurse hours. The nursing input to each category is costed. The patients are aggregated into diagnostic related groups (DRGs), and along with their costed nurse hours are then analysed to provide a cost per DRG. This is probably the most popular method in the USA, perhaps because it was used originally to roster staff. It is patient-focused, can be related to a medical model and can be linked to available staffing. However, it is detailed and labour intensive in the initial stages. Most hospitals in the USA are now using this method, as it is

found to be accurate enough to adequately charge for the nursing service, whilst requiring minimum information about the care process, which is complex to cost.

Skills

In many instances costs are related directly to skills, as it is assumed that a higher paid (and therefore higher grade) nurse will have more skills. This ignores the variety of skills within grades: not all E grade nurses have the exact same expertise or abilities. A nurse's ability to deliver the care required, or even to determine the best route of care is dependent on personal competence, and achieving a particular level of competence also requires investment in training and reflective practice. The competence the nurse brings to the patient's problem will affect cost in terms of an overhead for all patients in relation to staff development, and the pay scale awarded to ensure that that nurse is competent. Thus a measure that costs the nurse's time and relates that to competence is required. The nearest that anyone in the UK has come to relating skills to quality and cost has been the University of York Report on Skill Mix (Centre for Health Economics 1992): this stands as an example of what careful research can achieve.

Productivity

This is the activity or number of patients treated in a given period of time. In terms of nursing it would be the numbers of patients admitted and discharged, the total number on the caseload and the length of time patients stay on the caseload. This sits most comfortably with case management approaches such as Primary Nursing or Team Nursing. It must not be judged in isolation from the other key output – patient outcomes. There is no point in discharging patients to meet productivity requirements if their health suffers as a consequence!

Outcomes

In the new models of nursing, outcomes must relate to target outcomes agreed between the patient and the nurse. As mentioned previously, patient motivation and priorities should influence goal-setting in relation to outcome. 'Simple' clinical outcomes can be measured by assessing the patient's perceived and actual problems using validated assessment criteria for variables such as pain or functional mobility. Outcomes can also be measured against known clinical indicators of care such as pressure sore incidence, incontinence and leg ulcer healing rates.

Once the patient has been assessed, the joint expectations of the patient, nurse and other professionals in improving the assessment can be recorded. The patient is then reassessed on discharge. The difference in health status from admission to discharge, and any difference between expectations and actual achievement, can then be used as a measure of patient outcome and as a tool for audit. This should be linked to patient satisfaction through interviews, and satisfaction used as an outcome. Outputs should also be compared to what can be expected of the staff employed. For instance, it may be the case that all the nurses used an outdated method of caring for leg ulcers, which prolongs healing. Only by auditing the nursing care against national good practice can we be sure that we are getting the optimum outcome.

Dependents

However, this picture understates the patient's experience. There are other factors besides costs and skills that affect the overall outputs, described in the model as 'dependents'. These seek to recognize the world in which we live, and our desire to provide a personalized service for empowered patients. Thus a nurse's ability or willingness to achieve the desired outputs for a particular patient group will be determined by six factors:

1 *Nurse morale and motivation.* There is plenty of research that supports the theory that motivated and valued staff enjoy their work and produce better service for patients. However skilled the nurse may be, and however much he or she is paid, if their contribution is not valued their work will be of a lower standard. Staff motivation and morale can be measured using proxies such as sickness and absenteeism rates, and through staff interviews and questionnaires. Simple measures like listing the 10 worst things about working on the ward, and the 10 best things in priority order, may provide a valuable snapshot of staff opinion of the service and its environment.

2 *Involvement of the carer in providing care.* This can affect the overall workload of the nurse and the ability of the nurse to discharge the patient. If carers are willing and involved they may take over the whole of the patient's care. However, if carers are unhappy with the overall outcome they may refuse to take over the patient's care. Carer involvement should be recorded in the patient's record.

3 *The individual patient's personal choice in care planning, and expectations of the outcome.* To take an example, a patient may present with both a physical and an emotional problem. The doctor or nurse may perceive the former to be the most important and devote time and resources to it. But the patient may perceive the emotional problem to be the most important and feel let down by that care received. This brings in another dimension to the equation: appropriateness. The question must be asked, 'Did the care given solve the patient's problem?' In many cases only the patient can provide the whole answer. Moreover, the patient may choose not to comply with the recommendations of the nurse (e.g. to give up smoking prior to surgery), thus increasing their length of stay or contributing to a poor outcome. We can all sympathize

with the anecdote of the district nurse who goes into the old lady's house to dress her ulcer. As soon as she leaves the old lady pokes her ulcer with a knitting needle. The old lady wants the district nurse to keep visiting her, and so she does not want the ulcer to heal! Solving the whole problem is integral to achieving the best patient outcomes. Patients' expectations should be built into agreeing the overall objectives for care. All patients should be involved in their care planning.

4 *The service environment.* The environment in which the patient is being cared for will have an impact on a nurse's ability to achieve a good outcome. Nursing costs may be higher if the nurse is expected to undertake low skilled, non-patient-focused work, such as clerical work. Organizational audits might be appropriate instruments to assess the environment, as are health and safety reports.

5 *The patient's home environment.* The ability to discharge a patient is dependent on home circumstances, including the layout of their home, its accessibility and (above all) the amount of support from carers. This point and the last one emphasize that the degree of co-ordination between social, private and NHS care will affect both the inputs and outputs.

6 *The organization's priorities.* The organization may view one type of patient as a relatively low priority, or choose to channel resources towards a particular area of its activities. Devoting detailed nursing care for one patient will be to the detriment of other patients. The nursing staff must know the objectives of the organization in determining resources to meet patient needs. Any assessment of a patient's progress through the service will include those things that most impact the organization's agenda, principally contract agreements on cost, quality and volume.

The process of care

The ability to track a patient's progress is ultimately dependent on the written (or printed) record of care. In nursing this has traditionally been the care plan. However, at present, hand-written records rarely cover all the patient's care, nor do they prioritize nursing interventions. This challenges the Nursing Care Planning System (the Nursing Process) approach to determining care requirements. Batehup and Evans (1992) question the validity of care planning, saying that it does not determine priorities and, because it is time-consuming to complete, nurses side-step some assessing or recording areas of care assuming that they will take place anyway. As the Ombudsman only too often points out, it may happen, but if it isn't recorded nobody will know it for certain. Systems for setting expected standards such as protocols or critical paths seek to get over this problem. However, they too may have their problems, as they can too easily become task-based inventories of activities that have to happen to the patients, rather than outcomes agreed with the patient. Protocols typically document the standard process of care each day for patients by category, which might be a DRG, health-related group or local classification. Thus a patient admitted for hemicolectomy could have several protocols related to (for instance) general surgical admission, hemicolectomy and 'stable diabetic for surgery'. Critical paths go one step further in defining those instances that are critical to the patient being discharged on the agreed date (Fig. 6.2). Standard data on the process of care are identified, with additional space for non-standard problems. Daily reporting then relies on exceptions, where events are recorded if the agreed protocol is not achieved.

Critical paths as developed in the USA have been criticized for being too task-oriented. Thus audit should involve a review of patient outcomes and, where these do not reach expectations, a review of the exception reports and the dependents within which the process took place. It seems that standards for practice in a care setting, alongside protocols with exception reporting can provide a route to achieving a complete record of the nursing care.

Patient-focused information

The model depicted in Figure 6.1 leaves open the question of recording and analysing information so that the patient perceives care to be integrated, and so records are also integrated. The integrated record facilitates tracking of the patient through the whole of his or her stay. Of course, any information systems devised must support the effective delivery of care. It is likely that it will pivot on communication systems to support the rapid relay of patients' investigation results and of messages, designed so that data are tied into the central patient record. Hospital-wide order communication systems and electronic mail would speed up communications, and thus the professional's ability to adjust care appropriately.

A patient-based system will ensure that the hospital is in a position to best advance care whilst determining the parameters in which that care is delivered. Moving from a discipline base to a patient focus to information gathering will ensure that the information is meaningful and usable. Some of the data will be best captured on a computer. For example, a solution to nurse rostering, if patient-focused, will ensure that rostering is matched to activity to optimize the use of available staff. However, not all the data discussed above will be retrieved from computer systems and, if they are used, they should be developed on the back of tried and tested manual systems. This in itself would be a radical departure from current practice. Nurses seem bewitched by IT to the detriment of finding an information system that best meets the patient's needs for care and the hospital's needs to track the management and delivery of care. This has the potential to drag nurses away from patients. Any IT that is not flexible enough to support the care delivered by 'new nurses' will hinder progress to patient empowerment. If IT takes nurses away from patients, without demonstrable

Figure 6.2 Critical path for an abdominal hysterectomy.

ABDOMINAL HYSTERECTOMY

Patient's Name:
Case Note Number:
Admission Date:

Co-ordinated Care Contacts:
Jenny Brown ext 2004
Lyn Simpson ext 2059

	OPD	DAY MINUS 1	OPERATION DAY	DAY 1	
M E D I C A L	History, allergies etc Chest X-ray, ECG if indicated FBC, Group and Save Check smear Anaesthetist	Review medical history Physical examination and check allergies Obtain consent Complete anaesthetic sheet Prescribe antibiotic DVT Prophylaxis and night sedation	Audit form and Vital signs and urinary output IV regime Medication /analgesia	Review analgesia and IV regime Prescribe oral analgesia Check bowel and bladder function Commence oral fluids when satisfactory Check general condition and wound daily	
N U R S I N G	Urinalysis and MSU Pulse and BP Admission sheet Discharge planning commenced Weight	Nursing assessment Measure for TED stockings Order PT medication Shave Check bowel function	Prep for theatre Pre-op medication Complete check list Check valuables Check documentation BP, pulse and responses PCAS observations Observation of wound sites and drainage measurements Observe general condition	Continue 4 hourly measures TDS observations Observe wound Remove drain Commence 30 ml fluids hourly Review PCAS and IVI Vulval toilet with sterile water Check bowel and bladder function Review PV loss	
P H Y S I O		Breathing exercises Post-op exercises Circulatory exercises Pelvic tilting Discuss abdominal exercises and back problems		Assess chest Breathing exercises and mobility Back care as appropriate	
P A T I E N T T E A C H I N G	Info pamphlet to patient Admission and LOS details Health education re diet exercise and smoking	Patient informed of surgery time Counselling pre- and post-op care Reinforce patient teaching information	Nil by mouth for 6 hours pre-op	Assist patient out of bed and encourage exercise General hygiene	

PLEASE INITIAL IN SPACE PROVIDED WHEN TASK COMPLETE

ABDOMINAL HYSTERECTOMY

Patient's Name:
Case Note Number:
Admission Date:

Co-ordinated Care Contacts:
Jenny Brown ext 2004
Lyn Simpson ext 2059

	DAY 2	DAY 3	DAY 4	DAYS 5–7	OPD
MEDICAL	Review analgesia and IV regime; Check general condition and wound daily	FBC; MSU; Prescribe discharge medication; Check general condition and wound daily	Check general condition and wound daily	Complete audit / discharge form; Check histology; Check general condition and wound daily	General review examination; Letter to GP
NURSING	Discontinue TDS observations; Expose wound site; Increase fluids; Discontinue fluid balance; Discontinue IV and PCAS; Review PV loss	Microlaxenema if BNO; Review wound site; Arrange OPD appt; Review PV loss; Order discharge medication	Observe progress; Review wound site	Remove staples or clips; Discharge check list; Discharge form for GP; Nursing documentation	
PHYSIO	Breathing exercises and mobility		Mobility exercises; Abdominal exercises; Advice re post discharge activities		
PATIENT TEACHING	Encourage short walks with rest period; Patient teaching and counselling; General hygiene	Increased independence and mobility; Commence light diet; General hygiene	Continue patient education; General hygiene	Post hysterectomy discussion; General hygiene	

PLEASE INITIAL IN SPACE PROVIDED WHEN TASK COMPLETE

returns – as so often happens now – then some searching questions will have to be asked.

References

Bagust, A. and Burroughs, J. (1992) 'Quality or quantity', *Health Services Journal*, 6, 23–5.

Batehup, L. and Evans, A. (1992) 'Nursing development units: a review strategy', *Nursing Times*, 88(18), 40–1.

Beardshaw, V. and Robinson, R. (1990) *New for Old? Prospects for Nursing in the 1990's*. London, King's Fund Institute.

Buchan, J. and Ball, J. (1991) *Caring Costs*, IMS Report No. 208. London, Institute of Manpower Studies.

Centre for Health Economics (1992) *Skill Mix and the Effectiveness of Nursing Care*. York, York University.

Edwardson, S. and Giovannetti. (1987) 'A review of cost accounting methods for nursing services', *Nursing Economics*, 5(3), 107–17.

Frater, A. (1992) 'Health outcomes: a challenge to the status quo', *Quality in Health Care*, 2, HFMA/CIPFA Database, 3 Robert Street, London.

Keen, J. and Malby, R. (1992) 'Nursing power and practice in the United Kingdom National Health Service', *Journal of Advanced Nursing*, 17, 863–70.

NHS ME (1992) *Skill Mix in District Nursing*. London, Value for Money Unit, HMSO.

Pearson, A., Durrant, I. and Punton, S. (1989) 'Determining quality in a unit where nursing is the primary intervention', *Journal of Advanced Nursing*, 14, 269–73.

Read, J. and Benson, T. (1986) 'The Read Clinical Classification', *British Journal of Health Computing*, 3, 22–5.

7　Contracts: managing the external environment

John James

Historical perspective

The purchaser role has in most areas developed rapidly since it was unveiled in *Working for Patients* (Secretaries of State 1989) and amplified in succeeding working papers. At that stage most emphasis was placed on trusts and GP fundholders, with the purchasers' role rather more opaque. Yet the purchaser role was every bit as new. District Health Authorities (DHAs) had been planning and resource allocation bodies operating through line-management relationships with their units, but certainly not concerned with purchasing health care for their populations. Indeed most found, when the new arrangements came into operation, a substantial mismatch between the services they provided locally and local usage of those services.

April 1991 was the first visible milestone with the introduction of capitation-based funding of DHAs, the launch of first-wave trusts and fundholders and the need to have in place the first round of contracts. The eminently sensible 'steady state' principle (where existing patterns of services were to be retained) meant in practice that most of the issues that had to be addressed in relation to 1991–2 were technical in nature. They centred on the availability and reliability of the data about previously ignored patient flows that underpinned a district's or a GP fundholder's allocation, and providers' expectations that their income would match their historic expenditure levels. Those DHAs who had turned their directly managed units (DMUs) into viable self-managing organizations or, better still, first-wave trusts, and who had brought together multidisciplinary cadres of individuals to create the nucleus of a purchasing team working closely with GPs and Family Health Services Authorities (FHSA), fared best.

Box 7.1

Contracting brought to light the plight of physically disabled people lying for years in beds acute wards, blocking beds and receiving no rehabilitation.

Parkside DHA withdrew both patients and the associated resources from those acute providers and has invested in dedicated rehabilitation services and more suitable long-stay care.

Even the best prepared, however, found as 1991–2 progressed, that their plans were forced off course by referral patterns that proved to have no relation to the ones derived for 1989–90 from the National Clearing House, or by an upsurge in extracontractual referrals (ECRs), excess medical negligence claims or perhaps belated recognition that local fundholders had been given too large a share of the cake. Late availability of data and failures by providers to understand or to use the contractual mechanisms (especially the extracontractual) properly, bedevilled in-year monitoring. Software that should have been in place prior to April 1991 straggled in as the year progressed, and indeed continues to do so. The lessons from 1991–2 are all about surviving in a period of chaos. It is hoped that they will have less relevance by 1994. Their importance is principally that they brought into sharp focus the need to have clear management systems, supported by timely and meaningful information in order to obtain the full benefits of the purchasing role.

April 1992 proved to be an equally significant milestone, though it was approached on the whole with less nervousness. DHAs and the substantially larger number of fundholders were free of the steady state limitations (which most had observed in 1991–2) and could contemplate more noticeable alterations in referral patterns. Late availability of provider prices, partly incompetence, partly tactical, hampered those DHAs that had hoped to make price a major factor in decision-taking, but quite a number of constructive ideas were introduced. Boxes 7.1, 7.2 and 7.3 give some examples which should have continuing relevance. DHAs, in particular, were also able to unleash on their providers a range of quality standards, going in many instances well beyond the Patient's Charter, to sit alongside the quantified targets in contracts. One provider solemnly signed up not to have anyone waiting longer than 24 months for its maternity services – in general quality monitoring has not gone beyond its infancy.

Quite a number of DHAs insisted on provider-specific increases in the proportion of cases carried out on a day basis. Providers countered with more complex price structures, exclusion clauses and hidden extras. Not surprisingly, in an environment of change and uncertainty, late signing of contracts and recourse to arbitration were commonplace. Lack of negotiating skills, failure to understand the implications of contracts and differing

Box 7.2

Harrow DHA found it had five local hospitals providing orthopaedic treatment, one of which might have had to withdraw. A competitive tendering exercise was carried out, with independent clinical advice.

As a result, the DHA ended its contract with one of the other providers and renewed its contract with the vulnerable provider, which proved to be a significant competitor.

Box 7.3

Harrow DHA recognized many limitations in its initial foray into clinical tendering. It subsequently incorporated improvements into a tender for continuing care for elderly mentally ill people reprovided locally.

The tender was secured by a private company with substantial experience in another part of the country. The local Community Trust proved uncompetitive in cost and other terms.

interpretations of contracts have become very apparent. With hindsight, the immensity of the tasks for 1992–3 was not sufficiently appreciated.

By contrast, April 1993 was recognized early on to be a very difficult milestone, because it would see the full impact of the decision to give local authorities lead responsibility for community care. The need for jointly-owned community care plans, DHA endorsement of local authorities' care assessment and management plans and the need to survive in an increasingly tight financial climate have forced the health–social divide rapidly up the purchaser's agenda. At the same time there is an increasing push towards integration of DHAs and FHSAs into Commissioning Agencies, a process that recognizes that the main focus of purchasing in the years ahead will be on a shift from secondary to primary care, which is best achieved by pooling both the endeavour and the resources of DHAs and FHSAs. The same thrust lies behind the increasing number of locality purchasing projects, focusing either on local health needs assessment or on enhancing the responsibility of GPs in a particular small area, in the most ambitious cases also involving social services funding. At the same time, the health improvement agenda that finds expression in *The Health of the Nation* (Secretary of State for Health 1992) and its targets is pointing out the need to involve all of the agencies that are, however unwittingly, in a position to influence the health of a local population. Healthy alliance initiatives (Box 7.4) illustrate the sheer number of players that may be involved; together with the wealth of studies of the effectiveness of health

---

Box 7.4

The healthy alliances programme with the City of Westminster covers, *inter alia*, the following:

- home safety
- safety at work
- road safety
- emergency services
- coronary heart disease
- noise
- Legionnaire's disease
- water monitoring
- air pollution
- dogs
- HIV/AIDS
- substance abuse

---

interventions that are now emerging, all of these are fighting their way on to the purchasing agenda and will be influential in the years ahead.

The purchasing role has therefore changed rapidly from a largely mechanical approach, acute-sector-dominated with short time horizons, to a much more broadly based approach with a substantially more ambitious strategic and alliance-building approach. Nor will those alliances be confined to other purchasing-style agencies; the lessons of the contractual disputes and failures of 1992 clearly need to be reflected in the development of more longstanding relationships, often called preferred-provider relationships, between those providers and those purchasers who have no alternative but to continue to do business with each other. But, at the end of the day, it will be the external environment shaped by the changes introduced in April 1993 that will most influence what purchasers have to manage.

The purchasing cycle

Figure 7.1 illustrates a standard description of the purchasing process in the broadest sense. With the proviso that it reflects both an annual cycle and a rolling long-term cycle, it none the less provides a useful framework within which to consider the information, and hence the IT requirements, that underpin the complex and subtle process that purchasing has become. It should also be recognized that at April 1991 we broke into the cycle at stage 5, with the requirements of steady state. Only those (rare) districts which are effectively self-sufficient with small external flows could say honestly that their referral flows were the conscious outcome of stages 1–4.

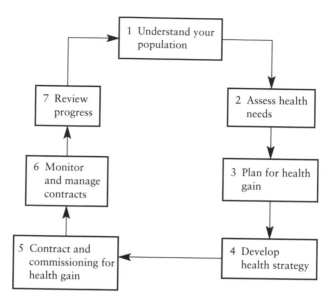

Figure 7.1   The purchasing cycle.

That said, it seems a reasonable aim for all purchasing or commissioning authorities to seek to get the circle to flow. At each stage information will play a key part in achieving the activity involved. The term 'information' in this chapter, while inevitably used much of the time to denote hard data, is used also to cover the much broader range of soft information and understanding that, of necessity, has to be built up between purchasers and others operating in the NHS environment.

Understand your population

In many ways this could be the most under-rated of the tasks. Population analysis is such a standard feature of health care planning that the difficulties of applying it within a purchasing framework may be underestimated. Not only does a commissioning agency need to know the numbers, composition and location of its resident population, and to project future trends taking account of demography, ethnicity, migration, and mobility, it also needs, if it is to achieve its health gain objectives, to know a great deal about the factors which determine the population's approach not only to the use of health care services but also to health generally.

Information has to be aggregated from a variety of sources of varying reliability. OPCS census data is the key resource, and for the immediate future we will have the 1991 data at its least imperfect. Access to FHSA registers is improving and has the capacity to enhance data at locality (however defined) level. For inner-city agencies, whose residents are highly

---

Box 7.5 Understand your population – inner-city issues

Ethnic composition is usually more varied in inner cities. This may have consequences for health need, but also implies cultural values which may be material to use of health services or personal or family responsibility for health care. Language and religion are also key. Immigrant groups, especially refugees, are likely to have fewer elderly people – now, but for how long? The anonymity of hospital A&E departments may be welcomed by various groups who feel outside society. They may avoid what we regard as more appropriate services.

---

mobile and may often have an aversion to registration, both sources are less reliable. Data on homeless people (street-dwelling or bed and break-fast) or on refugees may be at its most reliable from voluntary or outreach agencies, while local authorities and voluntary organizations may maintain registers on other groups. The tasks, therefore, will be centred around aggregation of information from a variety of sources and seeking to make sense of it notwithstanding its limitations. Box 7.5 picks out some typical inner-city issues.

The DHA has a responsibility not only to amass information about its population, and to seek to understand it, but also to disseminate knowledge gained thereby. This role is sometimes called information-broking. GPs, providers, pressure groups and other statutory and non-statutory bodies are entitled to share in the DHA's knowledge, quite independently of their entitlement to be involved in subsequent decision-taking.

Assess health needs

Everything already said about the variability of information sources in relation to understanding your population applies with greater force to assessment of the health status of the population and their capacity for health or health improvement. Incidence and prevalence of disease are notoriously hard to pin down and, with some exceptions, most planning has to proceed on assumptions that the findings of specific epidemiological or research studies can be applied to a given population with some adjustment for known relevant population or socio-economic characteristics. The position is gradually changing with improved computerized primary care data, and the 1991 census question on longstanding limiting disability potentially fills an important gap, but, for the most part, it is likely that we shall continue to be reliant on extrapolations of specific studies. The main exceptions are those conditions where a registerable event is a reliable indicator; in other words birth, death, cancer or notifiable diseases (though the latter is of questionable reliability, e.g. for AIDS). Box 7.6

Box 7.6   Assess health needs – extrapolation

The incidence of end stage renal failure among people of Asian or Afro-
Caribbean origin may be five times higher than among Caucasians. Parkside
District calculated that it should, on this ground alone, anticipate 240 new
cases annually per million population, compared with its current figure of
143 and an average of 80 nationally.

A general health questionnaire showed that 45 per cent of homeless people
reported mental health problems compared to 20 per cent of the general
population. This ratio can be used to estimate the additional service impact
of street dwelling or bed and breakfast homeless people. Over a 6-month
period, 20 per cent of all admissions to one acute unit were homeless people.

contains examples where extrapolation is reasonably reliable. Availability
of fully coded contract minimum data sets, which from April 1993 include
outpatient episodes and ethnic origin, will potentially provide a rich source
of data on condition-specific hospitalization rates that can be mapped back
to target populations, whether geographic (catchment, ward, locality) demographic (children, women, older people) or ethnic groups. While recognizing that current referral patterns may not reflect what is necessarily
appropriate, they are none the less a useful measure of currently met
demand to add to the matrix of assessed met and unmet need.

Health status, or data on incidence and prevalence, is however, incomplete without comparable data on potential for health benefit. The Department of Health is currently co-ordinating (very helpfully) a great deal of
work to draw together the best understanding of effective health care
interventions in different spheres, and many of the best-established are, or
are being, reflected in targets. It is to be hoped that the centre will continue
to recognize that targets for a particular agency, or locality within it, need
to take account of where that agency or locality is *now*. Health promotion
and immunization rates are classic instances where target levels that are
readily attained in one place are impossibly ambitious in another.

Plan for health gain or improvement

An agency which has reached at least provisional conclusions about the
current and potential (target) health status of its population needs then to
address the issue of how best to proceed. It will need to assess the requisite
pace of improvement, taking into account resources, distance from target,
knowledge of the effectiveness of health care interventions, knowledge of
the influence of external factors on health (see Box 7.4) and both professional and consumer views. In the area of professional views co-operation
with actual and potential providers will be crucial.

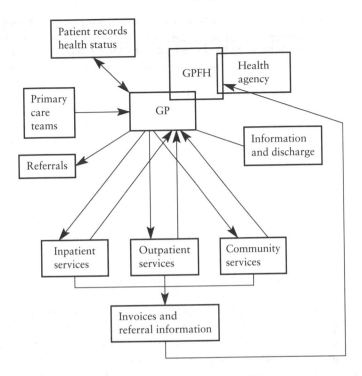

Figure 7.2 The GP as the information focus.

It is probably in this general area that the information to support deci-sion-taking, planning and monitoring effects is at its weakest, and systems and procedures to support the flow of such information as is available are least developed. Specification of minimum data sets for primary and community care is unlikely to meet purchasers' full requirements for re-cording and monitoring the effectiveness of interventions. Indeed 'contacts' with community staff are probably currently the least well-regarded activ-ity statistic in the whole Körner repertoire (DHSS 1982–4). One sugges-tion, illustrated in Figure 7.2 is to try to focus on the GP as the main repository of information. Thus it is the GP who initiates a referral and receives a report from the agency to which the referral has been made; it is the GP who hears from the patient or carer how the referral went; it is the GP whose knowledge of the patient, hopefully replicated in his or her records, covers both previous and following health status, and increasingly, through the development of primary care teams, there will be a range of soft data about the patient which will supplement the bare record of referral. To the extent that general practice can suitably aggregate such data it may assume or complement the DHA's information-broking role.

Thus, where the system is working well the general practice, fundholding or no, may be uniquely placed to put together an overview of the total patient experience which, with the advent of computerized record systems may provide an important analytical tool. It has to be acknowledged, however, that this probably asks too much of the majority of GPs and is also open to the objection that it does not address outcomes, other than at the simplistic level of immediate events such as re-admissions. Whether or not this pessimism proves well-founded, it is likely that DHAs will increasingly rely on information from GPs in this area of their work.

The term 'health gain' has entered the language comparatively recently and does not yet have an agreed universal meaning. It is used in this chapter to denote that most, if not all, of a purchasing authority's population have a potential ability to benefit in health terms from the consequences of decisions to purchase health services, but for the authority the issue is how to maximize the gain in health for the population as a whole within finite resources. To be able to address this issue, the authority needs to be able to measure, and to place relative values on, a myriad of potential health gains. Some other aspects of health gain require mention. First, in an ideal world, potentially beneficial developments ought to be evaluated before dispersal, but in practice both commercial pressures by the developer and clinicians' desire to improve standards of care militate against waiting for the outcome of evaluation of the new technological development. Breast cancer screening is a relatively unusual exception, and perhaps surprisingly the favourable evaluation results have not commanded universal support (Forrest Report 1987). Another factor in random dispersal is the desire of hospitals not to be left out. A recent study of ten district general hospitals in an area of outer London showed that four had embarked on installing an MRI scanner at about the same time, all assuming that they would be increasing market share by so doing. Another dimension to health gain that will increasingly have to come into play is assessing which of any number of approaches offers the best overall return. An agency with wide internal variations in morbidity may find that focusing attention on specific wards appears to give the greatest return, but raises difficult ethical issues in relation to the remainder. Many agencies, experimenting with forms of DHA/FHSA integration or of locality purchasing, or of healthy alliances working with boroughs, may also have to evaluate the potential health gain from forms of investment with no clear precedent. There will necessarily be a heavy emphasis on pilot projects.

Develop health strategy

Developing a health strategy for a commissioning agency is not really like developing a provider-based strategy, though both are intrinsically demanding and difficult. The purchaser will want to set a broad framework for a number of years ahead, reflecting the resources it expects to have available (a crucial issue, but even more so when a substantial shift upwards or downwards is anticipated); the broad assessment of health need that has been carried out, together with identified health improvement targets; the strategic shifts, between client groups or service areas, that it expects to want to achieve; and anticipated changes in relation to service providers in the foreseeable future. How far ahead the agency should look is open to argument. Health improvement targets looking less than five years ahead would in most instances have little validity, whereas resource prospects more than 1 year ahead can be very difficult to anticipate. Similarly, changes on the provider front will occur more quickly in a true market situation than in a managed market, and if a non-interventionist stance is adopted a given provider may not be in existence by the end of, say, a three-year contract period.

These difficulties do not obviate the need for a strategy, they merely suggest the need for it to be flexible, developmental and, where it cannot be definitive, indicative. The broad strategy should be revisited annually, both to update it for changes in the environment and to use it as an input to decision-making about priorities for the year ahead. The strategy should be quantified in all meaningful respects, though the cautions as to the reliability of any given data sets should not be omitted.

Authorities' strategies should be in the public domain if they are to secure commitment and legitimacy. This may be done through the medium of annual reports (from the Director of Public Health or the whole agency) and/or the medium of consultations on purchasing intentions. As health and local authorities work more closely together, the relationship between their strategies will also need to be addressed. If the timetable could be synchronized it is not inconceivable that a single document could encompass both community care and health plans.

Agencies are now beginning to have available modelling tools to enable them to examine alternative scenarios both at a tactical and a strategic level. However, they will vary greatly both in terms of in-house modelling skills and in their capacity to utilize the results. This seems likely to be an area in which collaboration between a number of adjacent authorities will be necessary to make effective use of scarce skills and to achieve economies of scale, and where funded pilot projects would be helpful. For those purchasers making significant use of providers not within their boundaries there will also be practical advantage in modelling that is based on collaboration with neighbours, whose assumptions may also be relevant to the behaviour of the model. Work done on behalf of London purchasers has illustrated the importance of collaboration in respect of both data and assumptions. In 1992 a model capable of exploring, on the basis of a range of assumptions, how purchasers' decisions over a series of years might affect the viability of teaching hospitals in central London was created. The full potential of the model has not, however, been realized because of difficulty in obtaining data from a sufficient number of purchasers away from the centre about either their known purchasing intentions or the criteria that would underpin future purchasing decisions, both of which were crucial to the model. None the less, this remains an area of key importance in relation to management of the implementation of change in London's health services.

Contract and commission for care

Purchasers and providers alike negotiated contracts for 1991–2 ignorant, in large measure, as to what they meant. The form and availability of the data extracted nationally from 1989–90 activity to create final templates or final cut, and the principles of steady state, necessarily circumscribed freedom to construct or use data differently. The significant problems surrounding the obtaining of numbers precluded any real thought of their meaning before contracts were due to be signed, while the poor quality and slow arrival of contract monitoring data during 1991–2, and the painfully slow progress in developing and/or introducing district information systems, gave little time for contemplation.

The result was that attempts to improve on data definitions, either as to price or volume, in the 1992–3 contracting round were of limited effectiveness or credibility. Providers' attempts to change price structures, to charge separately for outpatients, or to exclude certain conditions from the main contract, were regarded by purchasers with extreme suspicion. Purchasers' wishes to reduce contracts with local acute providers, even where they were apparently in line with 1991–2 activity level, or to end or reduce contracts with more distant but expensive providers, regularly foundered on disputes about the underlying information, with allegations of obduracy on both sides.

For the future it is clear that purchasers and (at least) preferred providers will have to work hard, at the time of negotiating contracts, to ensure that they are using a common language to describe the expectations one has of another. Reliance of inpatient contracts on the concept of completed consultant episodes (CCEs) or day cases provides a salutary lesson on this point. Many acute providers have shown substantial rises in CCEs and/or day cases in both 1991–2 and 1992–3, compared to the contracted values and/or the previous year. For the provider these rises caused anxiety that costs would over-run; for the purchaser they raised the question whether part at least of the increase was attributable to changes in recording behaviour. This has led to the development of some new methods of analysing activity. Boxes 7.7 and 7.8 describe two analyses carried out in late 1992 by one purchaser concerned about apparent major activity over-runs in two local providers. The concept of building future contracts on explicit assumptions about the ratio between discharges and CCEs has followed.

Other areas in the acute field which at first were covered sketchily in contracts were case mix and day care. It is reasonable to expect both purchasers and providers to want to develop greater sophistication in specification in these areas. Both are also areas in which the requirement to be able to *compare* performance is likely to lead to pressure for con-

---

Box 7.7

An acute provider contract for 1992–3 over-ran by 13 per cent in the first half year. The purchaser analysed data and became convinced that a proportion of the increase was not increased caseload but more assiduous identification of completed consultant episodes (CCEs). Analysis showed a steady rise since April 1991; in four selected months the CCE/discharge ratio (%) was: 105.6, 107.1, 107.8 and 109.4.

Subsequently data for the same four months was analysed for three other local acute providers, with the same net upward drift, albeit less consistent:

Provider 2	104.8	106.6	104.3	109.2
Provider 3	106.9	102.8	111.6	107.6
Provider 4	106.6	107.0	106.2	108.5

The conclusion was reached that 1993–4 contracts had to include an element reflecting CCE/discharge ratios.

Box 7.8

The acute unit and district jointly commissioned a senior registrar in public health medicine to study case notes for a sample of patients with *inter alia* two or more CCEs in a period; 119 patients satisfied the criteria, but the sample was limited to the 47 (39.4 per cent) whose case notes could be found, with a total of 140 CCEs. Within this restricted sample 39 CCEs (27.9 per cent) were considered questionable. It was accepted that the results could not be extrapolated to the whole multiple CCE category.

---

sistency of approach and for the development of contract management systems capable of evolution to support the more complex contract structure involved. In the community field it will certainly be necessary for both purchasers and providers to seek to build contracts on a more meaningful concept than 'contacts', but in addition there will be a quite specific need to be able to use common definitions and systems for the respective contributions of GPs and the staff they employ, and for staff employed or managed by community trusts. In time, in both fields, it is also to be expected that purchasers will want to see, and providers to demonstrate, information about the effectiveness of services provided – in other words outcomes. In the interim, however, it will probably be necessary to rely heavily on process measures, such as demonstration of the existence of clinical audit systems, and simple measures such as readmission rates. In this latter area readmission to the same provider can now be readily tracked (see Box 7.8) but repeat admissions involving more than one provider may also need to be brought on board. This is a development that will be greatly assisted by the introduction of a revised NHS number/unique patient identifier.

Monitor and manage contracts

Part of the discussion in the last section is germane to the issue of *monitoring* contracts, as it was concerned with improved specification of contractual obligations, as a result of experience to date. There are, however, additional points that need to be emphasized. First, the acknowledged problem of poor quality, incomplete or late data has to be addressed before purchasers can monitor effectively. While some authorities have sought to include in contracts a financial penalty for failure to meet data quality standards, it may be better to introduce the idea of a reward for good quality data, in other words give the provider an inducement to meet standards, rather than a punishment for failure to do so. The evidence of the GP contract is encouraging in this regard. Second, however, there is an obligation on the purchaser not to specify the unattainable or devalue key data requirements by immersing them in a list that is of dubious provenance and over long.

Quality targets are a case in point. Setting large numbers that cannot be measured, chased or analysed meaningfully is unhelpful, and may lead to nothing more productive than box-ticking. Indeed, there is a real danger to providers in agreeing to contracts with such features. When (inevitably) something goes wrong, the purchaser may sidle out of any share of responsibility, even though the contract patently did not contain the resources for implementation of all the targets. Third, there is indeed room for anxiety at a tendency, from which the NHS Management Executive is not exempt, to overload the contractual mechanism. It should be the means by which the obligations of provider to purchaser are expressed; it is not, and cannot be, the means by which all aspects of the provider's business are monitored or controlled.

Having determined what data requirements the contract should specify, and obtained agreement of providers, the purchasing authority also needs to give attention to the way in which it will analyse this data. Box 7.9 suggests the key features which will need to be addressed. To date, few authorities have given enough attention to this aspect, with the result that overlong and indigestible papers lead to unfocused discussion in health authority meetings, or, worse still, to no discussion at all. The NHS is a long way from being reducible to the simplicity of a Moody card; but agreement on key indicators in relation to contractual or extracontractual performance will go a long way towards enabling a focus on essentials.

Managing, as opposed to monitoring, the contract is less dependent on data and much more a matter of developing relationships between purchaser and provider. In the case of small contracts (value and activity)

Box 7.9   Performance analysis

The agency needs to know:

- How overall activity and resources compare with plan (including ECRs).
- Key individual variances from plan.
- How each provider's performances compare with plan and with each other.
- Position on key developments.

The agency requires:

- Trend data, covering also past years.
- Interpretation of effect of external changes.
- Simple, clear messages, intelligible without reference to a morass of appendices.

---

there may be insufficient time to do this, but the higher the degree of interdependence between purchaser and provider the greater the need for co-operation and trust. Take, for example, the familiar problem in 1991–2 and 1992–3 of over-performance against an acute contract. Agreeing how, and to what extent, to rein back activity can put a great strain on the best relationships and can be next to impossible if the activity levels were accepted with bad grace by a provider convinced they would be exceeded. Financial common sense would indicate the need for determined management of the contract throughout the year in order to ensure that the provider keeps expenditure under control, but both weaknesses of activity control systems within providers, and a reluctance to believe that the purchaser will not come up with some extra resources at the end, have come into play. Typically, therefore, restraint mechanisms have had to be introduced late in the year, hitting inevitably at non-urgent elective admissions and potentially endangering waiting time policies. The question of what to say to the GPs can be very divisive. Unquestionably, the best approach is a letter from the provider that carries the explicit support of the purchaser, and which stresses the points of continuity – that emergency and urgent admissions are being given priority, that upper limits on waiting times will not in any circumstances be breached and that patients not able to be admitted in the immediate future will be given, indeed preferably have been given, firm dates for their appointment or admission at a later stage. If this approach is to contain the situation, however, it must command a degree of confidence from both hospital clinicians and GPs. If, in practice, there has been a relative shift in favour of referrals to that particular provider, the purchaser may also find it helpful to indicate earlier rather than later that this shift will be picked up in the following year's contract. For the future, both purchasers and providers have to learn to work together to improve the way in which services are managed to meet need while remaining financially viable. The in-year crises in 1991–2 and 1992–3 reflect failure on both sides to achieve this, and it is only realistic to expect difficulties for a number more years before both parties learn how to manage the process effectively.

Review progress

As indicated earlier, the review needs to cover both the annual cycle and whatever longer-term cycle makes sense in relation to particular objectives. The annual cycle will focus principally upon the delivery of the contracts, extracting lessons for the balance between different areas of activity, between different providers and between different specialities, as well as more strategic issues concerning the level of reserves generally and the balance between contracted and non-contracted work. Where the authority has been able to implement developments in year it will also want to assess how these have gone, both to decide whether to continue to support them or whether to extend them, as well as to enable it to judge whether to fund further new developments that have been projected. Failure by a given provider to spend, or to spend as intended, a given sum painfully extracted from elsewhere, is likely to reduce enthusiasm for going through the same process a second time. An annual cycle is likewise an opportunity to review specific needs assessment work completed over the last 12 months and to assess its suitability for reflection in either the plans for the coming year or for consultation with a view to inclusion in the year after that, and to progress moves towards truly joint and actively promoted community care plans.

It is likely for the immediate future that analysis of health outcomes or of health improvement targets will require a longer timescale, and while annual updates will in time be possible, trends over a longer time period will be required. Analysis of infant or perinatal mortality data at district level, which has of course been possible for a significant time, illustrates how the small numbers per district make meaningful year-on-year comparisons impossible; 3-year rolling averages give a better picture. When we seek to evaluate, for example, the effectiveness of measures to reduce premature deaths from coronary heart disease, we shall not only have to cope with statistical variability but uncertainty as to timelags. Justification for changed spending priorities will be slow in emerging; data helpful to future decisions on spending priorities, other than by extrapolation of wider experience, will be slower still.

This caution on the speed at which the longer-term data will become available in a meaningful form is not intended to suggest that the task should not be given priority. *The Health of the Nation*'s emphasis on health targets is an important counterweight to obsession with measuring activity or with process issues, such as those surrounding the *Patient's Charter* (Secretary of State for Health 1991, 1992). Each is important, but their ultimate justification must rest on a knowledge of their impact on health status. The dung beetle provides a helpful analogy. Pushing or pulling a large ball of dung requires great energy and determination by a creature mostly unable to see where it is going; the justification for using up all that energy lies in delivering the dung to its underground storehouse where it will provide more than enough energy to replace that which has been lost. Should the dung beetle fail to bury the dung before the noonday sun has dried it, there will be no return for all that activity.

Conclusions

Purchasing is still very much in its infancy, and those who have to watch over its development do not have Doctor Spock or any other work of guidance to tell them what they have to expect. As the task of purchasing is still evolving, so also are the information requirements and the systems to meet these new demands. Dissatisfaction with the limitations on both the availability and the meaning of existing hard data, particularly that derived from Körner, has not yet given way to clear or unanimous views on what is required in its place. Faced with these uncertainties, and with the high degree of dependence of purchasers on data produced by a range of providers, it is clear that there remain uncertainties as to the IT solutions that will best meet purchasers' requirements. In the light of these uncertainties, purchasers will need to negotiate with IT systems suppliers on specifications and development paths to ensure sufficiently flexible, interactive and open systems.

Against this background of general uncertainty, the major lessons for purchasers at this stage are probably these. First, develop a strategic framework encompassing the whole of the purchasing cycle, annual and longer-term, and assess the tasks that have to be carried out at each stage. Second, be prepared to exchange experiences with other health agencies both about what has worked and what has not. Third, seek to work with regular providers, both in the interests of constructive working relationships and in the interests of mutual self-support, to improve contractual mechanisms and data definitions, so that each has confidence in what the contract seeks to achieve. Fourth, if existing data, hard or soft, does not meet needs, change it, or, if it is a national requirement, seek to persuade others of the merits of change. Fifth, and last, remember the dung beetle.

References

DHSS (1982–4) *Steering Group on Health Services Information* (Chair: Edith Körner). London, DHSS.
Forrest Report (1987) *Breast Cancer Screening.* London, HMSO.
Secretaries of State for Health, Wales, Scotland and Northern Ireland (1989) *Working for Patients*, Cm 555. London, HMSO.
Secretary of State for Health (1991) *The Patient's Charter.* London, HMSO.
Secretary of State for Health (1992) *The Health of the Nation.* London, HMSO.

Section 3
The academic
perspective

There is a vast academic literature on the role of information in organizations and the development and application of IT. It would seem the height of folly to ignore it – though a disappointing aspect of the NHS in this area has been that it tends to apply yesterday's rather than today's thinking. Perhaps it is time that changed. The six contributions in this section offer a range of commentaries.

James Raftery and Andrew Stevens discuss the information needs of purchasers, emphasizing the need for a structured approach to data collection and purchasing of services. Then the editor addresses the politics of information. The NHS is an environment where information is often not made available when requested, or acted upon when it is. Managers may know that operating theatres are underutilized but choose not to act; published papers may show that particular treatments are of no value or actually harmful, but doctors and nurses continue to provide them locally. Some possible reasons for this are explored.

Brian Bloomfield and colleagues then argue that the way in which IT is used in organizations does not fit a simple model wherein people 'use information to improve their practice'. Rather, IT is subject to continuous negotiation, and it is the outcome of these negotiations that affects how systems are used. Similarly IT strategy formulation is not a simple process, but something that has to take into account a variety of political and other factors. Bob Galliers discusses the process of formulating strategy and points to the problems that the private sector has experienced in this regard: the NHS can learn much in this area.

Next, the editor looks at an issue which has caused NHS staff considerable confusion: the evaluation of IT. It is suggested that the confusion may stem from a misunderstanding of the way that IT influences organizations, and suggests approaches which practitioners might find fruitful. Finally Mike Smith looks to future technical trends in IT, and considers the impact that technical developments will have on the NHS.

8 Information for purchasing

James Raftery and Andrew Stevens

Introduction

This chapter examines the information required by purchasers in the quasi-market initiated by the NHS reforms. The necessity for, and limitations of, such information are discussed. The process by which health-related data becomes information is outlined. Existing information sources are critically reviewed in order to suggest how they might be improved in both the short and medium term.

The NHS reforms

The NHS Review, which culminated in the NHS and Community Care Act 1990, revolved around a single dominant theme: the separation of *purchaser* and *provider* roles of health care. District Health Authority (DHA) purchasing was separated from the day-to-day provision of hospital and community care services.

The DHA – the principal purchaser – was financed to purchase services for its *resident* population rather than, as hitherto, funding providers for its *catchment* populations (Department of Health 1989). Purchasers and providers are linked through contracts. The initial round of contracting in 1991–2 (the so-called 'steady state') aimed to reproduce pre-existing patterns of services via 'block' contracts, under which purchasers paid roughly the same money for access to the same services as previously. More sophisticated contracts were envisaged to follow, in tandem with improved information. Providers of healthcare were encouraged to take up increased freedom in managing their own affairs by obtaining NHS trust status.

While DHAs are the main purchasers of secondary health care, primary

care continues to be financed through the Family Health Service Authorities (FHSAs), but with little power for manoeuvre, given the central
government framing of the GP contract. Better integration of primary
and secondary care has been given a stimulus as DHAs and FHSAs are
now both accountable to regional health authorities (RHAs). Some group
practices (with a list size greater than 7,000) have opted to become GP
fundholders. Fundholders are able to purchase certain hospital services on
behalf of their patients. These services include not only various specific
surgical procedures, but also outpatient visits and a variety of other
services (NHS ME 1992a).

If the purchasers are to achieve the optimum improvement in the health
of the population they serve (NHS ME 1991a), they must know what
those needs are and what services are being provided. These two basic
conditions, which are far from being met, comprise the most urgent information requirements for purchasers. Of course there are also constraints
on purchasing. Critically, the size of the DHA's budget is outside the
purchaser's control, being allocated in turn by Parliament, the Department
of Health and the regional health authority. Additionally, while DHAs
may in theory move money between services (e.g. from surgery to mental
health) or between providers, in practice such changes are likely to be at
the margin.

The NHS and the market

The separation of purchasers and providers in a publicly funded health
care system with a population focus contains built-in incentives to greater
efficiency for both purchasers and providers. Such incentives in a publicly
funded service have been described variously as *quasi-markets* or *neo-
markets* (LeGrand 1990). This emphasis on markets provides a useful way
of clarifying both attitudes and information requirements for a market to
function. Although markets constitute for many an ideological touchstone,
the component parts of markets are seldom separated. Two aspects should
be distinguished:

1 The information processing aspects (Simon 1987), in which changes in
  prices signal changes in supply and demand automatically and rapidly.
2 The income and wealth distribution aspects, which in many market
  systems generate inequalities.

As much of the disquiet about the NHS reforms hinges on the distribu-
tional aspect of a quasi-market, it is worth stressing that these two aspects
are completely separate in the reformed NHS. The distribution of health
care resources in the NHS will be by need, however defined and assessed,
rather than in relation to income or wealth. The degree to which the
market-oriented reforms are successful in improving the health of the
population will depend on the ability of the NHS to generate and process

appropriate information. This can be seen by examining the conditions required for a market to function.

The conditions for a market

The conditions for a perfect market to operate are as follows:

1 free entry and exit
2 many buyers and sellers
3 homogeneous products
4 perfect information.

Each of these is worth discussing briefly here: Chapter 1 discusses the difficulties in meeting these criteria for health services.

Free entry and exit/many buyers and sellers

The existence of these conditions, which imply competition on both the supply and demand sides, may be seen as mainly a concern of those charged with regulating the quasi-market. Some criticism of the NHS reforms has focused on the limits to these conditions in the NHS, specifically the possibility of monopoly or monopsony elements. On the supply side, for example, outside the main urban areas, a local hospital may face little competition and, even within urban areas, many other factors contribute to the inertia of services. Nevertheless, providers' business plans show that trusts are starting to examine the competition they potentially face.

Several surveys (Prescott-Clarke *et al.* 1988; Raftery *et al.* 1990) have shown that certain categories of patients are prepared to travel to receive faster treatment, including parents who want their children to be treated, and many of those suffering from conditions which require cold or elective surgery. Culyer and Posnett (1990) have taken the notion further by suggesting that while some units might not face competition, their management might if management services were put out to tender. Further, competition between providers will increase as purchasers merge to cover larger populations – a trend already well established. On the demand side, a degree of competition exists between DHAs and GP fundholders, with the latter free to take over the financing of a considerable share of elective surgery and associated care.

More recent thinking stresses that for quasi-markets to work, it is the threat rather than the presence of many buyers and sellers that matters. Contestability (Baumol *et al.* 1988) is a key notion underlying the NHS reforms.

Homogeneous products

The products of health services seem at first sight to be infinitely variable, including prevention, diagnosis, a blend of treatments, rehabilitation and care, which are offered to patients with varying degrees of illness combination, severity on presentation and frailty. Some means of classification yielding workably homogeneous components is necessary if products are to be compared.

Without homogeneous products, price and quality comparisons cannot be made. While homogeneous products can be readily defined in manufacturing industry, the products of the service industries, and particularly health services, have long resisted satisfactory classification. Some resistance to classification can be expected. Clinicians have tended to the view that each case is different, reflecting partly the nature of the doctor–patient relationship, but perhaps also to resist scrutiny.

There have, however, been developments in classification in recent years. The impending changes in the International Classification of Disease (ICD10) in 1993 will provide an improved foundation for case classification. ICD coding still falls short of solving the homogeneous products requirement. Despite the great number of ICD codes, there can be a considerable range of patient types within each code. The development of diagnosis related groups (DRGs) and healthcare related groups (HRGs) (Sanderson 1992), both of which group cases on the basis of ICD and procedure codes, supplemented by data on complications and age, represent a move towards defining homogeneous products at least from the provider point of view.

The case-mix approach to product definition in terms of cases (which has made little progress outside the acute hospital inpatient sector), may be usefully complemented by detailed descriptions of health service structure and capacity. For some services with poorly defined 'products', such descriptions provide the only option. In mental health services, for example, the 'product' can be made more homogeneous by subdivision of services by type, for example, into adult, elderly, child, substance misuse and forensic services. Adult services can be further subdivided into acute, intensive care, long-stay, day-care and domiciliary; further subdivision would distinguish specific facilities such as wards and day hospitals (Stevens and Raftery 1992).

Although to date purchasers and providers are negotiating largely block contracts, some (mainly teaching) hospitals have moved towards more sophisticated contracts with their purchasers. Subspecialty price bands have been used to weight specialty prices for the activity in the various bands. Suggestions have been made as to how HRGs might be aggregated into 'contract categories' (NHS ME 1993). The logic of the reformed market-oriented NHS will further such developments as more homogeneous products evolve to cover the acute and the other sectors.

Perfect information
This final condition has emerged in recent decades in acknowledgement of the growing awareness of the role of information. Exploring the implications of information asymmetries has led to the development of new subspecialities

in economics. The central point of interest here concerns the key role that information plays in a market (Eggerstrom 1990).

Besides the lack of information on the effectiveness of the bulk of health care products, or indeed of treatment options, health service information systems are complicated by the information asymmetries between doctor and patient. Information deficiencies at patient level ('Am I ill?' 'with what?' 'how should I be treated?') combined with the specialist nature of medical knowledge imply an information asymmetry between patient and doctor. These information asymmetries have been argued by health economists to justify regulation of markets in health care, ranging from legal regulation through public finance to public provision of services. Although the trend towards greater individual responsibility for health, along with improved education in many countries, may improve patients' understanding about their diseases, changes in medical technology may work against these trends.

Perfect information refers to the existence and availability of information on prices and quality of the products in the market. As applied to the NHS, the following six stages may be distinguished in the process of turning data into information which can be used to effect change:

1 health and health service events
2 data capture
3 data structuring
4 data publication
5 data acquisition
6 use of information to effect changes.

Each stage can be seen as acting as a filter in the process of transforming data to information which can be used to effect changes in health and health service events.

Data capture
In the NHS, this is carried out well, badly or not at all, depending on the type of activity. For example, the Census of Population and certification of deaths both capture data well, but the number of contacts that people have with various services is inadequately collected in *ad hoc* ways that make it difficult to follow a patient's itinerary (so-called 'patient-linkage') and with virtually nothing collected on the patient's health (except when they die). Overall, the data collected nationally on demography, mortality and fertility is much better managed and more reliable than those on health service contacts (Knox 1991).

Data structuring
This depends on the languages used to describe events, such as ICD coding. ICD codes, however, are limited for two main reasons. First, they cover only those events which are adequately described by diagnosis, thus excluding many community-oriented services and, to a lesser extent, mental

health services. Second, ICD codes were designed to shed light on the aetiology of disease and not the success or effort involved in treating it. (The development of Read Codes obviates a third limitation, to do with the translation between the language clinicians actually use and the ICD terminology.)

Data publication

This has traditionally, although not exclusively, been by the Office of Population Census and Surveys, which necessarily publishes selectively, with a historical emphasis on demographic rather than health service events. The Department of Health has commissioned an independent unit to make OPCS health-related data available to DHAs via the Public Health Common Data Set (PHCDS). Aggregated data on health service events have been made available to DHAs since 1983 via the Health Service Indicators (HSIs) (formerly Performance Indicators or PIs).

Data acquisition

Other than that made available free to all DHAs in the form of the PHCDS and the HSIs, data acquisition depends on the indigenous capacities of the purchasing organization, many of which have information personnel who have traditionally focused on hardware and data rather than on information. More recently, some DHAs have set up library and information systems (NHS ME 1991b).

Use of information

The use of such data as information by purchasers remains constrained by the limitations involved in the above process, which provides data that tends to be of little use in answering the kinds of questions purchasers face.

Although to some extent such hurdles exist in many information systems, they acquire particular importance in the reformed NHS, whose state of development can be compared with the countries of Eastern Europe following glasnost and perestroika. These stages are particularly significant in the NHS because the system (particularly regarding end-users' needs) is very much in evolution, and there is considerable mis-selection of data at each stage. As high quality health service information could incur considerable costs, the NHS must decide on optimal levels in terms of cost effectiveness of data collection and use. To take an extreme contrast, stock exchanges in the industrialized countries provide virtually perfect information about the financial markets, with each stage of the sequence integrated and feeding back rapidly on the world about which the data is captured and turned into information.

Purchasing healthcare

Purchasing involves defining what is required and then using contracts to implement the necessary changes. This process is outlined schematically in Figure 8.1, which shows a purchasing strategy as made up of three elements:

1 the district's purchasing strategy
2 baseline contracts
3 needs assessment, comprising epidemiological needs assessment, comparative analysis and a corporate view (NHS ME 1991c).

Figure 8.1 shows the translation of the purchasing plan into contracts via service specifications, some of which might involve modifications to existing services, while others require more fundamental reviews. Two elements of this process require information – the establishment of baseline services and needs assessment.

Baseline services

Establishing baseline services, that is establishing what and how much of each type of service is currently being provided to DHA residents, constitutes one of the major challenges to purchasers. Much of the data available is simply of the wrong kind. The services currently purchased by DHAs vary widely, ranging from preventive education campaigns, community contacts, diagnostic work-ups and outpatient consultations, to inpatient stays and major operations. To encapsulate this, the purchaser needs to define the dimensions and units of health care. Although this can be relatively straightforward in routine elective surgery where the number of operations is a clear measure of what is going on, almost none of health promotion, disease prevention, primary care and general medical secondary care can be described so easily. Even in the acute sector, the dominant process measure – the finished consultant episode (FCE) – is also only stable for a fairly homogeneous condition for which there is a consensus and reliable treatment (Clarke and McKee 1992). Other process measures, such as health visitor contacts, are even less stable and reliable measures than the FCE.

Rapid development of more homogeneous products, whether via case mix measures or service description, is necessary if purchasers are to purchase effectively. The most useful structural components will depend on the circumstances. Outside the acute hospital sector, the best description of a service is often some measure of capacity: the number of beds or day places or number of open cases on the books of a domiciliary system. If capacity measures are compared with the cost of the provision, purchasers are in a powerful position to make comparative value for money judgements. Although there may be good reasons (such as differences in case mix) for the unit cost per bed to vary, at least having the information allows purchasers to question providers appropriately.

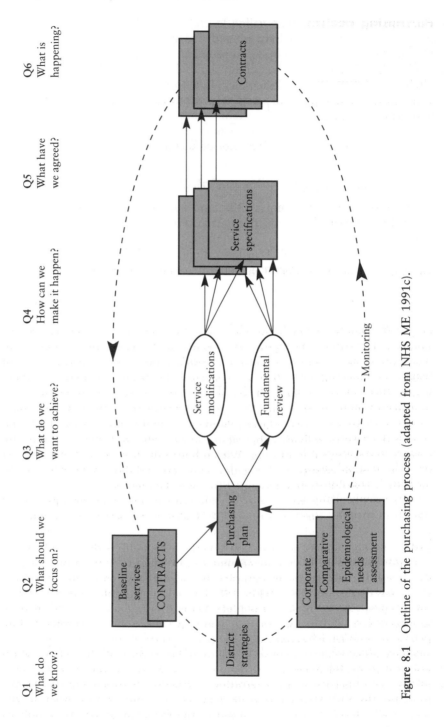

Figure 8.1 Outline of the purchasing process (adapted from NHS ME 1991c).

Needs assessment

Needs assessment can be seen (NHS ME 1991a) as comprising three elements:

1 epidemiological needs assessment
2 comparative assessment
3 a corporate view.

Each of these has information requirements.

Epidemiological needs assessment

From the purchaser's point of view the appropriate definition of need is: 'The population's ability to benefit from health care' (Stevens and Gabbay 1991). Given the inevitable constraints on the financing of the NHS, purchasers must aim to purchase cost-effectively. In the language of economics, a purchaser would maximize the health of a given population by purchasing each service/intervention up to the point where the marginal gain in health per pound spent was the same across all services/interventions, or, in the language of need, up to the point of equal marginal met need per pound spent. This clearly involves using some generic measure of health, incorporating mortality and morbidity: but these are reviewed elsewhere (Bowling 1991).

This definition of need for health care in terms of ability to benefit implies information on the level of the disease, the effectiveness of interventions and the costs of these interventions. Information is weak on all of these. Measuring the population's ability to benefit from health care generates two very specific information requirements:

1 The local prevalence and incidence of disease, ranged by severity.
2 The efficacy of the care and care settings available or potentially available to cope with it.

Together, these measurements, which form the basis of the epidemiological approach to needs assessment, present formidable information problems.

Local data is almost never available for most diseases. However, some national estimates can be made on incidence and prevalence, which can then be applied in DHAs if interpreted in the light of knowledge of local factors. Examples of work of this kind are the NHS ME-sponsored needs reviews on 20 topics (NHS ME 1991a). The collection of these and similar secondary sources suggests the need for each DHA to have a selective library facility as well as a routine information facility.

Information on the efficacy of health care and health care settings is at least as hard to come by. The development of health care has often been characterized by the adoption of procedures with poor accompanying evidence of their efficacy. Excellent summaries of efficacy are available in some fields, e.g. in obstetrics and perinatal care (Chalmers *et al.* 1989) and for some preventive strategies (US Preventive Services Taskforce 1989).

The latter adopted a commendable twin scale of efficacy assessment which was applied to the NHS ME's 20 reviews. (One scale describes the strength of a recommendation that a procedure be adopted, the other the quality of the evidence. Purchasers who can define care procedures on these scales will have accomplished half of the preparatory work for purchasing.)

The information base is even more deficient in relation to cost effectiveness, with the most recent compilation of cost per quality adjusted life year (QALY) estimates having around 400 interventions, with over half of them to do with prevention. Mooney *et al.* (1992) have gone further and argued that these cost per QALY estimates are of little use in purchasing for the following reasons: most of the estimates are based on average rather than marginal costs per QALY; the studies are of variable quality, leaving the reader in doubt as to how reliable the estimates are; many of the studies may be limited by the their location in time or space.

Comparative assessment
The comparative approach involves no more than making comparisons between districts, or even within districts of:

1 Morbidity and mortality, e.g. in the Public Health Common Data Set (Department of Health 1992) and in the General Practice Morbidity Survey (Royal College of General Practitioners 1986).
2 Service utilization and provision, e.g. in the HSIs (NHS ME 1992b).
3 Costs and outcomes (some crude data appears in the HSIs and the PHCDS but most will require local data and measurement).

Although comparative service use data at specialty level are useful, specialties do not link easily to diseases. The HSIs provide some limited data on service use by procedure/disease. Since 1987 data have been published on the policy tracer conditions (hip replacements, knee replacements, other joint replacements, bone marrow transplants, coronary artery bypass grafts, cataract surgery). The 1992 edition, which covers 1990–1, has extended this list to include a further 12 conditions (such as asthma, stroke and diabetes). In addition, average length of hospital stay is provided for some (but not all) of these.

Corporate view
The corporate approach to needs assessment involves the purchaser making use of the views of informed interests in local health care, including GPs (fundholders and others), other providers, clinical staff, local people and other local agencies (FHSAs, local authorities, etc.). Many of these sources, particularly providers, are in a position to alert purchasers to major crisis areas, reflecting unmet or evolving needs, much more quickly than a formal needs assessment could.

The importance of consumer voice has been accentuated by the Citizen's Charter and its NHS version, the Patient's Charter. The latter commits the NHS to meeting the following:

1 No hospital outpatient to wait more than 30 minutes.
2 Information with which to choose between providers, including GPs.

Many DHAs and GP fundholders have carried out consumer-oriented surveys of local populations. However, no routine source, other than occasional general surveys by bodies such as the Institute of Health Services Management/National Association of Health Authorities and Trusts exists.

Contracting

Purchasing intentions based on needs assessment methods will generally be based on diseases, procedures or client groups, whereas the baseline services are currently based on specialties. Attempts to show how the NHS ME-sponsored reviews might be applied in the form of local disease 'MAPs' (measurements of activity and prices) are outlined in a forthcoming NHS ME publication. Although local levels of service use and costs can be identified, the problem remains of how to specify changes within specialty contracts. Case mix measures may enable contracts to reflect the diversity of cases treated within specialties.

Information required

Existing information sources and the requirements for purchasing in the short and medium terms are summarized in the following summary tables, dealing with baseline services, epidemiological data, comparative analysis and consumer/patient preferences.

Baseline services

Existing information on baseline service capacity usually exists (Table 8.1), but with two shortcomings:

1 It is often seen as confidential (because commercially sensitive) provider information, despite providing the only useful description of services as discussed above.
2 It provides poor linkage between activity and costs.

Activity information tends to be constrained by a history of incomplete diagnostic coding, by interpretation problems (diagnoses can cover a wide variety of needs) and the inappropriateness of the consultant episode for many types of care. Both short- and medium-term progress require the disaggregation of data into meaningful measures of capacity and activity, and for these to be congruent with information on costs.

Epidemiological information

As shown in the overview of existing and desired information requirements in Table 8.2, the available data on the prevalence and incidence of disease

Table 8.1 Baseline services – available information and short- and medium-term priorities

	Available	*Required in short term*	*Required in medium term*
Capacity of service	Informal. Not available at all if purchaser is not host	Formal and disaggregated to relevant subunits	More refined and matched to cost data
Activity	FCEs (often incomplete coding but improving), HRG contract categories	Extended to cover range of services, including day cases and outpatients	Based on case mix and matched to costs
Function	ICD Codes, Informal knowledge of what services are used for	Case mix, measures. Formal designation of purposes of facilities	
Cost	Only at average specialty level	Formally available for relevant subunits of service	Formally available for case mix adjusted activity

is patchy, based on occasional survey estimates. The various health needs assessments have utilized these with varying degrees of success, leading in some cases to more detailed on-going survey work. Improved estimates of the major diseases constitute the main short-term requirement along with, in the medium term, estimates capable of taking account of local variations.

Only occasional and sporadic estimates of treatment outcomes are available in the literature, with many treatments never having been evaluated. Defining need as ability to benefit implies data on patient characteristics, such as the severity of diseases, as well as on age and sex. In the short term, the expansion of such information to cover the main diseases must rank as a priority, with extension to cover severity in the medium term.

Cost data by treatment remain confined to inpatient and day cases at specialty level and to the list of GP fund holder procedures. The extension of unit cost data to cover inpatient cases at subspecialty level (whether by HRGs or otherwise) must rank as a short-term priority, along with

Table 8.2 Overview of data pertaining to epidemiological health needs assessment

By disease	Available	Required in short term	Required in medium term
Prevalence and incidence	Best estimates based on surveys and estimates	Improved estimates, especially of sub-categories	Extension to take account of local variations
Treatment outcomes	Sporadic and partial efficacy evidence, – virtually nothing by severity	Systematic estimates for the range of diseases, by type of treatment	Further refinements by severity. Local routine outcome measurement
Costs	By acute inpatient/day case and GPFH procedures – by provider	By case mix group, inpatient and ambulatory, for major diseases and client groups	Extended to cover full range of procedures

extension of cost data to cover the range of ambulatory services and service settings.

Comparative data

Although relatively more data are available on comparative aspects, as shown in Table 8.3, obvious deficiencies remain. The best data relate to inpatient cases (FCEs), which are available by provider and by specialty in terms of number of cases and length of stay. More recently, the 1992 HSIs have distinguished elective/emergency FCEs and provided data on 20 diseases/procedures by age band. Waiting-list data are also available, by length of wait. In the short term, these data require to be extended to identify the major diseases, probably by HRG. In the medium term, patient linkages would be helpful, enabling purchasers to link patients across the range of services.

Day case data are available by provider and for the Audit Commission (1990) basket of 20 procedures (plus a limited list in the HSIs). These require extension to cover the major diseases in the short term, with scope for patient record linkage in the medium term.

Outpatient data will become available at specialty level in 1993–4. The short-term priority must be its disaggregation by disease/HRG-type

Table 8.3   Overview of comparative data

	Available	Required in short term	Required in medium term

Acute Inpatient admissions and length of stay	By provider and specialty
	By elective/emergency
	By consultant
	+ data by DHA on 20
	    conditions/diseases (HSIs)
	+ GP fundholder procedures
	+ waiting lists
	By provider by specialty
	+ Audit Commission 20
	    procedures
		All major HRGs	Patient record linkage

Day cases	By provider and specialty (from 1993/4)	By ambulatory group	Patient record linkage
Outpatients		By ambulatory group	Patient record linkage
Community Health Services	Minimal service contact data	By type of service, by ambulatory group	Patient record linkage
GPs	GP morbidity survey PACT data (Virtually unusable)	Updated and extended Improved linkage of prescriptions and patients	Patient record linkage

ambulatory group, with patient linkages acquiring importance in the medium term.

GP contact levels by disease are available in the General Practice Morbidity Surveys (RCGP 1986) whose 1981 survey is in the process of being updated and extended. In the medium term, the goal must be the provision of such data at local level, with scope for record linkage. Although the Prescription Pricing Authority processes some 400 million prescriptions issued by GPs each year (Harris *et al.* 1990), considerable difficulties exist in linking prescriptions to diseases and patients. Exploration of such links for particular diseases might be helpful in the short term, with extension to the range of diseases and with record linkage in the medium term.

Data on community health services are almost completely absent due to the non-implementation in most DHAs of data collection for community

Table 8.4 Consumer views – available information, short- and medium-term requirements

	Available	*Required in short term*	*Required in medium term*
Public attitudes	National survey, at general level	National/local comparisons	More detailed information on public priorities
Patient satisfaction	Occasional (but CASPE covers 50 units) GP practices doing surveys	Regular comparable yardstick information	National and local data

HSIs. Requirements in the short term include data on type of service by provider as well as by major disease or client group. As with the other services, patient linkage data would be helpful in the medium term.

Public/patient preferences

At present, very little information is available about public and patient preferences (Table 8.4). The various national surveys (IHSM, RIPA/SCPR) provide general data on public attitudes to the NHS, which are of little value to local purchasers. More useful would be surveys of sufficient size to allow comparisons between areas, with the addition of detail on particular types of services and illnesses.

Although more work has been carried out on patient satisfaction surveys, with many contracts specifying that providers develop systems for occasional or regular surveys, little comparative information is available. The CASPE survey, which has been validated in a follow-up study (Raftery and Zarb 1990) is used in some 50 units. As with public attitudes, more detail would be helpful in the short to medium term.

Conclusions

The UK model of purchasing health services is unique, and may well provide a testing ground for the type of market-oriented policies that have emerged in social policy in the last decades of the twentieth century. However, markets depend on information to function. Although NHS data has been, and remains, poor, the new quasi-market is leading to rapid improvements in the capturing and structuring of data. The degree to which these data can be processed into information capable of meeting the challenges outlined here will do much to determine the success or otherwise of these new policies.

References

Audit Commission (1990) *A Short Cut to Better Services: Day Surgery in England & Wales*. London, HMSO.

Baumol, W.J., Panza, J.C. and Willig, R.D. (1988) *Contestable Markets and the Theory of Industry*. New York, Harcourt Brace Jovanovich.

Bowling, A. (1991) *Measuring Health: A Review of Quality of Life Measurement Scales*. Milton Keynes, Open University Press.

Chalmers, I., Enkin, M. and Keirse, N. (1989) *Effective Care in Pregnancy and Childbirth*. London, Oxford University Press.

Clarke, A. and McKee, M. (1992) 'The finished consultant episode: an unhelpful measure', British Medical Journal, 305, 1307–8.

Culyer, T. and Posnett, J. (1990) 'Hospital behaviour and competition', in T. Culyer, A. Maynard and J. Posnett *Competition in Health Care – Reforming the NHS*. London, Macmillan.

Department of Health (1989) *Contracts for Health Services: Prices and Openness*. London, Department of Health.

Department of Health (1992) *Public Health Common Data Set*. Guildford, University of Surrey.

Eggerston, T. (1990) *Economic Behaviour and Institutions*. Cambridge, Cambridge University Press.

Harris, C.M., Heywood, P.L. and Clayden, A.D. (1990) *The Analysis of Prescribing in General Practice – A Guide to Audit and Research*. London, HMSO.

Knox, G. (1991) 'Information needs in public health', in W.W. Holland (ed.), *The Oxford Textbook of Public Health*. Oxford, Oxford University Press.

LeGrand, J. (1990) 'Quasi-markets and Social Policy'. Discussion Paper 9006, SAUS. Bristol, University of Bristol.

Mooney, G. *et al*. (1992) *Prioritising Health Services*. Birmingham, NAHAT.

NHS ME (1991a) 'Assessing Health Care Needs'. A DHA Project Discussion Paper. London, NHS ME.

NHS ME (1991b) 'Purchasing Intelligence'. A DHA Project Discussion Paper. London, NHS ME.

NHS ME (1991c) 'Moving Forward on Needs, Services and Contracts'. A DHA Project Discussion Paper. London, NHS ME.

NHS ME (1992a) *Executive Letter*, 92 48. London, HMSO.

NHS ME (1992b) *Health Service Indicators Handbook and Computerised Package*. London, Department of Health.

NHS ME (forthcoming) *Disease Mapping, Comparative Analysis and Purchasing for Health Gain*. Leeds, NHS ME.

NHS ME (1993) Costing for Contracting EL(93)26, Leeds, NHS ME.

Prescott-Clark, P., Brooks, T. and Machray, C. (1988) *Focus on Health Care – Surveying the Public in Four Health Districts, vol. 1, The Findings*. London, SCPR / RIPA.

Raftery, J. and Zarb, G. (1990) 'Satisfaction guaranteed', *Health Service Journal*, 15 November, 1692–3.

Raftery, J., Skingsley, R. and Carr, J. (1990) 'Preferential insights', *Health Service Journal*, 22 November, 1732–3.

Royal College of General Practitioners, OPCS, DHSS. (1986) *1981 Morbidity Statistics from General Practice*, Third National Study Series, MB5 No. 1. London, HMSO.

Sanderson, H. (1992) 'Measuring casemix', *British Medical Journal*, 304, 1607.

Simon, H. (1987) 'Politics as information processing', *LSE Quarterly 4*, 2, 345–69.

Stevens, A. and Gabbay, J. (1991) 'Needs assessment needs assessment', *Health Trends*, 23(1), 20–2.

Stevens, A. and Raftery, J. (1992) 'Information requirements of mental health needs assessment', in G. Thornicroft, C.R. Brewin, J. Wing and Gaskell (eds), *Measuring Mental Health Needs*. London, Royal College of Psychiatrists.

US Preventive Services Taskforce (1989) *Guide to the Clinical Preventive Services*. Baltimore, W&W.

9 The politics of information

Justin Keen

Introduction

A casual reader of much of the literature on information and information technology (IT) down the years might be led to think that it is a straight-forward area. Implement systems, collect data, offer it to people, and they will use it to improve their working practices. There are few hints that implementation may be vexed, or that people will fail to act on available information. This chapter, and those that follow, should help to set the record straight, and should strike a chord with the many practitioners who know that life is not that simple. The subject of this chapter is the politics of information: it is argued that one of the key reasons why information is not used is that it is bound up with organizational politics. If the NHS is to make use of the swathes of data and considerable knowledge available to it, political issues will have to be addressed.

The chapter is organized in three sections. The first deals with the conceptual confusion that surrounds the use of the term information. It is suggested that information is the victim of misplaced claims, and an alternative polemic is outlined. The second concerns the interaction of information and organizational politics. Information is, it seems, often used as an arena for negotiation between different stakeholders. The interaction is then further explored in the third section through closer examination of the governance of information in the NHS.

Information and mythology

The 1990s have been marked in some quarters by a sober reassessment of the value of investments in IT. There is plenty of evidence that organizations in both the public and private sectors are disappointed (Zuboff 1988; Grindley 1991). Technology has been oversold and has not delivered (Earl 1992). Yet there are others who continue to assert the vital role that IT can play in transforming organizational performance (Scott Morton 1991). There are indeed documented examples of successes, but they are distressingly few in number when viewed in the context of a ubiquitous technology. Earl calls for a more realistic approach to the role of IT, which should be based neither on hype nor on total cynicism. This would certainly be helpful in the NHS.

By analogy with Earl, it would also be helpful if information were better understood, and its potential and problems more widely appreciated. A fundamental problem is that information is difficult to define, and many writers studiously avoid defining it. No attempt will be made here either, save to say that a distinction can in practice be drawn between data and the product of interpreting data which is information. More helpful, perhaps, is to examine some of the claims made about information.

First, it is assumed by many people that information is a good thing. This ignores the problem that information is often a very awkward thing. If doctors discover through audit that they are having no effect on, or even harming, their patients, what do they do? They might react by changing their practice, but equally might not find it easy to accept the evidence. This is understandable: none of us likes to have it pointed out, publicly or privately, that we have made mistakes. So, information is good when the news is good, and perhaps less so at other times. It must be said, though, that the common secretiveness of the NHS in its internal dealings and its relationships with patients is not a good thing either. This suggests that the trend in the NHS to generating and using ever more information will have to be handled in a fairly sophisticated way if the benefits are to outweigh the costs of collecting it.

Second, many people implicitly believe that computers are the major source of information in an organization. They assert that everything will be well just as soon as the new computer is ready and they have the information they need. This simply doesn't bear scrutiny. It takes some explaining, for example, how the NHS has survived for so long without effective computer systems in many areas: high quality care is not ultimately dependent on computers, though they may help. It also ignores the fact that managers and service providers are highly educated, and so can bring to their jobs a wealth of learning and prior experience: of course they may also bring misunderstanding and prejudice.

One of the most helpful shifts in perception about information in the NHS would involve the appreciation that it comes from a variety of sources: knowledge lodged in people's heads, conversations with colleagues in other parts of the Service, journals and so on. Computers are simply one potential source of information, and indeed have to be justified on the basis that they add to an already rich environment. (This 'marginal' effect of IT is often underplayed by its proponents.)

Third, it is often asserted that information is a resource, that it behaves like a commodity which can be bought and sold. Again, this belief is open to challenge. In health services the value of information depends on context. Knowing that someone with abdominal pain does not have appendicitis (but probably has a pain which will eventually resolve without major treatment) is very useful before operating, and rather less useful two hours after the operation. Conversely, it may be that an apparently innocuous result of a test taken now will turn out to be highly significant next week, when combined with further information about a person's illness.

This emphasizes that there is no point in putting energy into data collection if it is late, wrong or will be ignored – but that it can be difficult to know which data are useful and which not. Perhaps this underpins the fourth assumption, that more data or information is better. Just like real commodities, such as copper or diamonds, a big pile is better than a small one. In their behaviour, especially in the desire to implement IT, many NHS staff appear to believe that more is indeed better. Again, though, this view does not square with evidence about the nature of decision-making (Tversky 1969; Todd and Bensabat 1992), which suggests that when people are presented with more and more data they do not use it all, but select what they think is most relevant and ignore the rest. That is, they make tradeoffs between optimal decisions and the effort they can or will put in. So more will be better only in those circumstances where people incorporate it into their decision-making processes: the trick is to achieve this.

These points might seem to be no more than common sense, as indeed they are. But the myth-inducing properties of information and IT, and their proponents, sow misunderstanding. Information cannot be conceived of as being isolated from organizational processes, and it is always important to take a broad view.

The information-based organization

Much has been made in recent years of the concepts of the information-based organization and the knowledge-intensive firm (see, for example, Keen 1991; Sproull and Kiesler 1991). On the face of it, health services should serve as models of both concepts. Information should flow freely between managers and all professionals as they deliver co-ordinated services, and there can be no denying the very high average level of education of health service staff. However, even the most myopic of observers could not fail to notice that the NHS falls some way short of these ideals. Information is as often cast as villain as it is hero: inaccurate, irrelevant and so on. The impressive knowledge base is manifestly not translated into the delivery of the most effective services: there is growing evidence that many services delivered by doctors, nurses and others are of no therapeutic value or are actually harmful. The question is, to what extent are concepts such as these appropriate and realistic models for the NHS to strive for?

Technocratic utopianism	A heavily technical approach to information management, stressing categorization and modelling of an organization's full information assets, with heavy reliance on emerging technologies
Anarchy	No overall information policy, leaving individuals to obtain and manage their own information
Feudalism	Information is managed by individual units or functions, which define their own information needs and report only limited information to the centre
Monarchy/ Dictatorship	The management board defines information categories and reporting structures, and may not willingly share information with the wider organization
Federalism	Information management is based on consensus and negotiation about information flows

Figure 9.1 Models of information politics (adapted from Davenport *et al.* 1992).

Davenport *et al.* (1992) have proposed five models which characterize the different ways in which organizations treat information (Fig. 9.1). These models are really caricatures, but do capture the flavour of different types of organization politics. Any one organization might exhibit aspects of more than one model at a time: all can be found in the NHS. Their appeal lies in highlighting the origins of problems – and possible solutions – in information management.

Technocratic utopianism remains widespread at the centre and in many hospitals. Information management is interpreted as a problem capable of solution through technical means, as evidenced by support for ambitious technical infrastructures within hospitals and across the NHS – an emphasis on data definitions and modelling, large databases for resource management, the national network for data exchange and even aspirations to a Europe-wide health network. The utopian tag refers to the belief that technology will solve problems, and that system implementation is a definable technical task which does not depend critically on wider management processes.

A proper technical infrastructure is essential for an organization of the size and complexity of the NHS. It is unimaginable that it could survive without any standardization of data or systems. But too many managers and clinical staff have been assured that all would be well when the new system arrived – and too many disappointed. An important reason for this disappointment lies in the fact that data generation by itself is a necessary but insufficient condition for good information management. Political and economic forces need to be harnessed to ensure systems are implemented successfully and data is used. And not all interesting information can be reduced to letters and numbers. Gossip and intelligence are often at least as important as computer-derived data: and they are obtained through formal or informal contact rather than technical processes.

The anarchy model of information politics is appealing to more cynical observers of the NHS. Anarchy implies that there is no overall model and individuals look after their own information needs. In contrast with technocratic utopianism, there is no common technical infrastructure and people collect data according to their own definitions and in their own systems. This describes parts of the NHS: the holding of many separate records – medical, nursing, paramedical and all using different terminology – for the same patient. In any one ward or clinic there are several parallel data collection systems: this must militate against proper co-ordination of services. There may be good 'informal' exchanges between different groups, which can overcome some of the limitations of anarchy. But at worst the result can be that people hide behind the jargon of their part of the NHS to prevent too much scrutiny, and find it impossible to review their own work (which is bound up with the work of others) in an intelligent way.

In the feudal model, individual functions control their own information flows and have a large degree of autonomy from the centre. They tend to have their own languages, which facilitate local communication but may be a barrier to wider discussion. In hospitals this model describes activities such as medical audit, which have come to be controlled by the medical profession (Kerrison *et al.* 1993). Similarly, surgical nurses and doctors can build up a helpful common vocabulary for use in operating theatres, where speed and accuracy are at a premium. The positive aspects of this model lie in the fact that some groups can exchange information efficiently through the use of specialized terminology. However, there are obvious shortcomings to feudalism, in that sharing of information across the organization is made more difficult and the same basic data may be collected many times as patients move between territories. A feudal model makes cross-group working more difficult and fragmentation of services is more likely; trends such as the increasing specialization of clinical service delivery will tend to exacerbate this effect. It is also more difficult for the hospital board to make decisions which increase the overall welfare of the organization, as it lacks information on which to base them. All may not be lost, though, if alliances can be struck: Davenport *et al.* (1992) suggest that, just as feudal barons could strike deals, so can their modern equivalents.

The hospital board may respond to the problems it perceives in the feudal model by imposing itself on the divisions. The term monarchy is used by Davenport *et al.*, but dictatorship seems more apt in the context of the NHS. Political forces are subdued by central dictate, with control preferred to empowerment. This is not entirely without merit: there are situations where an element of dictatorship is necessary. For example, the charge of secretiveness is one that much of the NHS does not seem in a hurry to contest, and it may be that greater openness to both staff and patients may itself have to be imposed: policies such as the Patient's Charter are groping towards this end.

In practice, much will hinge on the extent to which the dictatorship is benevolent. Benevolence involves striking a balance between the desire to collect information for central use and the willingness to share it once collected. If such a balance can be struck then a top-down approach may work, so long as there is general agreement as to its wisdom. At the level of individual hospitals, however, there may be little benevolence around, with the board tending to withhold information. This is a short-sighted policy, not least because staff may decide not to pass on accurate information about their own activities, leading to a situation where the board does not have the information it needs to manage.

The final model is federalism, and this comes nearest the Utopia that some management theorists advocate. It involves negotiation between parties with divergent interests, in order to achieve sharing of information and hence understanding: the negotiation occurs both between boards and units, and horizontally between units. The watchwords are co-operation and shared learning, stemming from a recognition of, and positive approach to, political forces. Empowerment of all staff (and patients) is preferred to top-down control. While utopian in its aims, the model does possess characteristics that seem desirable in practice, and it has been advanced in the Resource Management initiative and total quality management. Most importantly, there is a positive drive to exploit information from all sources in order to improve performance. Responsibility for data collection and action is devolved, but is carried out within a generally agreed framework. The dangers of fragmentation of services are mitigated by active central co-ordination: indeed co-ordination depends on the free flow of relevant information. This is consistent with the concept of the information-based organization, and exploits its rich knowledge base. However, real life tells us that federations have their limitations. The likely feasibility of this model for the NHS is returned to later.

The governance of information

The five models are entertaining, but by themselves might lead to superficial judgements about information politics. The insights can be rooted more firmly by considering the governance of information in the NHS. In Figure 9.2 one area is concerned with management and clinical processes, and the other with the infrastructure of data and IT. Different staff work within each: the management/clinical structure contains most staff, whereas the data/IT structure includes those for whom working with data or IT defines their jobs. The overlap between the two areas comprises those people who work in the wider organization but who either manage or use the data/IT resources.

In practice, many staff in hospitals and purchasing authorities sit in the

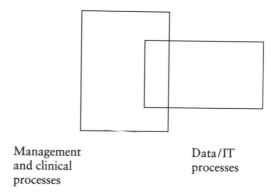

Management   Data/IT
and clinical   processes
processes

Figure 9.2   The governance of information.

intersection of the two areas: they both manage or deliver services and generate and use data. (In effect each group has its own structure, though the figure can also be taken to represent a whole hospital.) However, the data is often recorded on paper, in a number of different places, and controlled by those who record it. As other chapters emphasize, the data/ IT infrastructure (case mix systems, Körner data collection and so on) is only tangentially related to local management and clinical processes. Thus, in many hospitals there is no particular relationship between the overlap area and the main data/IT arena, save for longstanding services such as medical records. And the infancy of the purchasing function, with its severe information problems, means that much activity takes place in the management area. Fortunately this is now changing, but overall there is a long way to go.

Figure 9.2 is, of course, over-simple, and there are also differences between stakeholders, manifested in their skills and power and in the information they hold (Freeman 1984). Doctors, nurses and other groups will tend to defend their existing interests in their dealings with each other. Sometimes these interests are best defended through intransigence, at other times through co-operation. The tendency for particular groups to keep information to themselves, or fail to act on information produced by others, results in part from history. Each group of health professionals has traditionally held its own information on patients, and it is still rare for doctors to share clinical information freely with nurses and paramedics. If doctors or others retain information, especially if it is in a form that others find difficult to understand, it is more difficult to monitor their work. Such information asymmetries can be important buttresses of power.

The tendency to withhold information may also be exacerbated by more general forces. It was noted in Chapter 2 that central funding for IT has tended to be handed out policy by policy and tended to reinforce separate data/IT structures; the formation of NHS trusts and GP fundholders also tends to lead to fragmentation of services. So if different parties – say doctors and nurses – are to share information successfully they must co-ordinate both their clinical activities and their respective data/IT infra-structures. This is a major challenge, which requires attention both to the complex detail of harmonizing data collection and to the broader co-ordination of service delivery and review.

But there is also growing evidence of collaboration, often locally in-spired. Some NHS staff have grasped the nettle, as evidenced by some of the practitioners' chapters in this book, and have moved towards multidisciplinary working at operational, internal management and con-tracting levels. In the NHS, there has been a move from functional to directorate-based organization, and directorates would appear to be natur-al units for reducing information and other asymmetries between different professional groups. Indeed, directorates can be viewed as but one exam-ple of a more general phenomenon of devolved organizational units. The argument that doctors and – to a lesser extent – nurses should be involved in management now seems to be generally accepted, though achievement of effective collaboration is problematic. The idea that sharing of informa-tion is a good thing is no longer simply an assertion but accepted as necessary, at least by reasonable numbers of health professionals.

This tendency is bolstered to some extent by the contracting process, which depends on purchasers and providers, and staff within hospitals, discussing current and future plans. What is also clear, though, is that in some hospitals boards are holding on to power by negotiating contracts themselves. If management boards negotiate themselves they can retain control of the shape of contracts, but lose clinical input from the people who deliver particular services. The contracts may be clinically naïve; and it may be that in the long run failure to keep people on board will re-bound. (Withholding information may in the end be a naïve strategy, if failure to be open results in loss of contracts.) Conversely, if the board delegates negotiation down to directorates it should get better contracts, but the whole process is more complex. There are more people involved in the negotiation, each with their own interests, and so the process is more difficult to manage. The board has to co-ordinate a series of separate contracting processes. But more staff are involved in – sign up to – the result, and the discussions that take place can be part of the process of empowerment and reducing information asymmetries. Staff are better in-formed about the workings of their institution.

At present, then, there is evidence both of collaboration and sharing of information and of withholding and failures of exchange. This is not sur-prising in a transitional environment, where people are feeling their way towards new modes of working. This can be related back to the five models described above. The early models are characterized by a lack of co-ordination or collaboration, whereas the later ones depend on them (federal model) or at least on consensus (benign dictatorship). There are several possible arguments in favour of collaboration. One is that collabor-ative approaches to the delivery of care mean better services and better outcomes. A characteristic of such working is that service providers exchange information about patients (or clients), or discuss care plans with patients themselves. This has implications for the extent to which service providers and patients understand and are informed about wider developments. Another argument is that service providers no longer have any choice: the pressures on resources mean that collaboration offers the only means of arriving at allocations that make sense to both sides.

There are important consequences of sharing information. Increasingly public service organizations are dependent on information flows and relationships (Frissen 1992). As responsibility for decision-making has been devolved, it has become important for more and more people to inform one another of their intentions and actions. This trend towards 'informatization' has consequences which need careful thinking through. For example, many people would accept that a workforce which is well informed about the direction of an organization is desirable, but may well change the balance of power between workforce and management board. And better informed patients may, over time, change relationships with service providers as they demand more or different services.

Another way of looking at the consequences of collaboration is through analysis of incentives. The stark contrast between those areas where information is used (such as finance) and those where often it is not (e.g. medical audit) can to some extent be explained by the different incentives to use it. Analysis of incentives to collect data and discuss it is instructive (Keen *et al.* 1993). Evidence from hospitals implementing resource management suggests that both financial and non-financial incentives are important (Fig. 9.3): these need to be harnessed to encourage sharing of information. The challenge lies in designing incentives so that the interests of stakeholders can be aligned, a particularly difficult task in an organization with multiple objectives. Finance and other data will be used because the survival of individuals and the organization depend on it. Contracting necessitates review of ever more data. Equally there appear to be insufficient incentives to change practice as a result of service review, though this may still occur if local staff feel that change is consistent with professionalism.

There are other important potential problems. One obvious one is that the centre – Government or Management Executive – intervenes in an unhelpful way. This is not unheard of. They may remove local incentives to collaborate by, for example, imposing data collection requirements that service providers feel are inappropriate or too burdensome. If they feel that providing information to the centre seems only to result in cuts then they may put little effort into collaboration with managers (agents of the centre) or data collection. More generously, the centre has a legitimate need to monitor, and if necessary act as an enforcer of, local activities. This will often though, sit uncomfortably with local commitment to sharing sensitive information.

The fragmentation of management and services, exemplified by NHS

	Individual	Directorate	Hospital
Financial	Consultant merit awards linked to management	Service contracts	Service contracts Central finance for computer systems
Political		Service contracts	Service contracts
Prestige	Champion of new policies, e.g. NHS trusts, medical audit		Champion of new policies, e.g. NHS trusts
Professional			

Figure 9.3   Incentives to doctors in the provider market (from Keen *et al.* 1993).

trusts breaking their umbilical cords with district purchasers, also poses problems. Stewart and Walsh (1992) suggest that many of these newly free bodies will have a limited capacity for learning and therefore for adaptability, as information is held within separate units and as activities are governed by the terms of contracts. A third problem is that the increased transparency of affairs caused by both collaboration and formal contracts is uncomfortable for one or more parties. The explicitness of decision-making about prioritization or rationing of services, whether inside a hospital or between purchasers and providers, is difficult to handle.

The limits to the free flow of information in the NHS can now be better understood as involving tensions in the design of incentives and of governance structures which allow both empowerment (through information) and appropriate accountability mechanisms. The more one delegates, the more complex accountability mechanisms are required and the greater the problem of co-ordination. The more people are informed the more complex the processes that involve them in decision making.

Conclusions

So is the information-based organization attainable in the NHS? The answer seems to depend on where one stands. The separation of purchasers and providers does seem to require purchasers and hospital management boards to become 'information brokers': they are the negotiators and co-ordinators proposed in the federal model. However, there are a number of practical and political reasons to suppose that purchasers and hospitals may find it difficult to attain the federal ideal. They may, for example, suffer from the government and NHS Management Executive's desire (sometimes justified and sometimes not) to impose particular policies: so federalism will always be combined with dictatorship. The free flow of information will not be attained if the dictatorship is insensitive: local staff may not co-operate with the centre if they perceive that their own interests are not being met.

Currently the NHS exhibits elements of all five of Davenport *et al.*'s models, which emphasizes the overall lack of cohesion in information management. The federal model remains one to aspire to, but a combination of 'natural' tendencies to withhold information in certain instances, combined with the fact of the centre continuing to set priorities, means that the federal model will be difficult to attain. Yet some developments at the operational level within hospitals suggest that 'local federalism' may flourish if encouraged. Perhaps the realistic model for the public sector is a modified form of federalism, where it is incumbent on the centre to encourage as much as it directs.

References

Davenport, T., Eccles, R. and Prusak, L. (1992) 'Information politics', *Sloan Management Review*, Fall, 53–65.

Earl, M. (1992) 'Putting IT in its place: a polemic for the nineties', *Journal of Information Technology*, 7, 100–8.

Freeman, E. (1984) *Strategic Management: A Stakeholder Approach*. Boston, Pitman Press.

Frissen, P. (1992) 'Informatization in Public Administration: Research Directions'. Paper presented to Seminar on Information, Communication and New Technologies in Public Administration, 12 March.

Grindley, K. (1991) *Managing IT at Board Level*. London, Pitman.

Keen, J., Buxton, M. and Packwood, T. (1993) 'Doctors and resource management: incentives and goodwill, *Health Policy*, 24, 71–82.

Keen, P. (1991) *Shaping the Future: Business Design Through Information Technology*. Boston, Harvard Business School Press.

Kerrison, S., Packwood, T. and Buxton, M. (1993) *Medical Audit: Taking Stock*. London, King's Fund.

Scott Morton, M. (ed.) (1991) *The Corporation of the 1990's*. New York, Oxford University Press.

Sproull, L. and Kiesler, S. (1991) *Connections: New Ways of Working in the Networked Organisation*. Cambridge, MA, MIT Press.

Stewart, J. and Walsh, K. (1992) 'Change in the management of public services', *Public Administration*, 70, 499–518.

Todd, P. and Bensabat, I. (1992) 'The use of information in decision-making: an experimental investigation of the impact of computer-based decision aids', *MIS Quarterly*, 16, 373–93.

Tversky, A. (1969) 'Intransitivity of preferences', *Psychological Review*, 76, 31–48.

Zuboff, S. (1988) *In the Age of the Smart Machine: The Future of Work and Power*. New York, Basic Books.

10 A social science perspective on information systems in the NHS

Brian Bloomfield, Rod Coombs and Jenny Owen

Introduction

The NHS has always been fertile territory for social scientists, but the current changes taking place in the service have intensified this interest. Three features of recent developments can be identified which have particular relevance to this volume.

First, the NHS is sharing with most other organizations the experience of introducing information technology (IT) into a wide variety of its activities, ranging from the automation of clerical tasks to the analysis of the 'product-mix' and 'market position' of a hospital unit. Such uses of IT in complex organizations are already the subject of a substantive body of social science and management literature, and the question arises as to whether healthcare organizations are different. Second, and only loosely connected until recently with the first point, within the NHS there has been a relatively slow evolution away from administrative models of organization towards a more explicit concern with notions of effectiveness and efficiency, rooted in more managerial models of organization. Third, and most obviously, there is the current introduction of the internal market reforms in the NHS. This third feature gives an added impetus to the first two, but has its own specific origins in more fundamental attempts to reshape and reposition the NHS in the minds of employees, patients and the public in general. Added together, these three features create a compelling context in which to take a social science view of the inter-relationships between the way information systems are designed, and the organizational changes which are tied up with those information systems.

This chapter addresses the issue of information systems development and use in the NHS through three sections. First, we look at the fundamental question of the relationship between information technology (IT) and organizations. Second, we go on to consider the specific characteristics of IT, and especially information systems, which give them – as opposed to technology in general – a distinctive significance in terms of social practices within organizations. The argument here will be illustrated by reference to the changing boundaries between the professions of medicine and management. And third, we look at the construction of information systems, and give examples to show the inherent interpretative flexibility that exists in their fabrication. (These terms, with their origins in socio-logical studies of science and technology, emphasize the view that there is always more than one way to design a technical artefact, and that the social process of technological development is characterized by interpreta-tion and negotiation. In the third section of this chapter, we develop these points with specific illustrations in the area of information systems.) We will suggest that the boundary between the social and the technical is not given *a priori* but is negotiated during systems development and imple-mentation, thus casting light on our opening theme concerning the rela-tionship between technology and organizations. We should emphasize here that 'technology' does not refer solely, or necessarily, to fixed physical entities; any technology – from coal mining to computing – also encom-passes specific forms of knowledge, skill and organization.

The relationship between IT and organizations

A number of different social science literatures touch on the area of organ-izations, management and information technology (IT) and it is not possible to discuss all of them in the detail that they deserve. However, for our purposes there is one common thread which runs through them which is of particular interest – namely the fundamental question as to the nature of the relationship between technology and social (or organizational) structure. The different answers to this question can be usefully envisaged by reference to a continuum whose poles represent two extremes, charac-terized as technological determinism and social determinism. These repre-sent convenient labels which we can attach, with more or less severity, to particular schools of thought and their underlying assumptions.

According to technological determinism, what people do with IT, the way that it *impacts* on the structure of organizations, on the practice of management or on work design, is seen largely to be determined, or pre-ordained, by technology and its particular characteristics. With this view it is as if technological artifacts embody some inner logic *of their own* – that they fit into or are expressions of some unfolding evolutionary scheme to which there exist corresponding patterns of social relations, with the latter obtaining through a secondary process of adaptation to changing technical possibilities. Thus the course of societal or organizational change is seen to be anchored to technological imperatives. It is in this spirit that some writers have looked at the trends in the development of IT and sought to predict specific social or organizational developments accordingly. Within the social science literature, examples of this emphasis can be found in the work of Naisbitt (1982) and Toffler (1980). In a business context, surveys and reports from suppliers and management consultants in IT have also implied this kind of perspective on occasion (e.g. International Computers Limited 1990; Price Waterhouse 1991).

In contrast, a view underpinned by assumptions of social determinism would have it that IT, or any technology, can be moulded to a given set of social/political interests. On this view, technology has often been characterized as a mere instrument in the hands of a dominant class, gender, ruling elite, imperial power or management. For example, early studies in the labour process debate viewed technology as a resource which managers could use in order to control the workforce by expropriating their skills (Zimbalist 1979). Thus on this account, if technology is shaped by social interests then technological change may be seen as part of the broader pattern of social development. (In fact, the story is actually more complicated than this. Some work in the area displayed an uncomfortable tension between the idea that technology was politically neutral and the notion that machines were specific to particular forms of social organization – thus giving rise to the notion of capitalist versus socialist machines (Braverman 1974; Burawoy 1985).)

Between these two extremes lie contingency theories in which IT is regarded as just another variable in the organizational equation: something to be considered along with other contingent factors such as knowledge, organizational size and structure, or organizational goals (Kast and Rosenzweig 1981). Here one should also mention the socio-technical approach to the development of computer-based information systems: this aims to maximize organizational efficiency through participative methods toward job design, conceived within the orbit of a series of technical constraints. The idea is that in the end organizations must adapt to technology, to what are seen as its basically physical properties or characteristics; but there are, however, a number of conceivable or viable adaptations, and so the process of systems development must secure legitimacy through the involvement of those whose work is redesigned (Mumford 1981).

The approaches discussed thus far have their roots in discussions of technology in a very general sense, often taking manufacturing technology as a major reference point. Clearly, information technology raises some specific issues that may not be dealt with adequately from this starting-point. Thus in recent work on IT and organizations one finds that more attention is paid to the particularity and significance of information systems; that is to the informational aspects of IT. For example, consideration has been given to the ways in which information systems enable very detailed mechanisms of organizational control because of the enhanced surveillance possibilities which they open up. One finds, for instance, the idea of the 'electronic panopticon' in which, paradoxically, IT is used to increase the decentralization of decision-making while at the same time making possible a centralization of power. This is known as devolution-ism (Mosco 1989; Sewell and Wilkinson 1992). (The phrase 'electronic panopticon' represents a fusion of the surveillance potential of IT with Foucault's discussion of prison architecture; in particular, Bentham's model prison where prisoners could be observed from a central tower but could not be sure themselves as to whether or not they were being observed (Foucault 1979).) In short, IT is seen as a means of furthering management control. However, we shall argue that, because of the capacity for infor-mation systems to create rather than merely report organizational reality, coupled with the interpretative flexibility inherent in the design of tech-nological artifacts, the nature of management control may be changing as a result of implementing it through the medium of IT.

Another variant on this theme is adopted by Zuboff (1989), who argues a position in which traditional managerial control is actually seen to per-vert the potential of IT. Such control is seen as an expression of a rigid and outmoded form of organizational design (Orlikowski 1988; Rockart and Short 1991). Instead, Zuboff envisages new forms of networked organiza-tion, in which the workforce would be regarded as knowledge workers and in which IT would be used to enhance worker flexibility and auton-omy, and therefore the decentralization of organizational power.

Reviewing the ground covered so far, we have seen that there are related issues concerning IT and the structural changes in an organization, and concerning the role of IT in the exercise of managerial control. How do these arguments play out in the context of the NHS? Let us take the structure issue first. An analysis that leans towards a technological deter-minist stance might argue that IT systems, by virtue of their cheapness and their ability to capture information about activities as they happen and then to aggregate and analyse them, create a kind of 'decentralizing logic' for organizations. Use of IT can cut actual labour costs in the conduct of tasks that involve information, and yet make the performance of such tasks more visible to managers at a distance without the need for an additional management function 'on the spot'. This, it might be argued, makes organizations which use IT intrinsically more efficient, if they are configured in this structure of a core and a number of more autonomous but more visible peripheral units.

But from the standpoint of a social determinist, a choice to decentralize an organization in this way might be seen as derived from particular interests, ideas or values: for example, a view of the merits of markets in creating incentives for individuals to improve their performance; or perhaps from a quite different belief that only organizational units of small size can function effectively (and there are yet other possible theoretical perspec-tives which could underpin a decentralizing stance). From this perspective, the IT systems which support or permit decentralized approaches to organizational structure are simply particular forms of IT, whose design directly gives expression to the (prior) organizational choices. Other IT systems could equally well have been built as part of a more centralized structure.

But despite the various differences regarding the nature of the relationship between technology and organizations, it is interesting to note that these positions all share a fundamental premise, which is that technology either has agency itself – independent purpose or intentionality – or at least bears the attributes of agency by providing a vehicle for the expression and achievement of the interests of particular groups. In other words, the technology is conceptualized as possessing a directly mechanical kind of power which is seen as acting separately from, and indeed upon, the powers of individuals and organizations. Moreover, this assumed property is itself bolstered by the ways in which technology is frequently conceived of in the form of physical machines or equipment. At root the fundamental difficulty with these approaches is that they posit a dualism between the world of technological objects (e.g. machines) and the world of social objects (e.g. people, institutions). If we reduce technology to machines, as something other than ourselves as social beings, it is easy to fall into the trap of asking how such machines were socially determined, or alternatively, how such machines determine how we are socially.

In contrast, more recent thinking has exposed these implicit assumptions about 'the technical' and 'the social', suggesting that the boundary between the two is not fixed but subject to constant renegotiation, and that this process itself should be a central focus for social science analyses. It has even been argued for instance that technology 'is society made more durable' (Latour 1991).

To put the argument another way, the technological determinist and social determinist stances described above all depend on an implied separation in time between 'effects' which society might have on a technology, and 'effects' which that technology might have on society. This could enable us to argue, for example, that a particular coalition of interests in a hospital meant that a case mix package was designed with more emphasis on medical audit than on cost control (society shapes technology); but that the case mix system was incapable of meeting certain expectations because of the constraints of the UNIX operating system (technology shapes society). To some extent, such an analysis may be admissible. But in real time this is not how people behave. The 'constraints' associated with UNIX will only be made to act in the construction of the case mix system by those individuals who mobilize them and propose that they are in fact constraints of a particular form. Others who know little of UNIX might or might not believe these claims, with consequences for how significant they become. This is what is referred to in this literature as 'interpretative flexibility', to which we shall return in the last section of this chapter. But before this, we turn to the second of the three concerns identified at the beginning of this chapter – namely the distinctive significance of IT and of information systems.

The specific character of IT and information systems

Since the nineteenth century modern forms of organization, particularly administrative bureaucracies, have relied increasingly on textual information in order to secure the goals of internal co-ordination and management control:

> [T]he bureaucratic form routinizes the process of administration exactly as the machine routinizes production . . . a form of organization that emphasizes precision, speed, clarity, regularity, reliability, and efficiency achieved through the creation of a fixed division of tasks, hierarchical supervision, and detailed rules and regulations. (Morgan 1986: 24–25)

This description of course represents a classic Weberian analysis of bureaucracy. The pursuit of characteristics such as precision, speed, clarity, regularity, reliability and efficiency depend in part on the reduction of uncertainty through information and information processing. Thus we observe that inscriptions on paper, whether in the form of inventories, personnel records, sales forecasts, balance sheets, etc. have come to play an integral part in organizational life, constituting a picture of the past, present and future.

Similar developments have taken place in other forms of organization too. For instance, in medical practice the inception of the medical record provided a picture of the state of health of an individual patient (or, when aggregated together, of a population); and at the same time this knowledge provided a lever to help exert control in matters of health – whether in curbing disease or promoting hygiene. While in schools, the introduction of examinations enabled the classification and sorting of pupils (Foucault 1979). In each sphere the exercise of control depends in part on information; the more detailed and expansive the information, the greater are the possibilities that are opened up for control.

Against this (necessarily brief) historical perspective on the relationship between written records, bureaucracy and management control, it is instructive to view information systems in organizations as devices for inscribing organizational reality in order to make it visible and analysable (Latour 1986, 1987; Bloomfield 1991). Predominantly, the images and rhetoric surrounding IT carry revolutionary overtones and a sense of rupture with the past. In contrast, what is suggested here is a high degree of continuity – both with regard to the concern over organizational control and the use of information to reduce uncertainty. What is different derives from the particular characteristics of IT with regard to the information handling potential that it offers. More specifically, the greater the degree to which information is mobile, combinable and immutable offers a more potent organizational resource for persuading others about what is the case and therefore what should be done, who is deviating from the norm and who is in compliance.

To be sure, this may be taken as support for the idea of IT as a form of electronic surveillance system. But it is crucial to realize that, in some senses, information systems create organizational reality rather than merely report it. They do not reveal the world (of the organization) as it is in some neutral and objective way; rather, the information content of such systems involves partial choices, inclusions and exclusions, which construct a picture of what is happening in organizations. Put another way, information systems enable the generation and dissemination of information which informs or constitutes a picture of what organizational reality is taken to be. This picture, which is actually underdetermined by the goals of any particular group of actors, enters the field of interpretation through which organizational members/professions recognize organizational life; and to a greater or lesser extent it can monopolize the received view on matters of what the current situation is, what went wrong in the past, and what must be done in the future.

This brings us to our first example from the NHS – namely the role of information and information systems in mediating the changes in the boundaries between different professional groups.

Changing cultures and changing patterns of control

The ways in which information systems play a role in mediating and reinforcing organization realities are relevant to the changing relationships between the different professional groups within the NHS. Changes in the boundaries between different groups in terms of their responsibility and accountability are conditional upon changed understandings of organizational reality, which are themselves predicated on, mediated and reinforced by the forms of information which information systems make available. We might cite as (very abbreviated) examples the role of a case mix management system in changing the relationship between doctors and managers (the discourses of medicine and management); or the way that the requirement to input dependency scores for patients into a nurse management system might modify the boundaries between nurses and managers (the discourses of nursing and management). In each case, information systems are seen as a condition of making possible and sustainable new modes of organizational practice – the 'doctor–manager' or the 'nurse–manager' roles – which are determined or defined by the requirements of rational, efficient and modern organizations.

The aspirations of some of those responsible for driving forward many of the changes which the NHS has witnessed over the past few years clearly centre on the issue of management control of medical work, and the organizational and informational issues which surround it. Their aspiration is that efficiency and effectiveness can be highlighted and improved by generating sophisticated management information using IT, and feeding it into all levels of decision making in the hospital.

But there is some uncertainty and variety of practice on the question of how to establish the connection between this management information and the actual practices of doctors. In the Griffiths Report (DHSS 1983), the expectation was that doctors would be given budgets in which a planned volume of work and a related cash budget would be allocated at the beginning of the year. The doctor would be provided with regular information about actual work done and cash spent and would be responsible for adjustments in practice to ensure compliance with the budget. Thus, to give but one example of the underdetermination of current developments, it is interesting to note that while some managers think that the new information systems will enable them to monitor doctors' efficiency more closely and thereby exert some control, some doctors believe that the systems will enable them to prove for the first time just how efficient they actually are already (Bloomfield and Coombs 1992).

We can extend this argument with reference to the example of computerized care profiles. In prospect, a computerized care profile, available at the bed-side to clinical professionals, could be seen as tightening the control by seniors of juniors within the clinical professions, and perhaps also as tightening the financial control over senior professionals (as the care profile could have been influenced by cost considerations as well as clinical ones). But an alternative view would be to see the care profile as enabling for the clinician, inasmuch as it makes available a validated level of professional expertise for a situation, as a starting point for action, but still leaves discretion for individual variation of the profile on the basis of professional judgement of the actual case in question. Thus the profile could be seen as amplifying the power of collective, peer-reviewed practice in each clinical case, while preserving the traditional individuality of each interaction with a patient. In some sites, multi-disciplinary profiles, rather than profession-specific ones, have been initiated; this can prompt more fundamental levels of renegotiation (for a detailed discussion, see Chapters 5 and 6 of this volume).

The broad implications of resource management and all the associated organizational changes, such as the inception of clinical directorates, represent a radical change in the organizational position of doctors and nurses *vis-à-vis* the other parts of the formal management structure and represents a renegotiation of the boundaries between medicine and management. These changes encourage doctors and nurses to internalize more thoroughly certain norms and values concerning efficiency, and to regulate their own behaviour in accordance with those norms.

These changes in management control in hospitals arose as a centrally directed attempt at intervention in the culture (an intervention which was construed in instrumental terms), and therefore in the practices of doctors. While the upshot of this planned intervention cannot be predicted, it undoubtedly has the potential to lead to a long-term renegotiation of the received understandings of managerial and medical practices. What we can observe here is a convergence or, more correctly, a clash of discourses; a conflict between different ways of thinking and speaking about medical and management practice. Thus the conventional conceptions of patients and treatments are being challenged by the introduction of concepts from business – for example, terms such as efficiency, effectiveness, resources, etc. – in which IT is seen to play a fundamentally enabling role. But while these terms are becoming common currency throughout the NHS, the diversity of implementations of resource management indicates that in practice the meaning of these terms may be constituted differently in different locations.

This brings us to the third aspect of our argument, the processes involved in the construction of information systems and the underdetermination of these with respect to explicit goals and interests.

Fabricating information systems

The matter of the divergent interpretations of resource management and therefore the variety in the information systems which have been constructed in its name should not be read as some form of aberration; as if the 'true' course of information systems development had somehow been confounded by the very nature of the NHS as an organization. For just like ideas, we find that technologies too do not remain constant as they are passed from one group to another. Technology may not simply diffuse from one group of users to another but may undergo a 'translation' in terms of purpose and content (Latour 1987). Here translation is meant in the double sense: as an act of interpretation and as a fundamental movement from one condition to another. The process of translation can be considered in respect of two inter-related factors, namely interpretative flexibility and the properties of the networks which represent the different groups that come together to build technological systems.

Just as an idea may be received or interpreted in different ways amongst different audiences, so too there is more than one technical solution to a problem. Thus one of the key characteristics of technology is the interpretative flexibility inherent in the design of new artifacts (Bijker *et al.* 1987). Moreover, the degree of flexibility is connected to the nature of the relationships between the various groups of actors engaged in the construction of a technology. For example, in the case of resource management systems we have doctors, nurses, managers, computing/IT staff, management consultants, hardware and software suppliers, etc. Together these groups represent a form of socio-technical network – the network is obviously a social one because of the nature of the organizational interactions within it, but it is simultaneously and increasingly technical too, as the nascent information systems take shape. For example, different groups deploy various techniques or technologies (such as project management tools, or coding systems for medical diagnosis and practice) to argue their corner as to how a particular system should develop.

In accordance with this theoretical position and the arguments outlined at the beginning, it follows that in any attempt to look at the construction of an organizational information system it is impossible to impose rigid boundaries *a priori* around what are taken to be the 'social' and 'technical' aspects. The boundary between the technical (technical limits, potential or constraints) and the social (how organizational practice must change or adapt) is negotiated and renegotiated during systems development and implementation. Although organizational actors will frequently latch onto either social or technical factors when asked to explain how a particular system was implemented, their accounts must be treated as rationalized reconstructions which tend to reproduce the dualism between the technical and the social.

Let us take the resource management (RM) initiative as an example of this flexibility in the construction of information systems. Throughout the history of RM, some groups have emphasized its dual character as an initiative concerned both with information systems and with organizational change. RM is presented as being not simply about generating new sorts of information, but about getting clinicians involved in the management decisions that are informed by that information. Yet it is clear that not all participants view the balance between these two facets of RM in the same way. For some it is all about getting case mix software into place and connecting it to feeder systems. For others the information systems are less central than organizational issues, such as the establishment of clinical directorates. The presence of such differing emphases in RM project teams leads to actual implementations of RM which differ markedly from place to place (Bloomfield *et al.* 1991, 1992a). At a more general level, questions concerning the relationship between management and information were prompted by the Brunel Health Economics Research Group's own evaluation of the pilot phase of RM, but not tackled explicitly (Buxton *et al.* 1991).

On another front, the continuing evolution of IT systems and the arrival of the internal market has made those implementing RM later in the 'roll-out' see things rather differently from those who were part of the first wave. Some units look at the reported experience of others who have installed case mix on top of a rather fragile and underdeveloped assembly of feeder systems (a creaking PAS, perhaps, and no ward ordering) and have decided against what they now see as ill-advised 'top-down' IT strategies (Bloomfield *et al.* 1992b). They might then decide that IT needs, and even organizational requirements to get doctors more closely integrated into management, are better served by a 'bottom-up' strategy of investing in communications systems, ward ordering, improved systems in diagnostic departments or developing some IT support for medical audit. These differences in approach result in quite different operational requirements at the tendering stage for case mix systems; all of which means that there is some considerable room for manoeuvre in defining where the centre of gravity of RM and case mix lies.

Conclusion

It is always difficult to move from social science analysis of organization and management issues to implications for practice. It is certainly dangerous to try to do it in too direct and simplistic a fashion. At its best, social science should illuminate and enhance understanding, and influence practice through that enhanced understanding, rather than through a set of recipes and rules. Given that we are not proposing new recipes, what then are the main contributions to understanding of IT in the NHS which are being offered here?

The central point is this: received thinking tends to make us draw boundaries between the perceived properties of a technology and the perceived properties of an organization – boundaries which are drawn rather too sharply. This in turn fosters a kind of mechanistic or 'billiard ball model' of their interactions, in which they collide, exchange energy and spin, giving rise to a resultant new state of affairs. Put like this, it sounds implausible as soon as it is uttered; everyone knows from experience that in fact there were crucial points where choices were made which could have gone either way, where accidental factors produced outcomes which surprised everyone. And yet we persist in these ways of conceptualizing what happens because they seem sensible reconstructions after the fact, or because they are useful devices to try to mobilize several people in the same direction. In our account we have tried to bring to the fore and hold in focus the more fluid and open situation which exists as technology is being constructed, by contrast with the apparent fixity it acquires once it is in place.

Second, in the specific case of IT an extra feature of the situation amplifies this shading of the boundaries between the technical and the social. This concerns the specifically informational content of IT and the systems we build with that technology. We have emphasized the fact that the choice of the particular information categories which form the currency of these systems cannot be bracketed off as a merely 'technical' issue. Collecting data and presenting it in particular ways can never be done in isolation from the perceived interests and power relationships between those whose behaviour is referred to in the information and those who receive and consider the information. Such information categories – like the care profile, or the DRG, or the marginal costs associated with an extracontractual referral – create new categories of 'common sense' for those who use them. In so far as the categories for understanding organizational reality change, then the reality may be considered to have changed – reflecting a complex pattern of interaction, rather than the 'impact' of a single technological or organizational imperative.

References

Bijker, W., Hughes, T. and Pinch, T. (eds) (1987) *The Social Construction of Technological Systems.* London, MIT.

Bloomfield, B.P. (1991) 'The role of information systems in the NHS: action at a distance and the fetish of calculation', *Social Studies of Science*, 21(4), 701–34.

Bloomfield, B.P. and Coombs, R. (1992) 'Information technology, control and power: the centralisation and decentralisation debate revisited', *Journal of Management Studies*, 29(4), 459–84.

Bloomfield, B.P., Coombs, R. and Rea, D. (1991) 'Differences in a scheme of change,' *Health Service Journal*, 101(5235), 16–17.

Bloomfield, B.P., Coombs, R., Cooper, D.J. and Rea, D. (1992a) 'Machines and manoeuvres: responsibility accounting and the construction of hospital information systems', *Accounting Management and Information Technology*, 2, 197–219.

Bloomfield, B.P., Coombs, R. and Owen, J. (1992b) 'Top down or bottom up?', *Health Service Journal*, 102(5288), 20–2.

Braverman, H. (1974) *Labour and Monopoly Capital: The Degradation of Work in the 20th Century*. New York, Monthly Review Press.

Burawoy, M. (1985) *The Politics of Production*. London, Verso.

Buxton, M., Packwood, T. and Keen J. (1991) *Final Report of the Brunel University Evaluation of Resource Management*. Uxbridge, Brunel University.

Department of Health and Social Security (1983) *NHS Management Inquiry*. London, DHSS.

Foucault, M. (1979) *Discipline and Punish*. Harmondsworth, Penguin.

International Computers Limited (1990) *A Window on the Future*. An ICL briefing for management on the findings of the Management of the 1990s Research Program. International Computers Limited.

Kast, F.E. and Rosenzweig, J.E. (1981) *Organisation and Management: A Systems and Contingency Approach*. London, McGraw-Hill.

Latour, B. (1986) 'Visualisation and cognition', in H. Kuklick (ed.), *Knowledge and Society: Studies in the Sociology of Culture Past and Present*, 6, 1–40.

Latour, B. (1987) *Science in Action*. Milton Keynes, Open University Press.

Latour, B. (1991) 'Technology is society made more durable', in J. Law (ed.), *A Sociology of Monsters: Essays on Power, Technology and Domination*. London, Routledge.

Morgan, G. (1986) *Issues of Organization*. London, Sage.

Mosco, V. (1989) *The Pay-Per Society*. Toronto, Garamond Press.

Mumford, E. (1981) *Values Technology and Work*. London, Martinus Nijhoff.

Naisbitt, J. (1982) *Megatrends*. New York, Warner.

Orlikowski, W. (1988) 'Computer technology in organizations: some critical notes', in D. Knights and H. Willmott (eds), *New Technology and the Labour Process*. London, Macmillan.

Price Waterhouse (1991) *Information Technology Review 1991/92*. London, Price Waterhouse.

Rockart, J.F. and Short, J.E. (1991) 'The networked organization and the management of independence', in M. Scott Morton (ed.), *The Corporation of the 1990s*. Oxford, Oxford University Press.

Sewell, G. and Wilkinson, B. (1992) 'Someone to watch over me: surveillance, discipline and the just-in-time labour process', *Sociology*, 26(2), 271–89.

Toffler, A. (1980) *The Third Wave*. New York, Morrow.

Zimbalist, A. (ed.) (1979) *Case-Studies on the Labor Process*, London and New York, Monthly Review Press.

Zuboff, S. (1989) *In the Age of the Smart Machine*. New York, Basic Books.

11 Information and IT strategy

Bob Galliers

Background

There has been, with justification, considerable concern expressed over the expenditure on information technology (IT) in the NHS in recent years. For example, Wessex Regional Health Authority's Regional Information Systems Plan (Risp) was abandoned in 1990 with major write-offs of between £20 and £40 million. (Similar figures apply to other countries, e.g. USA (Martino 1983) and Australia (Galliers 1987a).) More recently, in late October 1992, the Labour MP for Southampton Itchen, John Denham, was reported as saying that a 'big question mark' hangs over the RHA's 1986 contract with a major management consultancy and major IT vendor. His intention was to find out whether the RHA was planning to recover any money paid out as part of the contract (Collins 1992). In the same article, it was reported that the RHA's IT Director had left her post suddenly despite having helped to restore some order to the RHA's IT management and strategy. It was expected that the post would remain unfilled.

Concern over investment in IT, and many tales of management disquiet over the lack of benefits achieved as a result, are not confined to the NHS, however (Galliers 1992a). Evidence along very similar lines as the above is readily available from the very largest of international corporations, which, one might expect, would get IT right. For example, Sir Denys Henderson, Chairman of ICI, is quoted as saying: 'I still worry enormously, both about the amount of money we spend on IT and the increasing difficulty of justifying that expense in terms of the bottom line' (Grindley 1990). Cost containment and integrating IT (i.e. with the business) have been identified as the top issues executives face in dealing with IT (Grindley 1992). One such executive is quoted as saying:

> We need to reduce overall costs [of IT] by 30 per cent to 40 per cent, and use the remaining 60 per cent to 70 per cent to focus on the core needs of the business. We want to simplify architectures, reduce infrastructure, increase systems development, and reduce operational expenses. (Grindley 1992: 7)

A report published by the Kobler Unit at the University of London's Imperial College (Hochstrasser and Griffiths 1990) lists findings from a range of studies on the subject, e.g.:

1 IT seldom leads to sustainable competitive advantage (Booz *et al.* 1989).
2 IT is not linked to overall productivity increases (OECD 1988).
3 Very few organizations succeed in educating staff to best use installed IT, let alone new IT (BIM/Coopers 1988).
4 70 per cent of companies indicate that management information systems (MIS) lead to confusion by generating what has been called information overload (Business Week 1989).

All this is in marked contrast to the kind of hype surrounding the claims made in recent years that IT can be a source of competitive advantage and a means of enabling and directing strategic moves (McFarlan 1984; Porter and Millar 1985; Scott Morton 1991).

So, can the NHS learn anything from the business sector, given this equivalent sorry state of affairs? The message of this chapter is 'Yes', provided that great care and attention is paid to the lessons that have been learnt from both the positive and negative experiences. The key point is that information and IT strategy needs to be incorporated into the strategic development process that has become part of management thinking since the NHS Review in 1989 (Eskin 1992).

The point is that the process of identifying and implementing strategically significant information systems is a complex one, which represents considerable risk to those organizations that are inadequately prepared for the task. In view of this, this chapter attempts to present guidelines which may help in improving management understanding of the process; deciding on an appropriate information and IT strategy given the particular circumstances that apply, and successfully implementing strategic information systems. A contingent, socio-technical approach to the strategy is proposed.

Information and IT strategy in theory and practice

There has been considerable attention paid to incorporating strategic thinking into our models of information and IT strategy formulation during the 1980s. Much of this arises from the work of Michael Porter and his colleagues at the Harvard Business School (Porter 1979, 1980, 1985; McFarlan 1984; Cash and Konsynski 1985; Porter and Millar 1985). Central to this kind of thinking is the attention paid to using IT to harness (or negate) the competitive forces identified by Porter:

1 potential entrants/new rivals
2 substitute products/services
3 suppliers
4 buyers/customers
5 traditional industry competitors.

While this may have only partial relevance in the NHS, clearly the position has changed radically since 1989. In any event, the greater focus on environmental factors is a key message here, given our traditional over-concentration on internally produced data in information studies hitherto.

To read the wealth of literature that now exists on the subject, one might be forgiven for believing that much of current strategy formulation practice reflects this kind of thinking. The reality is that many companies and not-for-profit organizations do not formulate strategy according to this rational/analytical model, nor do they adequately plan for their information systems, let alone incorporate competitive considerations into their strategy process. What is more, they experience difficulty in implementing their strategies, once these have been formulated. This is certainly true in the UK, and probably so in many other countries as well (Galliers 1987a).

The basis for this contention rests on survey evidence collected in the latter half of the 1980s by the author (Galliers 1986b) and by Tom Wilson of the University of Sheffield (Wilson 1989). Both studies indicate that in excess of 70 per cent of British companies have information and IT strategies but much current practice falls well short of what is the conventional wisdom for success in this difficult and complex field.

Part of the complexity relates to the terminology used. The field of information systems is populated by terminological opacity, and unfortunately that aspect of it concerned with strategy is no exception. The next section will therefore attempt to shed some light on this, before we go on to look at the lessons we can learn from research, previous experience and current practice.

Information and IT strategy: terminology and emerging concepts

I have decided to use the title information and IT strategy for this chapter. This is because IT strategy is a term in common usage in practice, and information strategy reminds us that our focus should be on the ends rather than just the means. In fact, Michael Earl provides us with a useful distinction between the different aspects of strategy in this context, with IT strategy being concerned with the how, information systems (IS) strategy being concerned with the what and information management (IM) strategy being concerned with the why (Fig. 11.1; Earl 1989: 63–5). In other words, Earl reminds us that our focus should not just be on how IT might be

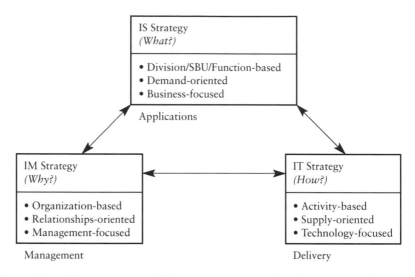

Figure 11.1 Three aspects of IT-related strategy (adapted from Earl 1989).

used, but just as importantly – if not more so – on what information systems are needed to support and direct the business and why we go about managing the information resource in the way we do. Essentially the latter 'comprises the policies, procedures, aims and actions' necessary to manage information and IT (Earl 1989: 64).

Two additional terms commonly in use are strategic and competitive information systems. Huff and Beattie (1985) provide a useful distinction between the two:

1 *Strategic information systems* – directly support the creation and implementation of an organization's strategic plan. The emphasis here is on information systems that enhance executive management processes and decisions. For example, according to this definition, information systems that test the assumptions underpinning strategic plans/business objectives would be classified as strategic.

2 *Competitive information systems* – directly support the execution of strategy by improving the value–cost relationship of the firm in its competitive environment. Here, the emphasis is more concerned with improving competitiveness through the use of IT in reducing costs or adding value to products/services.

It is also useful to consider how our thinking has developed over the years regarding the focus of information and IT strategy.

In the early writings on the topic, attention was concentrated primarily on improving computer efficiency and matters of computer management generally (Kriebel 1968). Information and IT strategy was seen as being a matter for the IS function, pretty well isolated from the on-going business of the organization. As time passed and experience of IS management developed there was growing concern on the part of non-IT management to have a business-driven process, capable of dealing with the business problem/issues they faced. Such approaches as IBM's Business Systems Planning (Zachman 1982) and Rockart's Critical Success Factors (Rockart 1979) became increasingly accepted. The approaches might be described as reactive in nature, given their emphasis on 'top-down' planning (Ng 1984), feeding off business plans/strategies.

While meeting with a measure of success, these were criticized in some quarters for not having a sufficiently strong link with business objectives and for concentrating too much on issues of the day, rather than on future goals/concerns (Davis 1979). Partly as a result of this, business-driven approaches began to focus more on the latter. Developments of, for example, the critical success factors approach also began to focus more on future scenarios with, using this example, efforts being made to identify the critical assumptions upon which business plans/strategies were being built (Henderson *et al.* 1984). While still being dependent on business plans (and, therefore, in this sense, reactive in nature), such approaches attempted to identify future opportunities for the application of IT, rather than simply focusing on current issues.

As organizations sought to identify IT opportunities through their information and IT strategies, so-called 'middle-out' approaches became more common (Henderson and Sifonis 1986). As indicated above, the seminal work here was that of Porter (1979) and colleagues (Porter and Millar 1985). In this context, information and IT strategy became more proactive, with attention being concentrated on an organization's business environment as much as on internal processes, and on technological advances that might be harnessed to good effect.

Current thinking recognizes that elements of each of these foci are likely to be more or less required in different circumstances, and in the mid- to late-1980s came calls for the adoption of 'eclectic' (Sullivan 1985) or 'multiple' (Earl 1987, 1988, 1989) methods. In fact, the very nature of information and IT strategy formulation is now seen to be more complex than formerly. Organizations should no longer be looking simply for a prioritized portfolio of information systems applications as the sole outcome of the process. Human, organizational and infrastructural issues (skills requirements and the manner in which information systems services can best be organized) are now seen as critical components of the task (see Fig. 11.4; Atkins and Galliers 1992; Galliers 1992a).

The above developments are summarized in Figure 11.2, which is based on a framework first proposed by Hirschheim (1982) and later amended by the author (Galliers 1987a,c) and by Ward (1988).

A note of caution, however: much of our thinking on information and IT strategy appears to be based on an overly optimistic, formal and

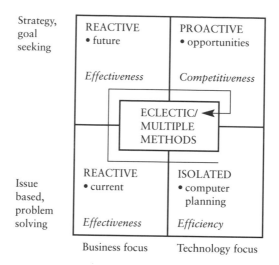

Figure 11.2   A development path for strategic information systems planning (adapted from Galliers 1987a,b; Ward 1988).

rational model of strategy formulation. As intimated above, in many organizations strategy is arrived at by a more informal and creative process. Indeed, it might be said that some companies have no formal strategy at all! The process must, therefore, take into account the prevalent style of strategy formulation in any given context (Pyburn 1983) and, moreover, should not adopt an entirely rational model itself, nor confuse strategy formulation with planning. As Eskin (1992: 24) points out:

> Planning does not depend on the possession of a vision of how the future could look, whereas inventing a strategic framework is entirely concerned with creating the future. There can be no strategy without vision, creativity and a sense of adventure.

Having summarized some of the developments that have taken place in our thinking on the topic, let us turn now to how practice compares with the 'conventional wisdom' for information and IT strategy success.

Conventional wisdom versus convention

In the author's 1986 survey of existing practice with respect to information and IT Strategy (Galliers 1987a), respondents indicated that, from an information systems management perspective, their efforts were either partially or highly successful in 71 per cent of the cases where a strategy was extant. Relative figures from a senior and middle management perspective were 68 per cent and 58 per cent, respectively. In Wilson's more recent survey of companies, 73 per cent of respondents indicated that they believed their efforts to be either reasonably or highly successful (Wilson

1989). The conclusions from the two surveys are remarkably similar, therefore, despite the intervening three years.

Where practice does appear to have changed, however, relates to the competitive component of the process, referred to above. In 1986, the author was able to report that competitor analysis was present in only 5 per cent of cases, while 6 per cent claimed that competitive edge was a focus for their planning efforts (Galliers 1986a). Conversely, Wilson reported 88 per cent of his respondents as claiming that competitive advantage was a feature of their information and IT strategies.

This comparison is somewhat misleading, however, in that Wilson reported 44 per cent (i.e. 50 per cent of those respondents claiming a competitive component to their strategy) as seeing the reduction of costs through the application of IT as a means to an improved competitive position. Likewise, Galliers reported 17 per cent of his respondents as seeing improved efficiency/cost reduction as being one of their objectives in undertaking information and IT strategy. Where the figures are radically different, however, relates to the use of IT to improve products or services. In 1986, Galliers reported this as an objective in just 4 per cent of cases, while in 1989, Wilson reported 73 per cent as claiming this (i.e. 83.3 per cent of the 88 per cent claiming a competitive component to their strategy process).

Hence, as a result of this comparison, it would be reasonable to suggest that competitive analysis has been a growing consideration over recent years in the strategy process of UK companies. Indeed, the 1990–1 Price Waterhouse IT review indicates that concerns about IT for competitive edge began to come to the forefront in 1987 (Grindley 1990).

A further useful comparison can be made in respect of the barriers that were identified as reducing the likelihood of successful information and IT strategy formulation and implementation. Wilson's findings are summarized in Table 11.1, while the viewpoints of IS planners as to information and IT strategy success factors, as reported by Galliers, are summarized in Table 11.2.

By referring to both sets of results, it is possible to group factors together to form a perspective on key considerations in the process of formulating and implementing information and IT strategies:

1 The attitude, commitment and involvement of non-IT management (to include debating the process and its outcomes to overcome resistance to change and the 'politics' of information ownership and management education).
2 The current status of the organization with respect to IT, in terms not only of the technology itself but also the manner in which the information systems function is organized and the skills available.
3 The ability to measure/review/assess the benefits of information and IT strategy (in terms of both the outcomes and the process itself).
4 Integrating the process with business strategy.

Table 11.1 Barriers to successful information and IT strategy

Rank		Barrier
I & IT strategy formulation	Implementation	
1	3	Measuring benefits
2	2	Nature of business
3	1	Difficulty in recruiting
4	6	Political conflicts
5	5	Existing IT investment
6	4	User education resources
7	11	Doubts about benefits
8	9	Telecommunications issues
9	7	Middle management attitudes
10	8	Senior management attitudes
11	10	Technology lagging behind needs

Source: amended from Wilson (1989).

Table 11.2 Keys to successful information and IT strategies

Rank (importance)	Success factor (IS planner viewpoints)
1	Senior management commitment
2	Senior management involvement
3	Senior and middle management involvement
4	Increased management understanding of IS/IT
5	Assessment/evaluation of IS planning (ISP)
6	ISP supported by IS management function
7	Business plans a basis for ISP
8	ISP outcomes/process debated by management
9	Middle management involvement
10	ISP outcome: prioritized applications portfolio

Source: amended from Galliers (1987a).

Management involvement and commitment

While the results of the Galliers survey suggest that the extent of involvement on the part of management in the process is often not a problem (Fig. 11.3), there is a weight of evidence to suggest that the attitude of UK managers to IT can reasonably be described, generally speaking, as one of disinterest, except in terms of concern about costs (Grindley 1990, 1992). Indeed, according to a PA Consulting Group report published in 1989, the commitment of senior management to managing IT issues is 'minimal'.

The very process by which the strategy is formulated can also have a negative impact on a shared commitment to, and vision of, the strategy.

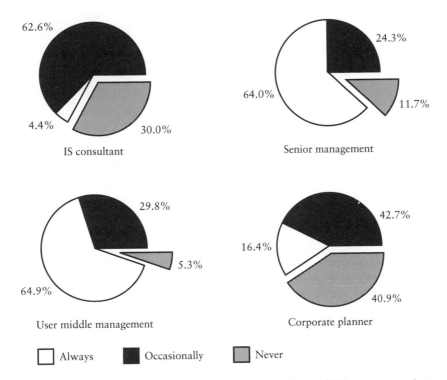

Figure 11.3 Management involvement in information and IT strategy projects (adapted from Galliers 1987a).

It is often the case that the approach adopted involves the planner/consultant interviewing individual managers, thereby reducing the opportunity for debate and sharing ideas and opinions. Further, despite a very large majority in favour of information and IT strategy projects being led by a senior manager, in practice it is most often the case that an IT executive will have to take the lead (Galliers 1987b). In other words, while it seems likely that management will often involve themselves in the process, the quality of that involvement, and the extent of their commitment to resultant change, may be called into question.

Current status

It is paradoxical that IT professionals are often criticized for developing information systems which too closely reflect the status quo. In other words, we all too often automate ineffective processes (Galliers 1987c). When it comes to information and IT strategy formulation, however, there is often a tendency to be overly optimistic in terms of what IT can deliver . . . and when! In addition, we often appear to be more concerned with where we want to get to, rather than the route that we need to take to get there. For example, Wilson (1989) talks of the process as '[bringing] together the business aims of the company . . . It is a plan for the development of systems towards some future vision'. Porter (1985), however, reminds us that business strategy is '. . . the route to competitive advantage'.

Strategic vision is, of course, critically important and, in the context of information and IT strategy, it is precisely this strategic vision in which it is essential that an organization's executives should share – non-IT and IT executives alike. However, it is also essential that the latter appreciate the alternative routes that might be taken in 'getting from A to B; and the implications of these alternatives. It is not sufficient that we know just A or B; we must know A *and* B. Just as importantly, B must be appropriate and achievable, given our A. In other words, the chosen strategy must be feasible as well as desirable (Checkland 1981), particularly when it is almost always the case that an organization will not be facing a 'green field' situation when it comes to IT.

Despite the reservations of academic researchers (Benbasat *et al.* 1984), so-called 'stages of growth' models have been used to good effect in helping executives to discuss and identify their organization's current status as regards aspects of IT utilization and management (Nolan 1979; Earl 1989).

One of the problems of earlier models relates to the fact that they referred to aspects only of the IT 'situation'. For example, the Nolan model focuses for the most part on database technology, the amount spent on data processing and the extent of user awareness with regard to IT. Because of this a revised model has been developed (Galliers and Sutherland 1991), which takes account of a number of broader issues associated with information and IT strategy formulation and implementation. These broader issues include the skills available (both on the part of managers and IT professionals), the manner in which information systems services are organized and the focus of the strategy effort. Because of this wider focus, the model has been used to good effect in identifying both feasible and desirable information and IT strategies. The revised model is described briefly on page 163.

Assessment and review

Reviewing both the process and outcomes of information and IT strategy is considered to be one of the most important success factors (Galliers 1986b, 1987a). However, while 84 per cent of respondents to the Galliers survey indicated that formal reviews did take place, an assessment of the benefits of the process were reported as occurring in only 16 per cent of cases. What is more, formal assessments of benefits occurred in just 9 per cent of cases. Given that measuring benefits is considered to be the single greatest barrier to the successful development of information and IT strategies (Wilson 1989), this is of major concern.

It is important to understand that benefits should be measured in the context of what is expected of the process in the first place. The Galliers study showed that what was important in terms of required outcomes to one stakeholder group may not be so important to another (Galliers 1987d). For example, while in general IT executives were looking for clear, achievable plans, middle managers simply wanted improved information systems as a result of the strategy process and senior managers sought an improved capability for justifying IT investment. Whatever the motivations, from whatever perspective, it is important that these are taken into account when deciding on which approach to take and what to measure when it comes to a review. Unfortunately, this occurs only occasionally. Indeed, in a more recent case study, Bayne (1991) found that in the companies he investigated there was often an absence of agreement as to what the IT investment was actually supposed to achieve in business terms, let alone a shared vision of the future arising from an information and IT strategy study.

When one considers the range of strategy approaches that can be used, many of which have a distinct type of outcome (e.g. information systems applications portfolio, database architecture, extent/type of IT investment required), an ability to assess likely benefits, associated with an ability to choose an approach likely to produce the desired outcome(s), appears to be significant. However, the Galliers survey showed that formal evaluation of alternative approaches took place in only 7 per cent of the organizations surveyed (Galliers 1986b).

Integration with business strategy

It is almost a truism to suggest that information and IT strategy should be integrated with the business strategy process (or failing that, that the two processes should at least be closely linked), and that it should therefore take very careful note of the nature of the business which is to be supported by IT. Nevertheless, it is a fact that as many as 58 per cent of those surveyed by Galliers were prepared to admit that their information and IT strategies were at best only tenuously linked with their business plans. Part of the reason for this is that business planner involvement is still relatively rare, with 83 per cent of respondents admitting that this takes place on an occasional basis at best (see Fig. 11.3; Galliers 1987a).

Given that there is now a greater commitment to strategy development in the NHS than was the case before the 1989 Review, there now exists a more promising environment to integrate the two processes. However, if the experience of the private sector is anything to go by, it is probably true to say that little attention is paid to information systems considerations when developing strategy.

The point should be made, however, that the integration is likely to come not from involving business strategists and planners in overly-technical discussions on IT *per se* (i.e. on the 'how' aspects of the strategy; see Fig. 11.1). The emphasis should be on the information and management aspects (i.e. the 'what' and the 'why').

Summary

This section has looked at how current information and IT strategy practice differs from the conventional wisdom of what is thought to constitute a successful strategy process. It would appear that we often find it difficult to put theory into practice when it comes to:

1 *Obtaining appropriate commitment to, and involvement in, the process from non-IT executives.* This is possibly due to the over-concentration on technical and technological, rather than management and organizational, issues associated with much of current practice (see Fig. 11.4). It may also be due in part to the fact that insufficient emphasis is given to management debate about the key issues associated with alternative information and IT strategies.

2 *Ascertaining an appropriate information and IT strategy, given current IT capabilities (human as well as technical), and future goals.* While it may well be possible in the longer term to introduce information systems applications which utilize the most up-to-date and complex technology and which promise to provide the organization concerned with a strategic edge, it may also be the case that the organization is not ready (e.g. in terms of skills, human resources and management practices) for such an eventuality. In these cases, such strategies may well represent a considerable risk (Ives and Learmonth 1984) and may well prove to be unimplementable. Frameworks for assisting in choosing an appropriate approach/strategy are introduced in the next section.

3 *Reviewing/assessing the benefits of the strategy process and choosing an appropriate approach in the light of the desired outcomes of the information and IT strategy process.* It is often said that this should be a continuous learning process, and very much part of on-going management activity. It is still often the case, however, that it turns out to be an annual budgetary, or a one-off 'special', exercise, which tends to be seen as being unrelated to key business processes. Even in situations where information and IT strategy formulation is undertaken in an on-going manner, the learning process is rendered less effective by a lack of assessment against desired outcomes/targets. In addition, the process itself suffers because inadequate attention has often been paid to the choice of an approach that is likely to be capable of delivering the required outcomes.

4 *Integrating information and IT strategy with the business strategy process.* While it is invariably argued that the two processes should at least be closely linked, it is still too often the case that the link is tenuous at best, with the two being undertaken in isolation from each other and with little business strategist involvement in the IS/IT aspects and vice versa. Again, part of the reason for this relates to too great attention being paid to technological, rather than business, management and organizational issues during information and IT strategy formulation.

This leads to a lack of committed management involvement, because the language used is most often that of the technologist, which in turn reduces the likelihood of any linkage with business strategy, thus compounding the problem.

A broader conception of information and IT strategy

It has been argued that part of the reason our information and IT strategies fall short of what is considered to be good practice is due to an overemphasis on IT strategy rather than information systems (IS) and information management (IM) strategy. As indicated above, Earl (1989) makes a useful distinction between the three components when he talks of IT strategy being more concerned with how to provide required information, while the IS and IM strategies are concerned with the what and the why. Note, though, that I am not arguing that IT strategy is unimportant – far from it. It needs to be taken very seriously indeed and, done well, can make all the difference. IT directors who are able to integrate IT strategy considerations with IS and IM, all within the context of business strategy, are hard to find – and worth their weight in gold! What I am arguing is that non-IT executive involvement in the process should concentrate on the key information requirements of the organization and on management issues associated with, for example, the organization of the IS services and the potential impact of IT in making core business processes more effective.

If one takes a socio-technical perspective of the topic 'information systems' (i.e. a more holistic stance), it can be argued that information systems are as much concerned with human activity and organization as they are with technology, if not more so (Checkland 1981; Land and Hirschheim 1983). If this argument is accepted, it follows that the strategy should contain not only IT strategy, but also strategies to deal with the change management and human resource issues associated with the introduction and utilization of IT in organizations. In other words, a strategy that takes into account the manner in which one might move from A to B, and the necessary organization, people and skills associated with this movement. Figure 11.4 illustrates this thinking.

It is important to reiterate the point that the information and IT strategy needs to be embedded in business strategy: it both feeds off, and feeds into, the business strategy process, which in turn is depicted in Figure 11.4 as having a two-way inter-relationship with the organization's business environment. The model is, therefore, in line with Earl's arguments for a multiple approach, with information and IT strategy, incorporating 'top-down', 'bottom-up' and 'inside-out' elements (Earl 1989).

Emphasis should be placed on the strategies located in the centre of Figure 11.4 (i.e. why? what? how? when? who?) when seeking management commitment, leadership and involvement, rather than on technological concerns (IT strategy) or the more technical issues associated with the

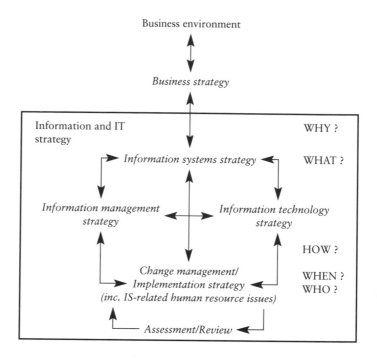

Figure 11.4   The components of information and IT strategy (after Earl 1989).

IM strategy, such as technical standards and infrastructure issues. All too often, it is the case in practice that the focus of debate is on what technology to purchase rather than on what information is required and what the technology might provide in terms of meeting these ends (and whether it has done so). As a result of an overly technological focus, there is often disinterest on the part of management regarding information and IT strategy, and where there is any, this is often misplaced.

As indicated on page 156, so-called 'stages of growth' models have proved a helpful means of locating a particular organization in terms of its growth in planning for and managing IS and IT. One such has been developed by Earl (1989) to give an indication in the development of the IS/IT-related strategy formulation process itself (Table 11.3). Another has attempted to take into account the broader view of information and IT strategy depicted in Figure 11.4 (Galliers and Sutherland 1991). This is summarized in Table 11.4.

As is evident from Table 11.3, Earl's view of the development of information systems planning expertise in organizations is in line with the development of information and IT strategy theory depicted in Figure 11.1, with attention being focused away from the isolated concerns of the information systems function to the organization as a whole and then to the organization and its relationship with its business environment.

Table 11.3 Earl's information systems planning in stages model

			Stages			
Factor	*1*	*2*	*3*	*4*	*5*	*6*
Task	Meeting demands	IS/IT audit	Business support	Detailed planning	Strategic advantage	Business-IT strategy linkage
Objective	Provide service	Limit demand	Agree priorities	Balance IS across business	Pursue opportunities	Integrate strategies
Driving force	IS reaction	IS led	Senior management led	User/IS partnership	IS/executive led; user involvement	Strategic coalitions
Methodological emphasis	*Ad hoc*	Bottom-up survey	Top-down analysis	Two-way	Environmental scanning	Multiple methods
Context	User/IS inexperience	Inadequate IS resources	Inadequate business/IS plans	Complexity apparent	IS for competitive advantage	Maturity; collaboration
Focus	IS Department		Organization-wide		Environment	

Source: Galliers and Sutherland (1991) (amended from Earl 1989).

Table 11.4 A revised 'stages of growth' model

				Stage		
Element	1	2	3	4	5	6
Strategy	Acquisition	Audit	Top-down analysis	Integration co-ordination	Opportunity seeking	Interactive planning
Structure	Informal	Finance controlled	Centralized DP department	Information centre	SBU coalitions	Co-ordinated coalitions
Systems	*Ad hoc* operational accounting	Gaps/duplication large backlog, heavy maintenance	Uncontrolled end-user computing	Decentralized approach some MSS	Co-ordinated centralized/decentralized Some strategic IS	Interorganizational systems IS/IT-based products and services
Staff	Programmers contractors	Systems analysts DP manager	IS planners IS manager Database specialists	Business analysts IR manager	Business and IS planners integrated	IS director (board level)
Style	Unaware	'Don't bother me (I'm too busy)'	Abrogation Delegation	Partnership	Individualistic (product champions)	Business teams
Skills	Individual Technical Low level	Systems development methodology	IS awareness Project management	IS/business awareness	Entrepreneurial marketing	Lateral thinking (IT/IS potential)
Superordinate goals	Obfuscation	Confusion	Senior management concern DP defence	Co-operation	Opportunistic	Strategy making and implementation

Source: Galliers and Sutherland (1991).

The latter leads to a consideration of inter-organizational systems and the possibility of systems that link directly with suppliers and clients.

The 'stages of growth' model depicted in Table 11.4 extends the concept still further, in line with Figure 11.4. In addition to what are taken for the usual components of information and IT strategy (i.e. those associated with the technology and the kind of systems that have been, and are being, developed), the model attempts to take account of the organization's superordinate goals (i.e. its culture/shared values – those values that underpin its business strategy) and the staff, skills and organizational structure necessary to implement the chosen strategy (Pascale and Athos 1981: 81).

The six stages of growth in this model are labelled:

1 *Ad hocracy* – characterized by a lack of control or, indeed, understanding, of the issues.
2 *Starting the foundations* – characterized by a developing IT 'priesthood' and increasing demand (inadequately satisfied) for their services, and a lack of involvement or commitment on the part of non-IT management in information systems management or IT projects.
3 *Centralized dictatorship* – best described as being a period of conflict during which the IT department begins to come under the senior management microscope, while striving to maintain control, and while, simultaneously, there is considerable – and growing – end-user computing taking place (as a result of the advent of personal computing and growing dissatisfaction with the central information systems department).
4 *Democratic dialectic and co-operation* – lessons begin to be learnt from the inefficiencies and ineffectiveness of the previous stage and more co-operative forms of working begin to emerge, with much greater emphasis on business-led approaches.
5 *Entrepreneurial opportunity* – having begun to gain the rewards from the previous stage, attention begins to turn towards not only improving efficiency and effectiveness, but also adding value to existing products and services through the use of IT, and to executive information systems and inter-organizational systems.
6 *Integrated harmonious relationships* – the lessons of the previous stages are brought together in this stage, with the emphasis being on quality, linkages between external and internal data and integration of IT into the mainstream.

Most models of this kind depict the final stage as representing 'maturity' – a stage of near perfection in which the hard-won lessons of the earlier stages are put to good effect. The 'maturity' label has not been used to describe stage 6 in this model. While it is true that this stage does represent a phase which incorporates the accumulated wisdom of the earlier stages, it does not represent an ultimate goal to which all organizations should aspire. For example, a stage 7 might be postulated, concerned with the provision of a flexible IT infrastructure and with integrating IT into both formal and informal organizational forms (Land, personal communication).

Similarly, it might be the case that, for a particular organization, stage 4 or 5 is a more appropriate goal.

The model has been used to good effect by a number of organizations over recent years. In particular, it has proved helpful in raising a number of questions about:

1 Those aspects of the current information and IT strategy which appear to require particular attention (i.e. those factors that appear to be lagging behind others).
2 Those organizational units or functions that appear to be lagging behind others with respect to IS and IT issues.
3 Plotting the location of the organization over time. For example, one might usefully ask whether one's organization has been 'stuck' at a particular stage at some point during recent years and, if so, what might the causes of this lack of growth have been? (Indeed, it may have been the case that an organization – or part of it – had reverted to a prior stage of growth for some reason or other: there is no God-given right for organizations to move smoothly from an earlier stage to a later one!).
4 The appropriateness, or otherwise, of revised or new information and IT strategies (i.e. in terms of feasibility as well as desirability).

With regard to the latter point, it has been noted that too little attention has been paid in practice to the choice of an appropriate approach to information and IT strategy, given the situation in which the organization finds itself and the views of key stakeholders as to what it is they are trying to achieve via their strategy. However, the above and other frameworks can help in this regard.

For example, McLaughlin et al. (1983) propose that an appropriate information and IT strategy can be chosen by reflecting: (1) on how IS/IT can impact on products and markets, and on the competitiveness of the company in the market, and (2) on the 'ability to deliver' of the company's IS resources (Ives and Learmonth 1984; Galliers 1987b; Ward 1988). The framework reproduced in Table 11.5 can assist in gauging the latter, while the work of, for example, Porter (1979, 1980, 1985) is helpful with the former. The McLaughlin et al. framework is depicted in Figure 11.5.

Briefly put, their argument is that organizations with good opportunities and strong resources should attempt to 'attack' their competitors by exploiting IS/IT. Similarly, in situations where there is both low potential and resources, they argue that the company concerned is 'safe' from attack. Conversely, however, should the situation exist where the company has good quality resources but potential appears to be limited, they should 'explore' all opportunities with a view to consolidating their IT assets and to being in a position to attack should the impact of IS/IT increase in their industry at some future time. Should opportunities be high but competence low, companies should 'beware' because they are vulnerable to attack at any time via the exploitation of IS/IT on the part of their competitors.

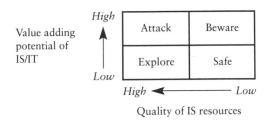

Figure 11.5 Choosing an appropriate information and IT strategy (from McLaughlin *et al.* 1983).

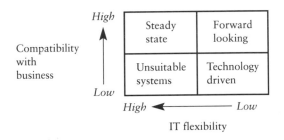

Figure 11.6 Estimating the current status of information systems within an organization (© PI Consultants Ltd. 1992; reproduced with permission).

They should also 'beware' attempting to use their IS/IT resources strategically because of the high risk involved due to the inadequacy of these very same resources.

A similar framework has recently been developed by PI Business Consultants Ltd. Their approach incorporates an attempt to measure the compatibility of existing systems with business imperatives and the flexibility of the existing systems in response to organizational and environmental change. The result of this analysis is an estimation of the extent to which an organization:

- has unsuitable systems
- is technologically driven
- is in steady state
- is forward looking (Fig. 11.6).

This analysis then provides a basis for further discussion as to an organization's appropriate next steps in relation to its information and IT strategy.

Another means of assessing the appropriateness of approaches to information and IT strategy formulation in any particular context is to review the motivations of various stakeholders in the process. It is likely that different stakeholders will have different reasons for wanting such a study

Table 11.5   A contingency framework for choosing an appropriate information and IT strategy approach based on stakeholder motivations

Motivation[2]	Information and IT strategy orientation[1]		
	IT	Organization	Environment
Efficiency, cost reduction	**	**	*
Effectiveness	*	***	**
Improved products/services	*	**	***
Applications portfolio	*	***	**
IT acquisitions	***	*	*
IT architecture	***	*	*
Competitive advantage	*	**	***
Improved management-IS relations	*	**	**
Resourcing decisions	**	**	*
Human resource considerations	*	**	*
Database architecture	***	**	*
Business process redesign	*	**	**
Information architecture	*	***	*

[1] Information and IT strategy orientation relates to the type of approach being considered, i.e. whether the focus is on the technology itself – 'isolated' – or on matters internal to the organization – 'reactive' – or on the business environment – 'pro-active'.
[2] The extent of likely utility of I and ITS orientation in respect of given motivations is indicated by: * minor; ** reasonable; *** major.
Source: amended from Galliers (1987f, 1991).

to take place, i.e. they may well be looking for different outcomes from the process.

As a result of the author's research into information and IT strategy practice during 1986, and more recent work (Galliers 1987d, 1992b), a number of different motivations have been identified. These can be compared with: (1) the prevalent motivations that exist amongst different stakeholder groups in any given situation; and (2) the kinds of outcomes different approaches are likely to produce. For example, certain approaches, such as business systems planning (BSP) and information engineering, concentrate attention on producing an applications portfolio or on a database architecture (Zachman 1982; Martin 1982). While these may well be entirely appropriate if these are the desired outcomes of the process, they are likely to be less helpful in, for example, identifying necessary organizational changes, IS-related skill requirements or opportunities to gain a competitive advantage through the utilization of IT. A matrix of the kind illustrated in Table 11.5 may be of use in choosing an appropriate information and IT strategy approach, based on the differing motivations that may exist at any one point in time, or are likely to at some stage in the future.

Conclusion

This chapter has attempted to introduce models of information and IT strategy that have principally been applied in the business world but that should have equal relevance in the health care sector. It has also attempted to show how current information and IT strategy practice compares with those factors generally agreed to be critical for its success. It has demonstrated that current practice is deficient, particularly in respect of:

- Gaining appropriate commitment to, and involvement in, the process on the part of senior and middle management.
- Implementing information and IT strategies, due to an inappropriate choice of strategy – from a feasibility as well as desirability standpoint.
- Reviewing/assessing the benefits of information and IT strategy in the context of the differing expectations of different stakeholder groups.
- The integration with business strategy.

Reasons for these deficiencies have been postulated, and a broader perspective of what properly constitutes information and IT strategy has been proposed. The resultant model aims to assist management in undertaking and implementing such strategies by circumventing some of the common problems encountered in applying theory in practice. Most importantly, however, the chapter has introduced contingent frameworks that assist in making an appropriate choice of approach/strategy.

Strategy formulation should not be seen as an entirely rational or formal process, however. It should in addition aim to capture creative, intuitive thinking. The contingent models introduced here should be used to question beliefs and bring key assumptions about current and future business to the surface. In so doing, it is hoped that they may assist creative strategy formulation and ease strategy implementation.

References

Atkins, M.H. and Galliers, R.D. (1992) 'Human resource development for IS executives', in *Managing the Information Provider/Managing the Information User. Proceedings: ACM SIGCPR Conference*, Cincinnati, Ohio, 5–7 April, pp. 129–35. Also published in the Warwick Business School Research Paper Series. 'Reconciling information systems' capability with the needs of the business: a research study among systems providers and business managers and users?

Bayne, T. (1991) Unpublished MBA Dissertation, University of Warwick.

Benbasat, I., Dexter, A., Drury, D. and Goldstein, R. (1984) 'A critique of the stage hypothesis: theory and empirical evidence', *Communications of the ACM*, 27(5), May, 476–85.

Cash, J.I. and Konsynski, B.R. (1985) 'IS redraws competitive boundaries,' *Harvard Business Review*, 63(2), March/April, 134–42.

Checkland, P.B. (1981) *Systems Thinking, Systems Practice*. Chichester, Wiley.

Collins, T. (1992) 'IT boss quits Wessex on eve of new strategy', *Computer Weekly*, 5 November.

Davis, G.B. (1979) 'Comments on the critical success factors method for obtaining management information requirements in the article by John F. Rockart', *MIS Quarterly*, 3(3), September.

Earl, M.J. (1987) 'Information systems strategy formulation', in R.J. Boland and R.A. Hirschheim (eds), *Critical Issues in Information Systems Research*. Chichester, Wiley.

Earl, M.J. (ed.) (1988) *Information Management: The Strategic Dimension*. Oxford, The Clarendon Press.

Earl, M.J. (1989) *Management Strategies for Information Technology*. Hemel Hempstead, Prentice Hall.

Eskin, F. (1992) 'Daydream Believers', *Health Service Journal*, 10 September, 24–5.

Galliers, R.D. (1986a) 'Information systems and technology planning within a competitive strategy framework', in P. Griffiths (ed.), *Information Management*, State of the Art Report, 14(7). Maidenhead, Berkshire, Pergamon Infotech.

Galliers, R.D. (1986b) 'Information technology strategies today: the UK experience' (Oxford/PA Conference, Formulating IT Strategies, Templeton College, Oxford University, 30 September–2 October), in M.J. Earl (ed.) (1988) *Information Management: The Strategic Dimension*. Oxford, The Clarendon Press.

Galliers, R.D. (1987a) 'Information systems planning in the United Kingdom and Australia – a comparison of current practice', in P.I. Zorkoczy (ed.), *Oxford Surveys in Information Technology*, vol. 4. Oxford, Oxford University Press.

Galliers, R.D. (1987b) 'Information technology planning within the corporate planning process', in A.D. Berry and T. Duhig (eds), *Integrated Project Control*, State of the Art Report, 15(2). Maidenhead, Berkshire, Pergamon Infotech.

Galliers, R.D. (ed.) (1987c) *Information Analysis: Selected Readings*. Workingham, Addison-Wesley.

Galliers, R.D. (1987d) 'Discord at the top', *Business Computing and Communications*, February, 22–5.

Galliers, R.D. (1991) 'Strategic information systems planning: myths, reality and guidelines for successful implementation', *European Journal of Information Systems*, 1(1), 55–64.

Galliers, R.D. (1992a) 'Information technology – management's boon or bane?', *Journal of Strategic Information Systems*, 1(2), 50–6.

Galliers, R.D. (1992b) 'Implementing strategic information systems plans: barriers and opportunities', *The University of Wales Business and Economics Review*, 8, 7–14.

Galliers, R.D. and Sutherland, A.R. (1991) 'Information systems management and strategy formulation: the "stages of growth" model revisited', *Journal of Information Systems*, 1(2), April, 89–114.

Grindley, C.B.B. (ed.) (1990) *Information Technology Review 1990/91*. London, Price Waterhouse.

Grindley, C.B.B. (ed.) (1992) *Information Technology Review 1992/93*. London, Price Waterhouse.

Henderson, J.C., and Sifonis, J.G. (1986) 'Middle out strategic planning: the value of IS planning to business planning', *Proceedings: 1986 NYU Symposium on Strategic Uses of Information Technology*, New York, 21–23 May.

Henderson, J.C., Rockart, J.F. and Sifonis, J.G. (1984) 'A Planning Methodology for integrating Management Support Systems'. MIT CISR Working Paper No. 116. Massachusetts Institute of Technology, Center for Information Systems Research.

Hirschheim, R.A. (1982) 'Information Management and Planning in Organisations – Part One: A Framework for Analysis'. Unpublished working paper. London, LSE, University of London.

Hochstrasser, B. and Griffiths, C. (1990) *Regaining Control of IT Investments*, London, Kobler Unit, Imperial College, University of London. Reprinted under the title *Evaluating IT Benefits: Strategy and Management*, London, Chapman and Hall.

Huff, S.L. and Beattie, (1985) 'Strategic versus competitive information systems', *Business Quarterly*, Winter.

Ives, B. and Learmonth, G.P. (1984) 'The information system as a competitive weapon', *Communications of the ACM*, 27(12), December, 1193–201.

Kriebel, C.H. (1968) 'The strategic dimension of computer systems planning', *Long Range Planning*, September.

Land, F.F. and Hirschheim, R.A. (1983) 'Participative systems design: rationale, tools and techniques', *Journal of Applied Systems Analysis*, 10, 91–107.

Martin, J. (1982) *Strategic Data-Planning Methodologies*. Englewood Cliffs, NJ, Prentice Hall.

Martino, C.A. (1983) *Information Systems Planning to Meet Objectives: A Survey of Practices*. New York, Cresap McCormick and Paget.

McLaughlin, M., Howe, R. and Cash Jr, J.I. (1983) 'Changing Competitive Ground Rules – The Impact of Computers and Communications in the 1980s'. Unpublished Working Paper, Graduate School of Business Administration, Harvard University.

McFarlan, F.W. (1984) 'Information technology changes the way you compete', *Harvard Business Review*, 62(3), May/June, 98–102.

Ng, M.W. (1984) 'Strategic systems planning should start from the top', *Australasian Computerworld*, 22, June, 12–13.

Nolan, R. (1979) 'Managing the crises in data processing', *Harvard Business Review*, 57(2), March/April, 115–26.

Pascale, R.T. and Athos, A.G. (1981) *The Art of Japanese Management*. Harmondsworth, Penguin.

Porter, M.E. (1979) 'How competitive forces shape strategy', *Harvard Business Review*, 57(2), March/April.

Porter, M.E. (1980) *Competitive Strategy*. New York, The Free Press.

Porter, M.E. (1985) *Competitive Advantage*. New York, The Free Press.

Porter, M.E. and Millar, V.E. (1985) 'How information gives you competitive advantage', *Harvard Business Review*, 63(4), July/August, 149–60.

Pyburn, P.J. (1983) 'Linking the MIS plan with corporate strategy: an exploratory study', *MIS Quarterly*, 7(2), 1–14.

Rockart, J.F. (1979) 'Chief executives define their own data needs', *Harvard Business Review*, 57(2), March/April. Reproduced in R.D. Galliers (1987) 'Discord at the top', *Business Computing and Communications*, February, 267–89.

Scott Morton, M.S. (ed.) (1991) *The Corporation of the 1990s: Information Technology and Organizational Transformation*. New York, Oxford University Press.

Sullivan Jr., C.H. (1985) 'Systems planning in the information age', *Sloan Management Review*, Winter, 3–12.

Ward, J.M. (1988) 'Information systems and technology application portfolio management – an assessment of matrix-based analyses', *Journal of Information Technology*, 3(3), September, 205–15.

Wilson, T.D. (1989) 'The implementation of information systems strategies in UK companies: aims and barriers to success', *International Journal of Information Management*, 245–58.

Zachman, J.A. (1982) 'Business systems planning and business information control study: a comparison', *IBM Systems Journal*, 21(1).

12 Evaluation: informing the future, not living in the past

Justin Keen

Introduction

The NHS is under ever increasing pressure to justify investments, including investments in information technology (IT). There is growing concern both inside and outside the NHS that investments are being wasted. The Audit Commission (1992) and National Audit Office (1990) have both published critical reports, and there have been headline-grabbing system failures. This has led to calls for explanations, and exposed the need for proper evaluation of systems. As things stand, there is a paucity both of clear guidance on how to approach evaluation of IT and of solid empirical evidence on the performance of IT in health services. This comes amid a more general trend towards evaluation of technology in medicine. Jennett (1992) has suggested that the rule should be 'no evaluation – no technology', and Eyles (1987) has pointed to the rise of the 'evaluative state', where increasingly all areas of public administration are being opened to formal scrutiny. It seems unlikely, therefore, that the pressures will abate.

This chapter reviews existing quantitative approaches to the evaluation of IT in the NHS and elsewhere, discusses pragmatic approaches to evaluation that might be used within the NHS and speculates on methods which might be incorporated into evaluations in order to assess the current and future value of systems. It begins with some very simple questions about the purposes of evaluation.

What are evaluations for?

Before embarking on any evaluation, it is as well to ask some questions. First, what is its purpose? This is a question that seems often to be omitted: there is a tendency to reach for an evaluation method, such as cost–benefit analysis, without careful thought about the questions that need to be answered, and which methods might help answer them. Is the purpose to identify financial or other benefits, to assess whether the system is acceptable to users, to improve financial control or something else? Different purposes may require different methods. Second, how does the political land lie? Who is the customer for the evaluation? If people at the top of the organization will accept a carefully argued report, then a relatively informal and subjective evaluation may suffice. If they will accept only 'hard' evidence, then a more quantitative study may be required. The political aspects of evaluations are often underestimated. In particular the capacity of senior management to ignore any findings is often an uncomfortable fact of life: and sometimes the messenger risks being shot. Careful thought needs to be given to the way information is collected and presented.

Third, what should be the balance of effort between pre- and post-implementation evaluation? In some cases, perhaps especially for systems whose 'effects' are poorly understood or where there are widely differing alternatives, the major focus might be on investment appraisal. A site needs to minimize the risk of failure through careful prior evaluation. In others, the concern might be with making sure systems are properly implemented and initial objectives achieved. Greater emphasis would be placed on evaluation during and after implementation. The special characteristics of IT, where benefits depend on wider organizational changes and where forward planning of implementation is usual, suggest that ideally evaluation should be undertaken before, during and after implementation. Resource constraints may make this impractical – hence the need to look before leaping.

Fourth, when are the answers needed? One of the most striking characteristics of the IT industry is its rapid rate of innovation and development. Organizations have a constantly changing array of new products to choose from. As organizations are themselves also subject to change, the general picture is one of a changing world. This is certainly true of health services, which are witnessing remarkable advances in medical technologies, with those technologies being implemented against a turbulent policy background. One has only to think of the differences between early Hospital Information Support Systems (HISS) sites with relatively large and expensive systems and the more recent 'second generation' sites. While it might be of some value to assess the 'full' costs and benefits of the early sites, the fact is that new sites will implement different technical solutions in a much-changed world. These new sites need to learn what they can from the pioneers now, even though the final tally of costs and benefits is not available.

And fifth, what will be the cost of the evaluation, as a percentage of the cost of the system being evaluated? Formal economic or experimental approaches can be expensive to undertake properly. In an ideal world, evaluation of IT would be simple and inexpensive, but this seems seldom to be the case.

The answer to these five broad questions should shape the nature and scale of any evaluation. It may be that a small-scale informal exercise undertaken by hospital staff will provide an adequate answer, or it may be necessary to commission a more formal and perhaps independent report. Whichever route is chosen, there is a variety of techniques available.

IT evaluation for the NHS

The principal IT evaluation techniques used in the NHS are based on investment appraisal and cost–benefit analysis (CBA). Investment appraisal guidance is concerned with choosing between different strategies and between particular systems, and hence with evaluation before implementation. The essence of investment appraisal is to make explicit valuations based on the extent to which each option is judged likely to achieve desired objectives. CBA can, in principle, be used at any stage, whether to predict the likely costs and benefits of a system or evaluate its actual costs and benefits in practice.

Until recently there was no IT-specific guidance, though general guidance was available (DHSS 1987). The DHSS (as it then was) published guidance on evaluation of large IT systems in 1988, based broadly on CBA. The guidance was financially oriented, and was concerned with identifying and measuring costs and benefits. More recently the HISS Central Team (1992) has produced guidance for large systems, as has the NHS Management Executive (1993) for both large and small systems. It is not clear how often these guidance documents have been used, or how effective they have been. Indeed, the environment in the NHS has not been conducive to careful selection, with central determination of which systems should be purchased. These included databases for medical audit and resource management, and nursing information systems. This, combined with some regions top-slicing monies for initiatives such as HISS removes local incentives for careful evaluation.

Both approaches are based on particular assumptions. One is that the impact of individual IT systems can be valued, that is, they can be considered in isolation. Another is that benefits can be measured and expressed in financial terms – given a financial value (Fig. 12.1). Indeed, there is an assumption that one of the benefits of many computer systems is that they will save money. As we will see, both assumptions are open to question.

The realization has increasingly grown that it is important to be able to review the value of investments during the course of implementation. Evaluation is, if not a continuous process, one that might be undertaken at any stage. Moreover, it is increasingly seen as part of the process whereby the benefits of IT are realized, a point appreciated by the HISS Central Team, who promote the concept of benefits management. As the name suggests, benefits management is concerned with the process of achieving benefits from IT implementation. It includes investment appraisal and the measurement and valuation of benefits, in parallel with guidance on

Figure 12.1   Routes to valuation of costs and benefits.

techniques for realizing identified benefits. System selection and implementation have to be integrated within general management processes. Underpinning this approach is an assumption that benefits will accrue from IT only if they are actively sought, and implementation harnessed to organizational change. This emphasizes the importance of the processes that occur before and during implementation: they may play a major role in the eventual success of a project.

The focus on benefits is illustrative of the growing awareness of the need to demonstrate them, and may also reflect an underlying concern that they have not been realized in the past. Perhaps as a result, the HISS team's documentation rather understates potential problems in identifying system-specific costs and valuing non-financial benefits, though it might be argued that guidance on these issues is available elsewhere.

There are three problems that must be addressed in any evaluation of IT. The first concerns the nature of the impact that IT has on organizations. If it were the case that IT simply automated existing activities, so that manual filing (for example) was replaced by electronic filing, then it might well be easy to identify IT-specific costs and benefits. The costs of running a department before and after introduction of a system might be attributed to the IT with reasonable confidence, as might any improvement or deterioration in service. However, modern systems are typically not concerned purely with automation. Even basic operational systems also provide information to users about their workload, and increasingly IT is viewed as a vehicle for organization change and so is an agent for transforming organizations (Scott Morton 1991). It is less clear that these information and 'transformation' effects can easily be captured in the conventional cost–benefit frameworks suggested for the NHS. And it is difficult, though perhaps not impossible, to estimate the potential of IT to act as an agent to transform organization processes for incorporation in investment appraisals.

This leads to the second problem, which is the difficulty of isolating the effects of IT from other, contemporaneous changes. Given the changes being wrought by advances in medical technology and by contracting and other government policies, any changes that do occur in a hospital might be due to any number of factors. Any changes might well have happened had the IT not been there. If one then adds the possibility that an IT implementation might be used opportunistically to achieve some desired change, perhaps a HISS implementation being used to review operational procedures in wards and departments, then the problem is compounded.

The evaluator is not faced with an IT system but a bundle of organizational and technological change, and perhaps a situation where 'purely' organizational effects seem to be greater than those due to the IT. In that case what is being measured and valued? It is difficult to attribute costs or effects to the IT with any confidence, as there is no simple traceable link between cause and effect. This problem of isolating effects is, to say the least, understated in guidance aimed at the NHS.

The third problem is that the future is unpredictable. Of course, investment appraisal and other methods are designed to help reduce uncertainty about the future. But prediction is a difficult business with IT. In many organizations the hoped-for benefits of new systems are not achieved, yet elsewhere there are often significant unanticipated benefits. So prediction of costs and benefits is likely to be vexed. This does not mean that investment appraisal should not be undertaken, but rather that any predictions should be general and treated with due reserve. Very detailed listings of costs and benefits are unlikely to be helpful. And evaluation against objectives for a system may be of limited value, not least because circumstances may change the objectives. What is required, though, is very careful thought about the way in which the IT can or should influence the way an organization works. Given that one organization can succeed with a system and another fail with identical kit, the effects of IT are probabilistic rather than causal. One task for the NHS is to work out the probabilities – a genuinely difficult exercise.

These three problems are not addressed in guidance to the NHS, so that its value is limited. This is not at all to say that economic methods have no value, but they need to be applied to packages which include IT, rather than just to IT itself.

Beyond the NHS

Has anyone outside the NHS fared any better? There are two main sources of evidence: other health-related guidance and techniques used in the private sector. They can be grouped under three broad headings: economic, research-based and accounting approaches.

The value of CBA is also asserted by a European Community Advanced Informatics in Medicine (AIM) team. They argue that the costs and benefits of systems can, straightforwardly, be identified, measured and valued. They do not hint at any problems of prediction or attribution of costs and benefits. Certainly, one potential advantage of CBA is that there are methods available for calculating past and future costs and benefits. In principle at least, calculation of net present values allows comparison of systems whose costs and benefits accrue over different time periods. But, as with the UK guidance, the onus is on proponents of this approach to show that these objections can be overcome.

Other economic methods may be useful in some circumstances.

Cost-effectiveness analysis (CEA) involves comparison of financial and other costs with effects measured in natural units, for example, years of life gained or relief from pain. No attempt is made to value effects: it is assumed that the effects measured are inherently valuable (Drummond *et al.* 1987). CEA is increasingly used in health services research, notably as an adjunct to clinical trials of pharmaceuticals. Like CBA, however, CEA often involves the commitment of considerable resources, and so is likely to be used in commissioned research rather than smaller scale local evaluations.

Cost utility analysis (CUA) involves valuation of different outcomes relative to one another: that is, subjective preferences are elicited for a range of outcomes associated with some intervention. The principal use of CUA in health services is to obtain people's preferences for particular health states: this can be used to inform decisions about priorities for different treatments. Broadly, the lower the value of the product of cost and utility for a particular outcome (often the cost per year of life gained), the higher the priority for the associated treatment. To date, CUA has not been used to elicit preferences for data or IT in health service settings. Others, though, have used utility measurement as a basis for new IT evaluation methods. For example, multi-objective, multicriteria methods use utility analysis as a starting point (Land 1976; Vaid-Raizada 1983). The analytic hierarchy process has also increasingly been applied in clinical settings (Dolan *et al.* 1989; Rabinowitz 1992).

Both economic and accounting approaches will often include a risk assessment. This can take a variety of forms (Birch and McEvoy 1992). It is striking, though, how seldom proper risk assessments have been undertaken for IT projects in the NHS. Given the high risks associated with IT implementation outlined in other chapters, this would seem to be a serious omission. Thought needs to be given to the nature and scale of IT-related risks, particularly for large systems.

A less 'formal' approach is information economics (Parker *et al.* 1988), an approach which starts with a broad economic framework but uses it to outline a method for attaching weightings to different, specified types of benefit. (It should be stressed that the title information economics is something of a misnomer – it is an evaluation approach which includes economic methods.) Rather than the explicit valuation used in utility analysis, simple weightings are used. It is thus more akin to investment appraisal than CBA. It incorporates the idea that IT exerts it effects in different ways, and seeks to capture each type. The authors point to three types of application:

1 *Substitutive* – automation, with machinery direct substituting for people.
2 *Complementary* – transformation, where systems enable new working methods.
3 *Innovative* – intended to create or sustain competitive edge.

Business domain
- Return on investment
- Strategic match
- Competitive advantage
- Management information
- Competitive response
- Project organization risk

Technology domain
- Definitional uncertainty
- Technical uncertainty
- Strategic information systems (IS) architecture
- IS infrastructure risk

Figure 12.2 Sources of value of IT in information economics (from Parker *et al.* 1988).

- Return on investment

- Management and clinical information

- Supports organization's strategy

- IS infrastructure

Figure 12.3 Simplification of value dimensions in information economics.

The authors list a number of sources of value of IT in supporting business processes and improving the infrastructure for data collection and analysis (Fig. 12.2). Their list seems elaborate, at least for the NHS, and a simpler classification may suffice (Fig. 12.3).

Information economics recognizes the variety of effects that IT has on organizations and offers a pragmatic classification of dimensions of IT value. It proposes that evaluators use subjective weightings, though calculations of net present value are also supported. It is not clear how far the approach might be taken in the NHS, but there is every reason to find out.

The second category comprises research-based methods. The experimental approach, and specifically the controlled trial, appears to hold a number of attractions. It has rarely been used in the evaluation of IT. The essence of the approach is to control for all variables that are unrelated to the technology itself. This is typically achieved through comparison of a number of experimental sites (with the system) with control sites (without it). Ideally, systems are also allocated randomly to sites, so that bias due to site selection is minimized. If 'extraneous' sources of variation can be eliminated, then any remaining differences can be attributed to the system. Perhaps the most celebrated trials have been conducted by de Dombal and colleagues of a system to aid diagnosis of acute abdominal pain (de Dombal *et al.* 1985). They showed that doctors performed better with the computer than without it. (The system is now used in a number of hospitals, but wide application seems to have been held back by a mix of factors, including resistance to the idea of IT as a decision aid and the perception that it takes too long to feed data in. This serves as a reminder that successful efficacy trials will not by themselves lead to widespread adoption of a system.) This approach raises an important general point, in that it focuses on individuals' performance – in this case at making diagnoses – rather than solely on the IT.

This approach is expensive because the number of sites involved may have to be large to demonstrate statistically significant effects. There are also fundamental problems related to the way in which IT is implemented. For systems of even moderate complexity, it is likely that they will be modified to suit local needs, making comparison difficult. Sites would in fact be implementing different systems and using them for different purposes. In addition, it is difficult to control for the variety of implementation strategies to be used, and differences in local styles of project management. That should not stop it being used for many IT systems, though the expense again points to a need for central funding for this kind of work.

The practical difficulties of properly controlled trials, particularly for larger systems, have led some to adopt quasi-experimental methods (Coffey 1980). The basic approach is the same, but is used where it is not possible to control for all important variables. Measures are made before and after implementation at a single site, or broad comparisons are made across a number of sites. This means that any effects observed may be due either to the technology or some other variable, but in practice, qualitative observation of developments can help to identify important IT-related events.

Of course, researchers use many other methods, as indicated elsewhere in this book. One that merits particular attention is the case study based on interview and observation (Rossi and Freeman 1987). It should not be forgotten that some questions can be investigated only through 'soft' methods, and are not amenable to analysis with any of the more quantitative approaches listed here. It is not always appropriate to reach for a quantitative technique – they all have limitations, and may not produce the answers required. It is perhaps too easy to be blinded by the lure of scientific and economic methods.

The theoretical and practical shortcomings of economic and other research-based approaches are recognized in health technology assessment (HTA). HTA is a basket of methodologies and methods, aimed at assessing a wide range of health technologies – from digital imaging to district nursing, as it were. Sometimes formal economic or experimental approaches will be appropriate, but often not. It may combine any of the methods already described. HTA has not been applied to any significant IT system in the recent past, but the reason for mentioning it lies in its catholicity. It recognizes that:

- different technologies require different approaches
- it will sometimes be appropriate to use a variety of methods to evaluate a single technology.

These points will be returned to later.

Another set of evaluation techniques can be grouped under the broad heading of accounting approaches. Calculation of return on investment is widely known: it is not clear how often it is actually used in the NHS or other health services. A related approach is SESAME, developed by IBM (Lincoln 1986). Another technique is return on management (Strassman 1990), designed specifically to relate IT inputs to outputs. This has been applied in the private sector, but not so far to the NHS or (as far as I am aware) other UK public sector organizations. Strassman argues that the contribution of IT is manifested principally in changes in management productivity. It should be possible to isolate management from other costs and compare this to financial results; this gives a ratio, in a way which avoids measuring system 'effects' directly. An objection to this method is that IT does not contribute only to management but to labour as well (Symons and Walshman 1988). Certainly in the NHS one would hope for benefits at both operational and management levels. Strassman is, though, pointing to the potential value of performance indicators in the evaluation of IT. Such indicators have been developed for comparative purposes in the private sector (Carlyle 1990).

This brief review is not comprehensive. Evaluation approaches have been developed for different types of system, and to fulfil different functions. Many authors, including Blackler and Brown (1988), Hirschheim and Smithson (1988) and Willcocks (1992) explore issues and approaches in more detail.

The approaches described in this section offer plenty of food for thought for the NHS. For whatever reasons, guidance to the NHS is backward-looking, focusing as it does on relatively unsophisticated notions of how IT affects organizations. Evidence from elsewhere shows that the NHS is not alone: ROI and SESAME seem similarly outmoded but are still used in the private sector. But there are several more interesting approaches which merit attention. We simply do not know how useful they may be in the NHS, but now would seem to be the time to find out.

Accounting for the future

Theoretically, it is desirable to wait until the full costs and benefits of any new system are known before acting. In the case of new pharmaceuticals or surgical procedures this would seem to be essential, though in fact many new procedures are introduced without any formal evaluation. But in the case of evaluations of government policies the situation is different:

officials and practitioners often want results before any clear end-points have been reached. There is a dilemma here. Policy makers may wish to build in lessons from on-going initiatives (at least, that is what academic evaluators tell themselves), but results may not be clear-cut and so liable to misinterpretation. But failure to take note may result in missing important information.

So knowledge of the value of an investment is needed before and during implementation. Waiting too long after implementation is fruitless, since in all likelihood the world will have moved on and so investment decisions would be different anyway. It would seem, then, that in practice evaluation needs to be undertaken before and during implementation, and at the latest soon after a system has gone live. In the latter case, if organizational change is co-ordinated with implementation then benefits may be accruing but the bulk of any benefits may remain to be realized. This makes it important to employ methods that allow judgements about future benefits, alongside measurement of those that have already occurred.

The implication, for evaluations to be of value to practitioners, is that they need to balance assessment of progress to date with prediction of future costs and benefits. The foregoing discussion suggests that:

- different systems require different types of evaluation
- in many cases a mix of methods should be used
- these methods might combine quantitative and qualitative measurements with more judgemental analysis of future changes.

This raises in turn the problem of how to predict future developments. This ideally requires a clear conceptual understanding of the relationship between IT and management processes, even though IT futures are inherently unpredictable. But it is important to address the issues of change and uncertainty.

Some systems designers would argue that it is possible to account for the future by implementing flexible systems. This in turn leads to a little-noted issue: what is flexibility? Would that there were a simple answer here. Social scientists recognize the importance of flexibility as a characteristic of organizations. Commentators on business have suggested that decentralization of decision-making affords greater flexibility, and that this flexibility is desirable in a turbulent world. Engineers and others now recognize the importance of flexibility in systems design processes. But it is not clear how to include it in evaluations. The fact that technology futures are often unpredictable is an uncomfortable fact that many prefer not to dwell upon. Yet it is crucial if some technologies are more adaptable to, or consistent with, change than others.

So for now we need something else. Clearly, some of the approaches outlined in the last section can be used. Economic and accounting methods are often used to calculate future costs and benefits – it is simply that they must be used with more insight and creativity with IT. The construction of performance indicators also merits attention. Equally, it would be sensible to re-examine the models used for evaluation. For example many new systems can be viewed as research and development (R&D) exercises. One could then appeal to the considerable literature on the management of R&D projects. This approach stresses the dependence of success on management processes as much as on the product under development. One might examine the relationship between the technology, technologists and wider management processes. The R&D analogy moves us away from judgement of costs and benefits and focuses on the successful creation of a new product. The significance of this analogy is that companies don't know for certain how their products will fare. In practice, the political risks entailed in having the NHS full of developmental systems are unacceptable, and the task for the NHS is to move key systems from R&D status to proven technologies.

Some authors advocate the use of futures exercises. Extrapolation from the present might be used to peer into the future: predictions might be made about technical, clinical and other developments to build up a picture of the future. More interestingly, one could work backwards from the future, by asking informed groups to imagine the nature of services at some distant point in time, then coming back to a point 5 or 10 years hence. This mid-distance view can be used as a framework for examining the relevance of particular systems in a changed context. Of course, this method is open to the serious objection that the scenarios created may be wrong. But perhaps accuracy of prediction is less important than finding a means of looking at future uses of a new technology.

This suggests another possibility, namely to use strategy formulation as part of evaluation (see Chapter 11). Imagine that you want to know the wisdom of your purchase of a ward nursing system. One way of answering the question is to examine current and future information and IT needs. If the system is still consistent with your strategy then continued investment is worthwhile. A key point about strategy is that it implies that the value of a particular system depends on the context in which it is implemented. A typical ward nursing system might have looked just the thing following the NHS Review, but if person-based systems establish themselves then it may increasingly appear to have been a poor investment. Value varies with place and time. Rather than single systems, it may be more sensible to evaluate portfolios of IT investments, to evaluate the costs and benefits of different strategic options.

Conclusion

The approaches that have just been outlined are a long way removed from the conventional approaches listed earlier on. Yet the reason for entertaining them as part of an evaluation derives from simple observations about the world. We all know that technologies can be rendered redundant by changing circumstances, and that some are easier to adapt than others. Given this, it seems sensible to find ways of taking account of flexibility and unpredictability in evaluations. Most existing evaluation techniques do not appear to lend themselves to busy practitioners taking account of them. New methods should be integrated with existing ones, to offer both data on first experiences of implementation and a view of the future uses of a technology.

References

Audit Commission (1992) *Caring Systems*. London, HMSO.
Birch, D.G.W. and McEvoy, N. (1992) 'Risk analysis for information systems', *Journal of IT*, 7, 44–53.
Blackler, F. and Brown, C. (1988) 'Theory and practice in evaluation: the case of the new information technologies', in N. Bjorn-Andersen and G. Davis (eds), *Information Systems Assessment: Issues and Challenges*. Amsterdam, North-Holland.
Carlyle, R. (1990) 'Getting a grip on costs', *Datamation*, 15 July, 20–3.
Coffey, R. (1980) *How a Medical Information System Affects Hospital Costs: The El Camino Hospital Experience*. Washington DC, US Department of Health, Education and Welfare, National Center for Health Services Research.
DHSS (1987) *Option Appraisal. A Guide for the National Health Service*. London, HMSO.
Dolan, J.G., Isselhardt, B.J. and Cappuccio, J.D. (1989) 'The analytic hierarchy process in medical decision making', *Medical Decision Making*, 9, 40–50.
Drummond, M., Stoddart, G. and Torrance, G. (1987) *Methods for the Economic Evaluation of Health Care Programmes*. Oxford, Oxford University Press.
Eyles, J. (1987) *The Geography of the National Health*. London, Croom Helm.
Hirschheim, R. and Smithson, S. (1988) 'A critical analysis of information systems evaluation', In N. Bjorn-Anderson and G. Davis (eds), *Information Systems Assessments: Issues and Challenges*. Amsterdam, North-Holland.
HISS Central Team (1992) *Benefits Management. Guidelines on Investment Appraisal and Benefits Realisation for Hospital Information Support Systems*. Winchester, HISS Central Team.
Jennett, B. (1992) 'Health technology assessment' (editorial), *British Medical Journal*, 305, 67–8.
Land, F. (1976) 'Evaluation of systems goals in determining a decision strategy for computer-based information systems', *Computer Journal*, 19, 290–4.
Lincoln, T. (1986) 'Do computer systems really pay off?' *Information and Management*, 11, 25–34.
National Audit Office (1990) *Managing Computer Projects in the NHS*. London, HMSO.
NHS Management Executive (1993) *Investment Appraisal*. London, NHS ME.
Parker, M., Benson, R. and Trainor, H. (1988) *Information Economics*. Englewood Cliffs, NJ, Prentice Hall International.
Rabinowitz, J. (1992) 'Collective decision-making: the analytic hierarchy process', *Social Policy and Administration*, 26, 87–97.
Rossi, P. and Freeman, H. (1987) *Evaluation*. Beverly Hills, CA, Sage.
Scott Morton, M. (1991) *The Corporation of the 1990s*. New York, Oxford University Press.

Strassman, P. (1990) *The Business Value of Computers*. New Canaan, CT, Information Economics Press.
Symons, V. and Walshman, G. (1988) 'The evaluation of information systems: a critique', *Journal of Applied Systems Analysis,* 15.
Vaid-Raizada, V.K. (1983) 'Incorporating intangibles in computer selection decisions', *Journal of Systems Management,* 34, 30–6.
Willcocks, L. (1992) 'Evaluating information technology investments: research findings and reappraisal', *Journal of Information Systems,* 2(4).

13 | IT futures in the NHS

Mike Smith

Health informatics past, present and future

Health informatics concerns the implementation of all aspects of information technology (IT) into the field of health care, including administration. Three main branches of health informatics have been identified (Shortliffe *et al.* 1990). The first branch, the oldest, involves embedding computers into medical instruments. Signals and images are the main types of data. Well known successes are CAT and MRI. This branch has succeeded in gaining a prominent and permanent position in mainstream clinical medicine throughout the National Health Service (NHS).

The second branch of health informatics involves medical information and administrative systems. Examples are general practice, patient information, hospital information systems (Blum and Duncan 1990) and certain types of decision support systems such as case mix and medical audit (Rigby *et al.* 1992). This branch of health informatics has proven its operational feasibility and is generally accepted as having value; it remains, however, peripheral to routine clinical medicine. In the NHS, the number of large, operational medical information systems probably numbers in the hundreds; the potential, however, is for tens of thousands.

The third branch of health informatics involves a knowledge-based medical system, typically employing artificial intelligence or expert systems techniques. The best examples are diagnostic systems (MacAdam *et al.* 1990). These systems have demonstrated their technical feasibility, up to a point, but remain largely experimental. Although work has been under way since the early 1960s, there may be no more than a few knowledge-based medical systems in routine use in the NHS.

The success (or lack of success) of the three fields of health informatics has been influenced greatly by the capability of the IT available. The first field, instrumentation, was suitable for the hardware and software of the 1960s and 1970s and so was practical. The advances of the 1980s simply made the field more successful. The second and third fields have been hampered for thirty years by insufficiently powerful computer hardware and software and, to some extent, are still affected. Technical and economic impediments to widespread medical information systems are likely to be swept away during the 1990s, healthcare organizations willing. The large-scale success of knowledge-based medical systems seems less likely with organizational and technical impediments unlikely to be fully overcome in the remainder of this century.

There is a fourth field of health informatics which should become apparent within the 1990s. This will be the integration of logically and physically disparate medical and administration systems and the establishment of high speed communications between these systems. Organizationally, integration will be fuelled by increasing commercialization (or quasi-commercialization) of NHS healthcare providers, and the consequent need to bill for services while containing administrative costs. Technically, integration is likely to depend on affordable high performance computers, large-scale distributed databases, technical standards, common or compatible clinical codes and digital communications.

Initial focus of healthcare systems integration is likely to be in support of financial transactions between purchasers and providers. Later, general practice and hospital systems should be integrated to provide benefits to patient care and commercial efficiency. Eventually, integration should extend to providing patient information across the entire spectrum of healthcare providers, including community care. Integration should not only provide greatly improved individual patient care but also significantly improve the effectiveness of healthcare organizations (Baldini and Heath 1991).

IT scene 1990s

During the 1970s and 1980s, the driving force in IT was advances in semiconductor design and manufacture. Progress was so rapid that many non-technical organizations and people had difficulty coming to terms with the rapidly moving technology or else became obsessed with it. At the same time, technology suppliers approached the marketplace naïvely, depending on a rapid cycle of technical obsolescence and spiralling price performance improvement to sell their products. Both buyer and supplier often overlooked real value in the rapid spiral of technology.

Throughout the 1990s, progress in semiconductors will continue to be a driving force for IT. Major technical breakthroughs are still possible in many fields. The difference will be that organizations and people should be much more used to rapid pace of change, less impressed by raw technology and more adroit in using IT, at least in a facile sort of way. An uncertain economy and the likelihood of major decline in the defence industry should inhibit uncritical investment. In this climate IT will enter a new phase: it will start to become a commodity – a high volume and routine technology. IT will be important, but it will no longer be an obsession for its users. The main emphasis will be on getting real value for IT investment during a period of economic stricture.

In this context of commodity IT, the major themes of the 1990s may prove to be:

- Strong, perhaps even harsh or unreasonable, emphasis on cost effective and business-oriented IT. Facilities management could become very popular with organizations who have managed to stabilize their IT requirements enough to be able to 'farm it out'.
- There will be strong demand for practical, reasonably standardized IT products, although not necessarily for products based on official standards. Computer standards will be more like those found in passenger automobiles: all cars use the same petrol, meet the same legal requirements and have their controls in more-or-less the same place. There remains, however, a constant desire for different body types and much cosmetic variation. Brand and image loyalty is strong, if not necessarily logical.
- Large, tightly integrated and business-critical applications will continue to be implemented. There will be strong emphasis on combining the computing and communication functions seamlessly.
- Unfortunately, many major traditional computer and communications suppliers, perhaps even the largest ones, will fail or be reorganized unrecognizably during the 1990s. Large, generalized software houses may not prove tenable without other major lines of business. Several-product software companies may survive well by focusing on their products and preserving their customer base.
- There will be intense competition among fewer IT suppliers. They will not necessarily compete, however, on raw price or technical features. For example, buyers may see imaginative 'price performance insurance' schemes and emphasis on gaining long-term business.
- Software quality, developer productivity and human skills will remain the single major limiting factor to even greater IT progress. These human limitations could be exacerbated by the harsh economic climate.

During the 1990s the NHS should become almost completely merged into the mainstream of IT. Economic constraints, changes in the nature of UK healthcare provision and the transformation of IT into a commodity suggest that even the NHS can no longer sustain an independent computing culture. This merging will, in general, be beneficial for healthcare computing, although probably at some loss of customized function.

Hardware

Unabated progress seems likely in all aspects of mainstream hardware technology (Madnick 1991). This will support IT progress during the 1990s but will not necessarily be the compelling force that it was in the 1980s. It could be argued that the expected economic problems of the 1990s may hinder investment needed to fund hardware research and development. The momentum of basic hardware technology development remains strong, however, and is not necessarily driven entirely by economic factors. There is probably considerable scope for reducing the very high investment and personnel costs of hardware research and development (e.g. shifting it to Eastern Europe).

By the end of the 1990s, hardware technology (Geisinger *et al.* 1990) may be expected to feature:

- Emphasis will be placed on even smaller sized and lower powered components as a means of increasing physical mobility and performance of computer systems and other electronic devices.
- Still greater levels of integration and fabrication will be achieved above the semiconductor device level. This will lead to even smaller, more robust, lower powered and more powerful computers of all types. Three-dimensional fabrication should become common.
- Reduced instruction set computer (RISC) and complex instruction set computer (CISC) technology. It is possible that CISC (e.g. 486, 68000) technology eventually will prevail as being able to provide the highest levels of performance.
- Both RISC and CISC microprocessors of 500 million instructions per second (mips), 200 million floating point operations per second (mflops) and 64 or 128 bit instruction and data address bus will be available.
- Specialized fixed point, floating point, graphical and communications processors should be standard and integrated with the general purpose central processing unit in higher performance computers.
- Symmetrical multiprocessors (SMP) with two to eight processors on a single semiconductor device will be possible. Fabrication of 'matchbox mainframes' and large-scale multiprocessors (more than 32 processors) is likely using three-dimensional techniques.
- Random assess memory (RAM) devices of up to 256 megabits will have been demonstrated in laboratories by the turn of the century. Commercially available RAM is likely to hover around the 16 megabit device until the end of the 1990s. Four megabyte cache memory may be typical in higher performance processors. Very large RAM memories, perhaps greater than 0.5 gigabytes, will become common in minicomputers and mainframes.
- Magnetic hard disk drive performance will keep pace with developments in processors and semiconductor memory. 1 gigabyte (Gbyte) magnetic hard disk drives will be commonplace, 16 Gbyte drives will be available.
- Controllers for redundant arrays of inexpensive disk (RAID) should be implemented on integrated circuits to improve cost, data storage performance and reliability dramatically.

- Small (e.g. 3 cm × 3 cm × 1 cm) removable, highly robust disk drives of 40 to 100 megabyte capacity could develop as a convenient means of transporting personal data.
- Magnetic cassette tape will continue to lack dominant standards. There will be no return to 9-track drives, however.
- Floppy disks probably only double in capacity. The 5.25″ format will disappear but the 3.5″ 1.4 megabyte format should persist for some time into the next century. Removable hard disks plus more convenient computer-to-computer communications could make floppy disks less of a necessity.
- Optical disks will be employed mainly for the commercial distribution of large volumes of data and software.
- High performance data compression technology, implemented in silicon, will become important to achieve desired levels of computer, disk storage and communications performance, particularly for sound and video information.
- Optical computer busses should start to appear at the high end (i.e. minicomputer and mainframe) of the market.
- Local area network (LAN) speeds of 100 million bits per second (mbps), operating over twisted pair wire, should be available (Eugster 1992) at a cost similar to 10 mbps LANs today. Wide area network (WAN) speeds greater than 2 mbps will be technically possible but commercially expensive.
- The cost, resolution and functionality of printers is likely to improve linearly. Laser printers should become the most popular type; 600 dot per inch resolution and ten pages per minute devices should become common at the price of today's 300 dot per inch, four page per minute lasers.
- Liquid crystal displays (LCD) should continue to be improved up to the quality and performance of present cathode ray tube (CRT) screens. Commodity graphics resolution may reach 1024 × 1024 pixels with 256 colours but seems unlikely to surpass that quality. Specialist displays will, of course, vastly surpass commodity resolution. Increased display size, using LCD devices, could become popular. Major reduction in display prices seems unlikely.
- The price of touch and pen input technology should decline significantly, driven by the popularity of pen-based portable computers. Keyboards and mice will remain popular, however.

The impact of continued progress in basic technology on healthcare computing should be improvements in performance of all aspects of IT at least as significant as those of the 1970s and 1980s. The last impediments of hardware technology as the limiting factor for implementation and integration of healthcare applications should disappear towards the middle of the 1990s.

Software

In general, a dull applications software scene seems likely during the rest of the 1990s. This will be caused by a decade of entrenched package software for PCs, fear of copyright litigation, economic downturn and a general sentiment against software development. This suggests widespread stagnation in commercial software development skills and culture which, by the end of the decade, may reduce the impact of hardware advances.

Software trends of the period could be:

- UNIX will dominate the minicomputer and workstation arenas and move into mainframe sized environments. Proprietary mainframe operating systems will persist so long as traditional mainframes remain. DOS and Windows will persist in the PC arena; successful introduction of another PC operating system or their displacement by UNIX is unlikely.
- Organizational sentiments will tend to discourage in-house development, even against growing evidence that externally developed software does not reduce the risk of installation failure.
- Weak standards in graphical user interfaces (GUI) will continue and hamper dominance of character-based applications. Display size will still be a limiting factor for applications; advanced input/output devices will not supplant the keyboard/screen combination in this decade.
- No direct replacement for COBOL will appear. There will be continued decline of use of all types of third generation languages (3GL) such as COBOL, BASIC, FORTRAN and C in favour of fourth generation languages (4GL) and database management systems (DBMS) in commercial programming. C++ is likely to be the most popular new 3GL.
- DBMSs will be refined during the decade but it is difficult to see major technical innovation on the horizon. Specialized processors for databases could become important, especially if the commercial range of DBMS offerings contracts or strong standards arise to stabilize the environment.
- Multimedia, virtual reality, expert systems, neural networks and object orientation bandwagons are likely to become niche technologies with useful aspects being adopted into normal development practice and software products. None of these technologies will subsume the commercial IT field, however.
- The popular applications software (wordprocessors, spreadsheets and DBMS) of the 1990s is already established and will persist in recognizable form well into the next century. Refinements of existing function and extensions to support integration may be expected, of course. Most popular PC software products will be ported to UNIX.
- Software engineering and CASE will still struggle against poor software development productivity and quality. Prototyping (Smith 1991) will become legitimate and subsumed into normal practice thereby rendering

it largely ineffective. Computer aided testing will become a major bandwagon.

Significant alteration or upgrade of software may be needed to effect the fourth field of health informatics, the wide-scale integration of healthcare systems. Anticipated needs are:

• Conversion of many systems, typically those originating from single user PC applications, to operate reliably and securely in large-scale, multi-user environments.
• Redevelopment of health care systems to accommodate the full range of NHS data set standards (NHS Information Management Centre 1990) and EDIFACT protocols.
• Incorporation of appropriate data communications functions into systems.
• Means of identifying patients accurately and economically in the absence of a NHS identification card carried by individuals. Existing patient databases without NHS numbers will need entry of NHS numbers. Systems with existing NHS numbers will need to accommodate the new NHS number.
• Implementation of standard administrative and clinical codes (Read 1990) or correlation of non-standard code sets with standard ones.

The move towards commercialization of healthcare providers in the UK implies that significant investment in software will have to be made to support new business objectives. In spite of this, a sharp decline in the number of healthcare software suppliers is likely. At present, there are too many firms competing for what is a small (presently no more that £350 million per year), erratic and 'difficult' market. Pressure for genuine integration of systems, use of effective standards and incorporation of new business requirements may result in many suppliers exiting the healthcare business rather than invest in redeveloping their products.

Computer systems

High performance commodity microprocessors matched mainframe performance levels by 1990 (Hennessey and Jouppi 1991). Throughout the rest of this decade, the present computer classes (i.e. PC, workstation, minicomputer, mainframe and supercomputer) will persist. They will, however, have roughly comparable processing power on a processor-to-processor basis. Differentiation will come from high-availability (resilience) features, parallelism, memory size/architecture, caching, physical packaging, bus capability and market positioning. Cost of acquisition and of ownership are likely to be the driving issues for computer systems in the 1990s.

Possible features of 1990s systems may be:

• Use of traditional mainframes and minicomputers will persist into the next century, even if sales of new mainframe and minicomputers and their traditional manufacturers may not. The need for powerful, central computers will increase, however, to meet the need for larger and more integrated applications.

- The 'logical mainframe' may arise out of the installed base of PCs, departmental minis, database servers and mainframes (Holbrook 1990). Disparate processors will be integrated through LANs and WANs. Logical mainframes will reflect the need towards centralizing computing but may not be sufficiently integrated or powerful to act in this capacity.
- Microprocessor-based minicomputers, typically multiprocessor configurations, could evolve into the 'neo-mainframe'. Neo-mainframes will provide efficient client-server services for workstations, PCs and X-terminals at a fraction of the cost of traditional mainframes. Neo-mainframes will also be capable of providing cost-effective time sharing for terminals. The neo-mainframe should be able to perform more capably than logical mainframes.
- Traditional minicomputers will largely give way to UNIX-based PCs and workstations configured for efficient time-sharing on a departmental or small organization scale. Local area networks (LAN) of PCs will supplant minicomputers to some extent.
- Workstations (i.e. UNIX-based) and PCs (i.e. ×86 and DOS-based) may be expected to converge in price and function. Workstations will describe the upper end of the market, PCs the middle and lower part. Workstations typically will have 16 to 32 megabytes of RAM, around 400 megabytes of hard disk, integrated LAN facilities, high quality audio input/output and video input; processor power should exceed 50 mips. Mid- and low-range PCs will be similar to those of today, although processors are likely to be 486s with memory large enough for Windows.
- Portables will have taken over much of the middle range business PC market. The A4 'clamshell' format will persist as being the most practical but portables will be thinner (1 cm) and lighter (0.75 kg). The typical portable will feature VGA resolution LCD, 8 to 16 megabytes of RAM, 200 megabytes of removable hard disk, track ball (in place of mouse), built-in AC power supply, integrated LAN/WAN and six to eight hours battery life. The popularity of palm top portables will be limited by their small screens and keyboards.

The decline of traditional mainframe and minicomputer suppliers, combined with financial and organizational pressures, should force the NHS to invest heavily in the new types of mainframe and minicomputers in the latter part of the decade. The cost, performance and functional advantages of this step will greatly assist the integration of health care systems later in the decade.

Communications

Communications are likely to be one of the IT 'hot spots' of the 1990s. Technical progress, deregulation, competition and affordable technology will be the driving forces. The blending of communications and computing should be the major focus of effort.

Likely communications trends of the decade are:

- Semiconductor technology will be as much a driving force for communications as it was for computers in the 1980s.
- Telephone supplier orientation will change completely to digital and data orientation worldwide before the end of the 1990s.
- Affordable integrated system digital network (ISDN), or something like it (e.g. frame relay), will be essential for teleworking, small business electronic data interchange and video telephony. There is no technical reason why ISDN should cost more than analogue communications. Look to the late 1990s for data volume, rather than time charging. Many users will adopt ISDN for convenience, rapid call setup and increased communications rates in spite of the increased premium (Stanislawski 1992).
- Data compression will be vital to providing increased data communications speeds beyond the capability of the physical elements of the communications systems. Standards for data, audio and video compression will be essential.
- Modem performance will approach 64 kbps communications rates to counteract ISDN. More competitive pricing may be expected, as well. Eventually, ISDN will prevail over modems but this may be well into the next century.
- Video telephones may prove to be the 'fax of the 90s'. Video conferencing is likely to be successful in the financially difficult 1990s, given the need for maintaining long distance contacts established in the economically dynamic 1980s.
- Present WAN standards (e.g. X.25, 'RS-232') should remain healthy for many years. OSI seems unlikely to be fully defined in this century and the need for it has been eroded by other protocols such as TCP/IP.
- Wireless and portable communications for computer communications could become very important as a means of conveniently connecting PCs and workstations to larger networks, particularly as an alternative to wiring existing buildings. Wireless communication is particularly relevant to healthcare because of the large numbers of old buildings and the particular needs for delivering computing to the bedside (Smith and Berry 1993).
- LAN capability will become an integral part of commodity PCs and workstations. LAN takeoff will not be as fast nor its effects as profound as expected, however, unless wireless LANS become inexpensive and reduce the scope of installation and increase physical scope of operation. Legislation and deregulation are key enablers for wireless LAN technology.
- Contending LAN software and standards (e.g. Ethernet versus Token

Ring versus FDDI, TCP/IP and UNIX versus Novell) will be a minor technical problem but will present a major marketing problem for buyers. The wired LAN base of the 1980s will be an impediment to further investment for many. Within healthcare organizations, however, LANs appear likely to make steady progress in facilitating local integration.

- Software problems and skill shortages will limit the growth and effective use of LANs and WANs within many organizations.
- Electronic data interchange (EDI) is a concept in which organizations transfer business information directly in computer form. EDI has been successful in many industries and is very important to healthcare organizations. EDI healthcare standards are being developed, although it is likely to take many years before full definition and implementation is finished. Healthcare organizations should track the progress of EDI and adopt it as soon as it appears practical.

Communications will become an essential part of healthcare computing integration and will be essential for effective business operations and patient care. The NHS made investments in the 1980s to provide wide-scale networking for the FHSAs. This, assisted by rapid technological and cost improvements in communications, can be extended to accommodate almost universal networking of healthcare organizations in the 1990s and beyond.

People and organizations

Max Planck is supposed to have said, 'Change never occurs any faster than it takes the older generation to die off.' For the first time in the computer business, natural retirements will begin to have an impact.

The 1960s and 1970s often suffered from too much technical skill, acquired because that was the only way to get computers to work. This skill was often used to stretch application boundaries to the breaking point. The 1990s' lack of adequate base technical skills for the new technology could be exacerbated by the 'computer semi-literates' and half-hearted careerists of the 1980s who swelled the ranks of genuine information technologists when the economic scene was good and entry into the IT field was easy. This could result in a new wave of technical failures.

The future for the 1990s' IT professional does not look particularly promising. The background for this is:

- Increasing technical complexity hidden from all but the most expert practitioner.
- Increasing economic constraints on all types of IT spending, including training and time to learn on the job.
- A generally declining educational base with increasingly superficial technical education.

- Plentiful entrants into the field of low to average ability and motivation but willing to work for low salaries.
- Concentration of genuine technical skills with a few IT suppliers having only a limited number of openings.

User organizations may not be able to make effective IT decisions in this milieu. Here is one gloomy scenario:

- 'Class of 1960' retires; classical mainframe decline can be strongly related to retirement of this cadre who were in upper technical echelons of many organizations until the 1990s.
- 'Class of 1970' takes over. This group was trained well on classical minicomputers and is generally familiar with the problems of implementing large, multi-user systems. Their arrival in the uppermost technical echelons causes a resurgence of neo-mini (i.e. UNIX-based RISC mainframes) adoption. This trend also is driven by business need for low cost and high integration.
- 'Class of 1980', trained *ad hoc* on PCs is now the mainstay of technical support and implementation. This cadre struggles with inadequate technical background and standalone system experience to meet demands for lower costs, large-scale applications and tight integration – disaster results.
- Consequent relegation of information technologists into blue collar status, commensurate with the commodity status of the hardware and software.

The poor outlook for IT professionals in the 1990s is both an opportunity and a danger for healthcare organizations. Given their reluctance to invest heavily in IT skills in the face of other demands on resources, healthcare organizations should be wary of totally losing their IT expertise. On the other hand, IT skills, if carefully selected, should be available at reasonable cost.

Fads, bandwagons and hot spots

A number of technologies and techniques will become prominent during the 1990s. Some of these may have relevance to healthcare organizations, others may not. Some prominent issues and their outcomes, in alphabetical order, are likely to be:

- Computer-aided testing is a development within software engineering to improve the detection of errors in software. This is an early technology and one which is likely to have minor direct relevance to healthcare computing, especially if the trend against in-house development continues.
- 'Data mining' is the use of artificial software techniques to extract new information from existing databases (Luck 1992). The technology is

new but the application of data mining could benefit areas such as epidemiology and medical audit.

- Executive information systems are software to present information, typically aggregated, in graphical form and to provide features for browsing or 'drilling down' through data interactively. Many existing EISs must be set up by skilled software developers and are inflexible. Current products are attractive, however, and could provide benefit to healthcare managers. More flexible EISs are worth evaluating as they appear in the market.
- Geographical information systems (GIS) are a means of presenting data on maps. There is considerable opportunity for this technology in epidemiology and healthcare planning; postcodes provide reasonably accurate physical location for individual patients. GISs remain relatively immature technically and suitable primarily for mapping specialists. The potential for GIS in healthcare will remain underexploited during the 1990s.
- Image processing and storage involves the digital manipulation of pictorial information. This technology is maturing and becoming economical through PCs with greater processing power and better graphical capability. The potential for storage and transmission of X-rays and documents (e.g. patient records) is enormous in terms of cost saving and improved patient care. The main impediment in the NHS appears to be conservatism.
- Neural networks supposedly emulate the logical function of neurons. Neural networks are trained empirically to give results which may be difficult to achieve through conventional computing techniques. Neural networks appear to have considerable promise for specialized functions within embedded instrumentation and knowledge-based systems. The technology seems unlikely to make a major impact on healthcare computing, although it may be of value for identifying patients and linking records.
- Object orientation is a software development technique for combining programs and data to reduce certain types of error and to improve the reusability of software. Object orientation appears to have little direct relevance to healthcare computing.
- Pen, touch, voice and other novel computer interfaces could eliminate the need for keyboards and keyboard skills. These technologies could have a major impact on healthcare computing, particularly where 'hands free' operation is essential. At present, however, these technologies are immature and expensive. Their actual performance and cost-effectiveness should be evaluated very carefully before adopting them.
- Robotics have widespread potential applicability in healthcare. There appear to be few cases of routine use of robotics, at present. Organizational resistance is likely to be great, costs are high and the technology is relatively primitive. While there may be experimentation, the potential for robotics seems unlikely to be realized for many years.

- Smart cards employ microprocessors and memory embedded in a plastic card similar to those used by banks. The use of smart cards in healthcare has been tested (Markwell 1991). The amount of memory available is relatively small, however, and it is difficult to see the advantages of smart cards in the face of universal networking of healthcare systems. A more likely form of personal data storage may be removable hard disks, which are physically robust and capable of storing entire patient records.
- Teleworking is the concept of having staff work from home by means of computers and audio, video and digital communications. Teleworking may begin to impact working practices in some industries before the end of the century. There is some potential for teleworking in healthcare, even for direct patient care. The concept seems unlikely to find favour within the healthcare sector for many years.
- Virtual reality is the use of multiple sensory inputs and outputs (sight, sound, touch), combined eventually with television quality graphics, to alter human perception of computer interaction. Virtual reality may become a major form of entertainment in the late 1990s and, possibly, a serious social problem. Experimental applications in specialized aspects of healthcare (e.g. surgery, psychiatry, medical education) are likely but it is difficult to see a major impact on health informatics as a whole, however.

Conclusion

What are believed to be significant developments for IT users such as the NHS during the 1990s?

- Technical function and price improvements similar to those of the 1980s or perhaps even greater.
- Practical, working standards taken for granted.
- Rapid progress towards affordable convergence of computing and communications.
- A stable, if not stagnant, software scene.
- A favourable climate, both in the technology and business sense, for user organizations who can maintain their technical competence and an adequate level of investment in the commodity IT scene.

What are the possible pitfalls of the 1990s?

- Frequent IT supplier business failures, perhaps even the biggest suppliers, and the consequent effects on buyers, especially non-commodity buyers locked into proprietary products, skills and knowledge.
- Disasters caused by ambitious, but naïve, implementations created by underskilled and undereducated user/developers who will attempt to create 'logical mainframes' from personal computer applications.
- Loss of technical capability within user organizations to the point where

they can no longer make valid technical decisions and thereby miss the exciting commercial deals waiting for canny buyers.

How should healthcare organizations prepare for this commodity computing future?

- Maintain a flexible position and avoid highly tuned technical solutions.
- Buy systems with a clear and standard upgrade path which permits third party suppliers. Buy hardware and software incrementally as needed and make irrevocable purchasing commitments as late as possible.
- Keep a reasonable base of technical knowledge and skills, even if organizational policy is oriented towards facilities management and outsourcing.
- Look for applications opportunities in the computing–communications interface but don't get too clever with the technology.
- Do not 'bleed' your chosen suppliers to death but do keep them 'lean and keen'.
- Exert pressure on communications suppliers to provide ISDN at a reasonable price.

The NHS seems to have been one of the organizations that did not take full advantage of the IT cost/performance improvements of the 1980s. It is hard to see that the IT position of the NHS will be greatly improved in the 1990s in spite of intense business pressures to do so. The reasons for this pessimism are:

- The 'farming out' of computing and technical management functions outside the NHS has become so pervasive that the organization may be unable to respond appropriately to the exciting opportunities of the 1990s.
- The widespread perception of high risk in healthcare computing and relatively harsh management controls devised to prevent failure may stifle initiative and innovation.
- The level of IT investment in the NHS, at £250 per employee (Allison, personal communication), may be an order of magnitude below that of many commercial enterprises. This level may not be sufficient to sustain the move towards commercialization of healthcare provision in the UK. Increasing localization of budgets and decision-making may not encourage the necessary investment either.

One must hope that the problems of NHS computing have not gone too far or that they are not irremediable. It is difficult to imagine the NHS reforms working without a much larger and more complex IT base. Help may lie in the upcoming generation of IT-knowledgeable clinicians and managers, who will be more demanding of IT than have been previous generations. Perhaps they will demand a rejuvenation of IT skills and progress within the NHS and be willing to pay for it.

References

Baldini, J.J. and Heath, R. (1991) 'Intelligent networking of information technology systems in healthcare', in B. Richards *et al.* (eds), *Current Perspectives in Health Computing 1991*. Weybridge: BJHC Books.

Blum, B.I. and Duncan, K. (1990) *A History of Medical Informatics*. New York, ACM Press.

Eugster, E. (1992) '100 Mbps to the desktop via FDDI over copper', *Telecommunications*, October, 68–73.

Geisinger, P.P., Gargini, P.A., Parker, G.H. and Yu, A.Y.C. (1990) 'Micro 2000 – a cpu with 50 million transistors', *Electronic Product Design*, April, 47–53.

Hennessey, J.L. and Jouppi, N.P. (1991) 'Computer technology and architecture: an evolving interaction', *Computer*, September, 18–29.

Holbrook, A.B. (1990) 'Global impact of new directions in connectivity', *Electronic Product Design*, April, 85–8.

Luck, M. (1992) 'Nuggets of information', *Computing*, 22 October, 34–5.

Madnick, S.E. (1991) 'The information technology platform', in M.S. Scott Morton (ed.), *The Corporation of the 1990s*. New York, Oxford University Press.

Markwell, D.C. (1991) 'Patient-held records: a card for all seasons', in B. Richards *et al.* (eds), *Current Perspectives in Health Computing 1991*. Weybridge: BJHC Books.

McAdam, W.A.F., Brock, B.M., Armitage, T. *et al.* (1990) 'Twelve years' experience of computer-aided diagnosis in a district general hospital', *Annals of the Royal College of Surgeons of England*, 72, 140–6.

NHS Information Management Centre (1990) *The Common Basic Specification: The Generic Model Reference Manual*. Birmingham, NHS Information Management Centre.

Read, J.D. (1990) 'Computerising medical language', in H. de Glanville *et al.* (eds), *Current Perspectives in Health Computing*. Weybridge, BJHC Books.

Rigby, M., McBride, A. and Shiels, C. (1992) *Computers in Medical Audit*. London, Royal Society of Medicine Services Limited.

Shortliffe, E.H., Perreault, L.E., Wiederhold, G. and Fagan, L.M. (1990) *Medical Informatics: Computer Applications in Health Care*. Reading, MA, Addison-Wesley.

Smith, M.F. (1991) *Software Prototyping: Adoption, Practice and Management*. Maidenhead, McGraw-Hill.

Smith, M.F. and Berry, G. (1993) 'Computing at the bedside: portable computers for ward information systems', in B. Richards *et al.* (eds), *Current Perspectives in Healthcare Computing*. Weybridge, BJHC Books.

Stanislawski, S. (1992) 'Supplying value-added services locally', *Telecommunications*, October, 36–44.

Index